Thatched Roofs and Open Sides

UNIVERSITY PRESS OF FLORIDA

Florida A&M University, Tallahassee
Florida Atlantic University, Boca Raton
Florida Gulf Coast University, Ft. Myers
Florida International University, Miami
Florida State University, Tallahassee
New College of Florida, Sarasota
University of Central Florida, Orlando
University of Florida, Gainesville
University of North Florida, Jacksonville
University of South Florida, Tampa
University of West Florida, Pensacola

Thatched Roofs and Open Sides

The Architecture of Chickees and Their Changing Role in Seminole Society

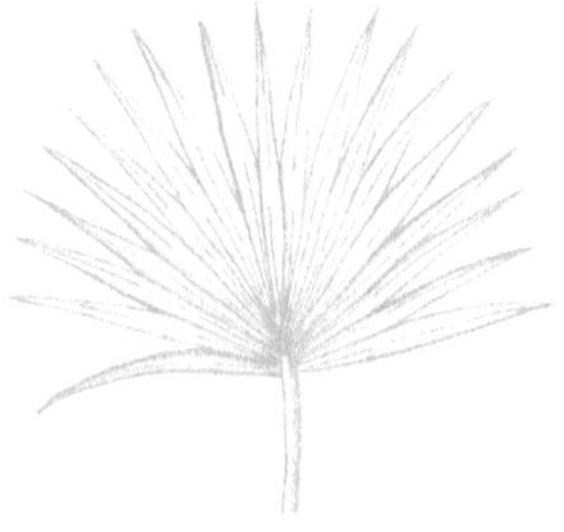

Carrie Dilley

Foreword by Paul N. Backhouse

University Press of Florida
Gainesville | Tallahassee | Tampa | Boca Raton
Pensacola | Orlando | Miami | Jacksonville | Ft. Myers | Sarasota

Publication of this book was made possible in part
by a grant from the Seminole Tribe of Florida.

Printed in the United States of America on acid-free paper

This book may be available in an electronic edition.

First cloth printing, 2015
First paperback printing, 2018

23 22 21 20 19 18 6 5 4 3 2 1

Library of Congress Cataloging-in-Publication Data
Dilley, Carrie, author.
Thatched roofs and open sides : the architecture of Chickees and their changing role
in Seminole society / Carrie Dilley ; foreword by Paul N. Backhouse.
pages cm
Includes bibliographical references and index.
ISBN 978-0-8130-6153-5 (cloth)
ISBN 978-0-8130-6492-5 (pbk.)
1. Indian architecture—Florida—History. 2. Seminole Indians—Florida—History. 3. Seminole Indians—Florida—Social life and customs. 4. Indians of North America—Florida—History.
I. Backhouse, Paul N. (Paul Nathan), Author of introduction, etc. II. Title.
E98.A63D55 2015
975.9004'973859—dc23 2015011679

University Press of Florida
15 Northwest 15th Street
Gainesville, FL 32611-2079
http://upress.ufl.edu

Contents

Illustrations

Foreword

As I sit in the Seminole Tribal Historic Preservation Office doublewide trailer to write this, the air is thick with moisture and afternoon downpours are inevitable. It is the beginning of the rainy season here on Big Cypress. The subtropical environment and climate of southern peninsular Florida is unlike anywhere else in the United States, and in these circumstances the chickee reigns supreme. Carrie Dilley has a unique perspective on these amazing examples of traditional craft. She has dedicated more than five years in situ, a period of residence, if you will, observing and measuring chickees and talking to master crafter tribal members who make these structures such iconic symbols of Seminole culture. Carrie has observed and photographed hundreds of chickees—working side by side with community members to document the variety of their forms and uses. She has stood under the thatched roofs of chickees on hot summer days, like today, and witnessed the remarkable weatherproofing as the palmetto thatch stands up to another beating—the same violent storms that have caused leaks in the asphalt roof of our modular trailer here on Big Cypress.

Carrie's work demonstrates an understanding of the importance of chickees as the products of a traditional industry that resonate as much with modern Seminole life and identity as they did in the past. More fundamentally, as an architectural historian, she brings a different set of eyes to a structure and subject that has until now received short shrift in the academic literature. Writing here to a general audience, she makes us think about these structures afresh, reassessing our preconceptions about what makes a structure important and perhaps the most poorly applied term—*significant*. I hope that readers are left with a sense of the history and cultural meaning that these structures represent and that when they explore the interior of southern Florida, they can themselves witness the indigenous beauty, craftsmanship, and culture that are manifest in these enigmatic buildings.

Paul N. Backhouse
Director of the Ah-Tah-Thi-Ki Museum and Tribal Historic Preservation Officer

Preface

When AMC's television series *Mad Men* (set in the 1960s) premiered in 2007, it had audiences across America swooning over all things mid-twentieth century. From clothing and cocktails to cars, furniture, and architecture—"Mid-Century Modern" made a swift comeback to the mainstream. Though the simplicity of the modern movement had fallen out of favor for several decades before this recent revival, one of the kitschier aspects of the movement never left South Florida—the tiki craze. With nearly endless summers, South Florida is the perfect place to live out a tropical fantasy without ever leaving the contiguous United States. Dreams of paradise could be realized under the shade of a palmetto thatched-roof hut.

Thatched huts are found all over South Florida. Some of the cypress and palmetto structures at beachside bars are simply tiki huts, and others are authentic Seminole chickees. Many people have no idea there is even a difference between these two types of structures, let alone understand the history and significance behind them.

Over six years ago, when I started working as the architectural historian for the Seminole Tribe of Florida's Tribal Historic Preservation Office (THPO), I never imagined I would be afforded the opportunity to write a book about Seminole architecture. I am not Seminole; in fact, I do not belong to any American Indian tribe. I was born and raised in southern Kentucky, educated at Western Kentucky University in architectural sciences, and moved to Florida in 2005 to attend the University of Florida for a degree in architectural studies and a historic preservation certificate. I had never in my life been immersed in Native

American culture, let alone indigenous architecture. Throughout this book I often use the term "we," and by that I am referring to the non-Native perspective that I represent—the perspective I challenged by writing this book.

I spent several years working on-reservation in Hollywood, Big Cypress, and Brighton trying to learn what makes a building or structure "significant" to the modern-day Seminole Tribe. It certainly takes time to try to understand the complexity of a radically different perspective that is, oftentimes, directly contrary to what I learned in the nonindigenous classroom setting. Architecture created for aesthetic reasons alone is practically nonexistent out here in the Everglades. Only in recent years did buildings pop up that I can imagine an architectural historian in fifty years will call "significant" upon first glance—all thanks to the booming Indian gaming industry. Nearly every building created before this recent turning point was more or less utilitarian, created to meet a specific need and not to make an architectural or cultural statement. Interestingly enough, the emergence of architecture designed by prominent local architects on the reservations also coincided with a mass resurgence in traditional architecture and particularly chickees.

I quickly learned that there has been very little written about Seminole architecture despite the fact that chickees are a significant fixture in South Florida—both on-reservation and off-reservation. The lack of ample historical documentation sent me straight out in the field to learn about chickees firsthand. The same structures that were classified as "primitive" or "outdated" by local newspapers or by area activists fifty years ago seemed fresh and timeless to me.

My two-year survey of chickees on the Big Cypress Reservation was the catalyst for the book you now hold in your hands. The survey revealed critical information about modern-day chickees—new (often nontraditional) uses, longer-lasting materials, and innovative techniques. As the architectural historian for the THPO, I was able to access the reservations and personally speak with tribal members who grew up in and around chickees and to gain insight directly from the chickee builders themselves. I did not simply conduct a "windshield" survey based upon what could be seen from the road. The interaction I had with Seminoles who build, own, and/or grew up in chickees generated a wealth of information that will be unique to this book. While no chickee builder has written a book about chickees from the first-person perspective, my goal is to convey the voice of the builders throughout this book. I have taken extreme caution, however, to keep much of the information general so as not to reveal aspects of culture that the Seminoles did not want to share.

The modern-day Seminole Tribe is made up of people who were traditionally two different linguistic groups, commonly called Creeks and Miccosukees. They spoke either Maskókî/Muscogee (Creek) or Mikasuki/Mikisúkî (Miccosukee or Hitchiti-Mikasuki). These two languages are still alive within the tribe today. Over the past fifty years, these "Florida Seminoles" have again divided into four different groups—the Seminole Tribe of Florida (comprised of members of these two linguistic groups), the Miccosukee Tribe of Indians of Florida, the Independent Traditional Seminole Nation of Florida (not federally recognized), and lastly the independent Seminoles, who are not members of any federally or nonfederally recognized tribe. The main difference between these groups today, however, boils down to politics, and it is important to keep in mind that the chickee was the primary home for all groups of Seminoles, not just the Seminole Tribe of Florida, for over one hundred years. I am writing about what I have learned from my time with the Seminole Tribe of Florida, though sometimes I do refer to chickees of Seminole people in general, or even specifically Miccosukees or independents.

On the Seminole reservations, it is obvious that chickees are evolving to meet current needs without losing their cultural integrity. Although most Seminoles no longer live in chickees, they are still an essential part of Seminole culture and identity. I aim for this work to help showcase an art, to help keep tradition and culture alive, and to prove the significance of the chickee. Many aspects of Seminole culture are meant to be kept private, but chickees have been proudly shared with the world.

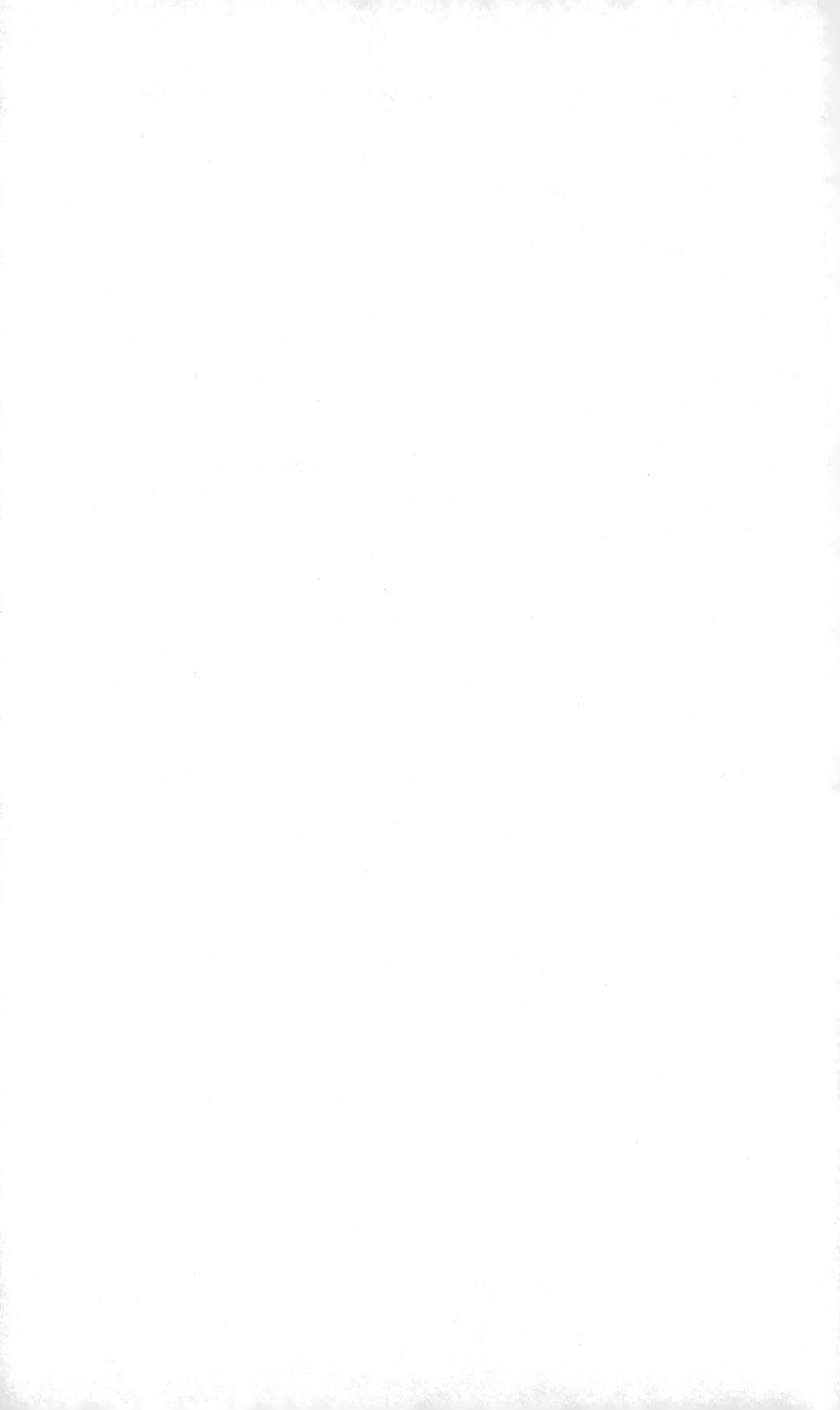

Acknowledgments

This book would not have been possible without the generous support of the Seminole Tribe of Florida, the Big Cypress community, and the talented chickee builders I interviewed. I hope that I have captured their voices in this book and have shown the beauty of Seminole chickees. I would further like to thank the Ah-Tah-Thi-Ki Museum and the Tribal Historic Preservation Office for allowing this project to take place. From the Tribal Historic Preservation Office, I'd like to send extra thanks to Paul, Kate, and Anne, who helped review the manuscript multiple times throughout the writing process. All of your feedback was invaluable. Willie Johns and Lewis Gopher, from the Brighton Reservation, also deserve my gratitude for reviewing the book for accuracy from the Seminole perspective. This research was further enhanced by materials and information provided by the Seminole/Miccosukee Photographic Archive.

Thanks go to Neal Downing, at Western Kentucky University, for teaching me there's so much more to architecture than designing buildings. Thank you for inspiring me to follow my dreams of becoming an architectural historian.

Last but not least, I would like to thank family back home in Kentucky for being so supportive throughout my life, including the time I've spent writing this book. Even though you are far away, you have never doubted me for a second.

Abbreviations

BCNP	Big Cypress National Preserve
BIA	Bureau of Indian Affairs
CBS	concrete block and stucco
CCC	Civilian Conservation Corps
CCC-ID	Civilian Conservation Corps–Indian Division
STOF	Seminole Tribe of Florida
THPO	Tribal Historic Preservation Office

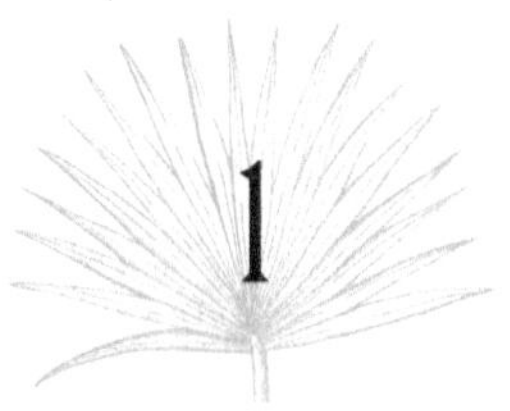

1

An Introduction to Native American Architecture

The Seminole chickee—a seemingly simple structure with a storied history. Perfected in the swampy Florida Everglades, this open-sided thatched-roof structure can be created from as few as two building materials. Cypress posts provide the framework, and interwoven palm fronds provide a covering. Despite this basic description, it should become clear throughout this book that both the architectural and cultural significance of the chickee lies beyond its outward appearance.

In perhaps the simplest of terms, and for purposes most befitting of this text, architecture can be described as "nothing more and nothing less than the gift of making places for some human purpose."[1] What is often misunderstood is that, in fact, all buildings can be considered architecture. The beauty of the above definition lies in the fact that it does not limit the use of the word to descriptions of grand monuments per se, but implies that it can also refer to the everyday buildings around us. As stated by the architectural historian Spiro Kostof, "all past buildings, regardless of size, status, or consequence, deserve to be studied."[2] I dare take this a step further and state that all buildings in general, not just those of our past, deserve to be studied because they hold some level of significance in that they help tell the story of humankind. The mistake many architectural historians of the past made was that they focused almost solely on "buildings of evident substance"[3] or world-renowned monumental works. Kostof points out that "delight is an elusive thing that may apply to the random and unstudied as it does to the calculated designs of the professional."[4] Many architectural historians in recent de-

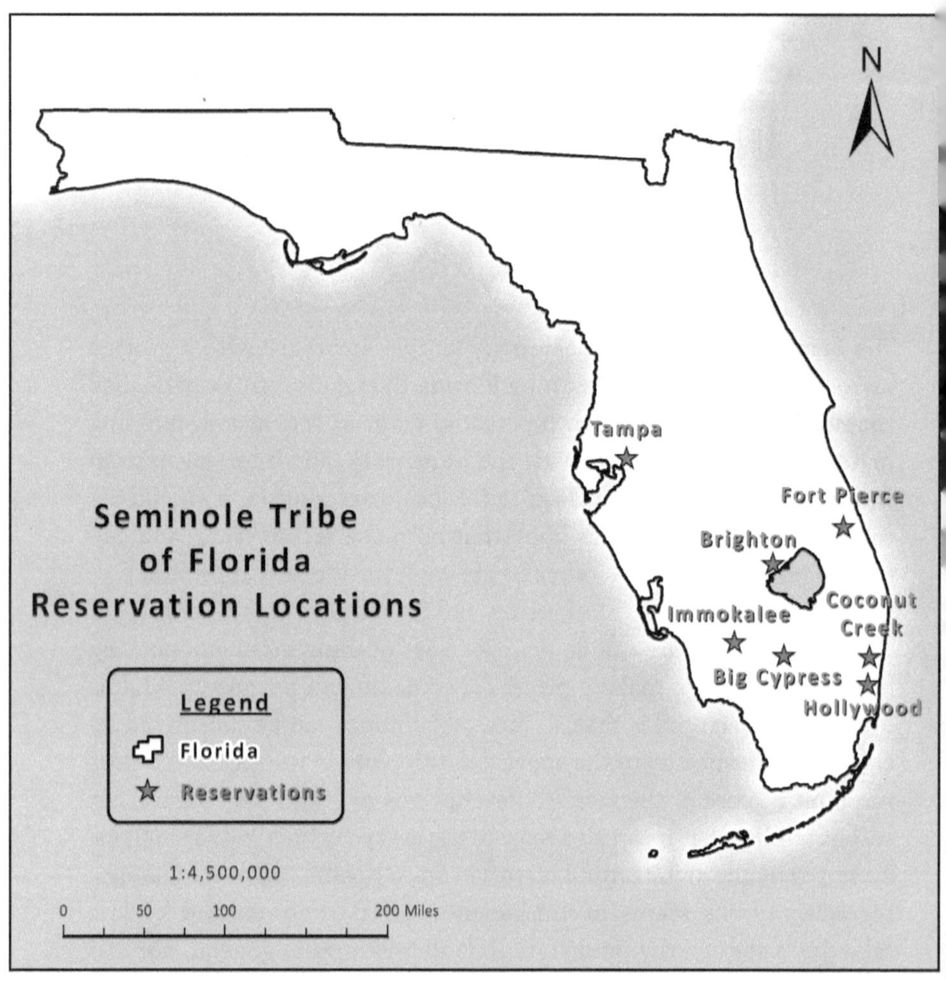

Figure 1.1. Map of the Seminole Tribe of Florida reservations. Created by Juan Cancel, Tribal Historic Preservation Office chief data analyst.

cades, myself included, have shifted our focus beyond what has already been studied, beyond the obvious, to other, perhaps lesser known, or at least less commonly studied, forms of architecture.

Notwithstanding a few "monumental" exceptions, Native American building types as a whole are often overlooked in the field of architectural history. These structures are not built by famous architects, they typically do not feature the most modern or advanced building materials or construction techniques, and often they are not even built to stand the test of time—all components that help make a building architecturally "significant." Instead of defining the significance of Native American buildings in these shortsighted terms, I suggest we take a further look at what truly makes architecture "significant" and successful. All Native American structures were crafted for a specific human purpose, often one that goes beyond a utilitarian shelter.

The anthropologist Peter Nabokov and the architect Robert Easton spent years studying the architecture of American Indians. In their comprehensive work on the subject, aptly titled *Native American Architecture*, they examine not only *how* structures were built (a typical way to evaluate architecture) but also, and perhaps more relevant, *why*. They break down stereotypes, including that these structures are too simple to be of architectural significance, to show the complexity of American Indian architecture. Throughout their decade-long study, they focused on the many ways in which structures varied from region to region and from tribe to tribe. They also highlighted the common threads that tie them all together yet make them stand out from non-Native architecture.

American Indians did not necessarily view their homes in terms of permanence as much as in terms of practicality. Many times the building techniques themselves were more significant than the end result because the ways in which structures were built were a direct reflection of cultural belief systems.[5] Since Native Americans more or less inhabited specific cultural areas and often had limited means of transportation, they looked to their environment for available building materials. Nabokov and Easton point out that "Indians had no choice but to build with raw materials from the land around them."[6] However, this does not mean that if other groups were given the same materials and environment, the outcome would be the same. Humans have different life influences, different tastes, different upbringings, different values, different opportunities, and different priorities. Whether these factors are conscious or subconscious, they are undoubtedly reflected in our buildings and in our homes.

Amos Rapoport discusses how culture, human behavior, and environment affect architecture in his book *House Form and Culture:* "Materials, construction and technology are best treated as modifying factors, rather than form determinants, because they decide neither what is to be built nor its form."[7] Many tribes had access to the exact same natural building materials, but their dwellings were different because they incorporated their cultural beliefs into the structures they created. As outsiders, it is often hard to pick up on these elements because they are not always straightforward. We might see the Seminole Tribe's seal or medicine colors incorporated in their buildings, for instance, but it could actually be the elements that are less obvious, the building techniques or arrangement patterns, that truly reflect a belief system. It is impossible to deduce these characteristics from a simple architectural survey where we focus on the physical or outward traits of a building. As Kostof points out: "And then the historian must go beyond this established reality of the buildings to understand what they are, how they came to be, and why they are the way they are."[8] That is to say, we must look beyond a building's physical attributes to truly understand the meaning of the architecture.

When conducting an architectural survey, it is common practice to focus on the character-defining features of a building—the exterior materials, structural system, architectural form or shape, windows, doors, porches, roofs, and the presence of any other stylistic details such as moldings, columns, arches, or brackets, to name a few. Since Native American structures are typically less ornate, we tend to look strictly to the building materials, structural system, and building shape when creating architectural descriptions. By failing to look beyond the surface, however, we often overlook the true significance of a structure.

As a study of a specific type of Native American architecture, this book examines both the physical and the undeclared. Not only is it important to describe what a building looks like, it must also be understood why it looks a certain way. As an architectural historian, it is second nature for me to break down buildings into their smallest physical components. This first step of describing architecture helps us to better perceive the question of *why*.

Basic Building Components

Understanding why a building stands up can be a complicated concept. It is the sum of building loads, strength and quality of materials, environmental factors, and a combination of compression, tension, and force. The main element that keeps a building standing up is the structural system, yet it is possibly the least understood component to the layperson. The structural system defines how a building is put together. Unlike the other building components (which I address in the following paragraphs), the structural framework of a building is often hard to determine from the exterior. Architects and builders go to great lengths to hide the "bones" of the building from the inside because building occupants do not want to see how their buildings are put together. Interior walls are covered with drywall, ceilings with plaster, and floors with carpet, all in an effort to hide what lies behind or beneath. Native American dwellings, on the other hand, are usually more undisguised in construction, making the building frame much easier to determine. We can quickly see the tensile or bent frame structure of the wigwam and wikiup, the compression shell frame of the igloo and tipi, or the post-and-beam construction of the Seminole chickee. We may not fully understand how these systems keep buildings standing up from an engineering perspective, but they certainly look like they do a great job of it, all unconcealed. To apply a phrase often used to describe the tenets behind modern architecture, in these structures it is accurate to claim that "form (ever) follows function."[9]

The exterior fabric protects the structural system and interior spaces of a building. The exterior components can themselves aid the structural system in holding the building up (as seen with load-bearing masonry walls), or they can simply clad the outside. The exterior fabric is also what often catches the eye; its materiality has texture and color that appeal to our senses. Two buildings with the exact same structural system, shape, and size can appear dramatically different if the exterior materials are different, say brick versus wooden shakes. In historic preservation, we know the value of staying true to original building materials. If you put vinyl siding on a brick Italianate home, you completely alter the look of the building. Using proper exterior materials is critical.

Indigenous peoples primarily covered the structural systems of their homes with parts of trees (wood, bark, leaves), plants (grass, reeds), earth (adobe, mud), snow, stone, or parts of animals (including the hide or bones) rather than relying on manufactured materials. It is most likely that they did not have much of a choice in the matter. The exterior fabric was determined by available resources, the logical choices that correlated with the limitations of the structural system, and the overall needs of the group. Imagine trying to clad the compression shell frame of the tipi with leaves rather than animal hide. You would create an entirely different structure, one that deviated from the inherent need of portability—a characteristic that makes the tipi such a success.

A building's shape can be one of its more distinguishing characteristics. Most buildings either take on the shape of a rectangle or a series of rectangles, but when the shape is anything other than the "norm," it captures immediate attention. Ancient Egyptians built great pyramids. Art nouveau architecture thrived through curved lines and floral inspirations. Organic architecture synchronized habitations with nature through nonlinear forms. Buckminster Fuller's geodesic domes relied on geometry to create spherical structures based upon polyhedrons. Deconstructivism is built upon fragmenting traditional shapes for new applications. Architects today are pushing the boundaries, creating buildings beyond imagination. These designs challenge the traditional ideas of what are acceptable forms for our structures. Sometimes these unique shapes are created to make a statement (to prove that an architect or builder "thinks outside the box"), sometimes they are built in a particular way to reflect a belief system, and sometimes they are created based upon scientific principles with the intent to produce much stronger structures. Regardless of the reason, uniquely shaped buildings make an impact on society.

Though many Native American structures are rectangular in form, domes and cones are also quite common.[10] Rectangular structures are by no means less impressive in their composition or construction (consider the large-scale cliff dwellings and adobe pueblo homes), but the domical or conical shapes of the igloo, wigwam, wikiup, ki, tipi, and earthlodge are often considered more distinctive. These structures take on irregular forms for a particular reason, not to make an architectural statement. Domes provide excellent protection from the wind due to their aerodynamics (wind flows around, not through), which is critical in regions such as the Arctic. Domes also enclose the most amount of space with the least materials and do not need interior framing supports, which frees up space inside. The conical tipi relies on less surface area of animal skin to cover it in its entirety compared to a rectangular structure. Form and function are united into one, much akin to the principles that drove the creation of organic, and later modern, architecture.

In addition to examining the physical aspects of Native American structures based upon the three factors previously mentioned, it is important to keep in mind that these dwellings were typically arranged in a specific manner. Nabokov and Easton note that "the way in which tribal people arranged their spaces and used their dwellings reflected the way they organized their society as a whole."[11] Everything was in a specific place based upon a cultural belief system. The Seminoles certainly practiced this type of strategic arrangement in their chickee camps (the focus of chapter 5).

Misconceptions

People unfamiliar with Seminole history and culture often do not know that their traditional house is called a chickee, and others assume that all Native Americans lived in tipis or wigwams. It might sound ludicrous, but tipis and wigwams are no doubt the stereotypical Indian structures most present in American culture. This is such a common misconception that the National Museum of the American Indian created a book entitled *Do All Indians Live in Tipis?* to debunk many popular Native American myths, including housing types.

Minnie Moore-Willson was a noted writer and advocate for the Seminoles in the late 1800s to the early 1900s. She and her husband, James Mallory Willson, developed a close relationship with the Seminoles through various hunting trips in the South Florida area during a time when the Seminoles were still very wary of outsiders. Moore-Willson culminated her observations in her 1911 book *The Seminoles of Florida*, which included a small glossary of words at the end. Although she considered herself a close friend of the Seminoles, Moore-Willson mistakenly calls Seminole structures "wigwams" on eighteen different pages of the book.[12] She does, however, record the word *cho-ko* for *house* in the vocabulary section itself, which could be a variation of the Muscogee (Creek) word *cuko*, or a house with solid walls.[13] Decades later, an *Orlando Sentinel* headline read, "Indians Eager to Swap Tepees for Plumbing." This article detailed how the Florida Seminoles wanted to "learn the civilized ways of the white man and trade in their tepees for houses with inside plumbing."[14] There are even instances today when the terms are being misused, as I have directly been asked if Seminoles lived in tipis or wigwams.

Common Themes in Native American Architecture

At first glance, it seems that the chickee has little in common with other Native American building types. It is true that it does not look like many indigenous structures found in the United States throughout the past or present. It bears a stronger resemblance, however, to the huts recorded before modern times and in other locales, a point discussed in later chapters. "Hut" should not be viewed as a derogatory term. A hut is simply a type of vernacular dwelling with its design based upon local craftsmanship. Huts are made from readily available materials and may or may not be temporary or portable structures. If you look beyond the physical appearance, beyond the shape and building materials, you will start to notice common themes running through various Native American building types.

In addition to food and water, shelter is one of the most basic human needs. People have been trying to fulfill this need since the beginning of time—whether it was seeking shelter in a cave or constructing a rudimentary hut. Most forms of shelter are inherently intended to protect their inhabitants from weather and other external factors; the structures built by American Indians are no different. Humans need more than simple protection; they also seek a certain level of comfort. In Arctic regions where the temperature can drop to -50°F, the igloo can provide an internal temperature of 20° to up to about 60° with body heat.[15] In the Mojave Desert, Colorado River tribes lived in sand-roof homes in the winter that had floors with radiant heat to provide warmth in the extreme cold and occupied outdoor spaces during the harsh desert summer when temperatures top 100°.[16] Pueblo homes are also cool in the summer and warm in the winter due to the thermal mass of the thick adobe mud brick. And, of course, the chickee, with its open sides and thatched roof, feels quite cool when outside temperatures reach the 90s in South Florida. These levels of comfort are all accomplished without electrical heaters or air conditioners.

Looking at various Native American shelters, we also notice another major similarity—scale. With few exceptions (such as the Pueblo house of the Southwest or the plank house of the Northwest Coast), Native American structures are scaled to their inhabitants without much excess space—a practice that could be attributed to a variety of factors. Many of these homes were intended to be temporary in nature, and building large structures would be an extraordinary waste of time and materials. One of the biggest determining factors, however, was that perhaps their cultural systems predicated against the material excess associated with large, European-style homes with subdivided rooms for different functions.[17]

Again, we revisit the point that buildings are often much more complex than they appear from the exterior. According to Kostof, "Buildings are not only physical presences. To study as fully as we can what they are does not exonerate us from asking why they are there, and why they are the way they are."[18] It is hard to deduce the *why* based upon the *what*, but this book seeks to explain both the physical and the unobvious characteristics that define the Seminole chickee.

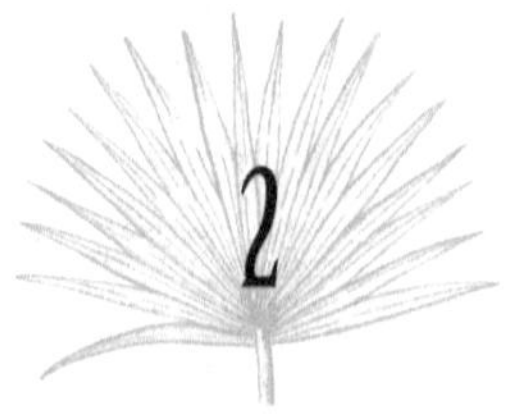

2

What Is a Chickee?

A chickee is the open-sided, thatched-roofed Seminole dwelling made from palmetto and cypress trees. Since the two distinct Seminole languages of Maskókî/Muscogee (Creek) and Mikasuki/Mikisúkî (Miccosukee or Hitchiti-Mikasuki) were traditionally not written down, there are a number of spelling variants for words within the Seminole vocabulary. The term is sometimes spelled *chiki*, *chikee*, *cheekee*, or *cheke*,[1] though *chickee* is the most common version seen today.

Chickee versus Tiki Hut

In the previous chapter, we looked at how people often think that all Native Americans lived in tipis or wigwams and have little knowledge about the wide variety of indigenous structures (including the chickee). Here, I unveil another mistaken counterpart to the chickee—the tiki hut. Though the chickee looks nothing like the tipi or wigwam, it has several similarities to the tiki hut.

The anthropologist Ethel Cutler Freeman developed an interest in studying the Seminoles during her winters spent in Naples, Florida, in the first few decades of the twentieth century. Although Seminoles were still very cautious of outsiders at this point, Freeman was able to convince W. Stanley Hansen (trusted adviser of the Seminoles in the late 1880s until his death in 1945) that she was qualified to conduct such a study. She made two initial visits to the Big Cypress Reservation on behalf of the American Museum of Natural History. Beginning in the winter of 1940, Freeman took her two children to the Florida Everglades and immersed herself in Seminole society. Freeman and her children lived with the Seminoles for the next eighteen winters.[2] In her 1942 article "We Live with the Seminoles," she included a photograph with the caption, "NOT SAMOA, but a typical thatched-roof village in the Florida Seminole reservation." She also refers to these thatched-roof homes as "chi-kis" in her article.[3] Although Freeman correctly identified Seminole structures, her article reflects the mistaken identity of the chickee and how similar chickees look to Polynesian-style thatched-roof huts.

Thatched-roof huts are a mainstay in most tropical locales. In hot and humid South Florida, thatched huts are everywhere—at beachside bars and restaurants, at hotels and pools, and in people's backyards. Some of these open-sided palmetto thatched structures are Polynesian-style "tiki" huts, while others are authentic Seminole chickees. People use the terms interchangeably because at first glance it is often difficult to tell the two types of structures apart. Chickees do share many similarities with the huts originating from the South Pacific islands—similar shapes, sizes, and materials. The major difference lies more in who builds them rather than the outward appearance. It is critical to differentiate between these two types of structures for several reasons.

Tiki culture in the United States gained popularity beginning in the 1930s in California with the opening of two "tiki bars": Don the Beachcomber and Trader Vic's. The fascination with Polynesian-style imagery, food, drinks, and architecture grew to become a phenomenon in the post–World War II era. Soldiers brought back souvenirs from their time spent in the South Pacific; Hawaii became a state and air travel started to the islands; and books, movies, and television shows (especially *Gilligan's Island*) gave Americans a taste of this tropical style. People hosted luaus in their backyards, donned Hawaiian shirts, and sipped sugary rum-based tiki cocktails. Soon "tiki palaces" popped up all over the United States. Though the tiki obsession was often a far cry from authentic South Pacific culture, what people saw on television or drank at their local thatched-roof watering hole infiltrated their minds. People yearned for an exotic escape from reality.[4]

During this tiki craze that swept America, the Seminoles residing in South Florida started to experience some interesting changes. As the pressure to move out of chickees and into modern homes was increasing, Seminoles started capitalizing on an aspect of their culture that had not before been sold en masse to outsiders—commercial chickee building. According to Chairman James E. Billie, Johnny Tucker and his brother Jimmie, in Hollywood, Florida, were perhaps the first Seminoles to start a successful chickee building business in the 1950s (though commercial chickee building technically began with the tourist camps of the 1920s). Chickee building became one of the more lucrative ways to make money during that time. It also allowed Seminoles to utilize their skills and showcase their culture while helping South Floridians live out their dream of having a piece of tropical paradise.

There have been many significant chickee builders over the years—those who have constructed hundreds, if not thousands, of chickees.[5] Many other Seminoles have made a name for themselves through chickee building businesses, both on-reservation and off-reservation. William McKinley Osceola (1883–1966), Miccosukee leader and head of the William McKinley Osceola Seminole Village on the Tamiami Trail, was featured in a 1952 Fort Lauderdale newspaper article written by Sam Hawkins. Osceola not only built the chickees in his tourist camp but extended his services to wherever there was a demand for chickees. Hawkins stated that ambitious people could harvest materials themselves and attempt to build a chickee, or that Osceola and his crew could deliver materials to a site if the homeowner wanted to construct the chickee him- or herself. Hawkins also outlined many steps in the construction process but pointed out the difficulties: "it is an interesting challenge to the craftsman to see if he can do a job comparable to Osceola with materials he can cut from the fields and swamps."[6] Even in the 1950s, it was apparent that Seminoles were superior chickee builders. Chickee building is an inherent part of Seminole culture.

Though the tiki craze of the 1950s and 1960s died down for at least a few decades, there remained a yearning for this tropical lifestyle in certain parts of the country. In an area such as South Florida, with its perpetual summers, plenty of palm trees, and tons of vacationers, this next incarnation of the craze, what tiki expert Sven A. Kirsten calls the "Jimmy Buffetization" of tiki culture,[7] has continued to exist. And while most of the country had moved on to the next trend in the 1970s, thatched-roof huts were still popular in South Florida. Though they were viewed as an antiquated form of housing for the Seminoles, they were viewed as trendy for non-Seminoles, as evidenced by an August 28, 1977, *Fort Lauderdale News and Sun-Sentinel* headline: "Chic Chickees Spell Success for Seminoles." The article draws attention to the success of Seminole chickee builders such as Johnny Tucker, Allen Jumper, Jack Henry Motlow, Jack Willie, and a young "Jimmie Billie."

Merely a few years before he was first elected chairman of the Seminole Tribe of Florida in 1979, James Billie thrived as a commercial chickee builder. He made a strong impression on the job site back in those days, especially when he pulled up in a Triumph TR7 sports car instead of a pickup truck. He stated: "I used to drive up in a truck and wear a little Seminole vest, and didn't make much money. . . . Now I've got a one-ton truck, and the little TR, and it seems that people say to themselves: 'Hey, he's a really successful businessman.' So business goes better."[8] Not only did he build chickees throughout Florida during that time, but while serving in the Vietnam War he used his thatching skills to help the Vietnamese build huts from coconut palm trees.

James Billie served as the chairman of the Seminole Tribe of Florida from 1979 to 2001 and again from 2011 to the present. When he was out of office, he fell back on his chickee building business for income. The name "Jim Billie Seminole Indian Chiki Huts" became synonymous with quality. Billie said in 2005, "A lot of people try, but only a Seminole Indian can build chickees correctly. . . . And the Chief's chickees are best of them all!" He went on to say that "every time in my life I've gotten down financially, I went back to building chickees and it brought me back up. . . . Long as there are wooden poles and leaves, I won't starve."[9] And "back up" he soon went, back to being the chairman of the Seminole Tribe. Many other Seminoles looked to chickee building for financial stability during the last few decades of the twentieth century, including tribal elder Bobby Henry.

The popularity of commercial chickee building has brought notoriety and wealth to many Seminoles but has come with its share of issues, particularly imitations. Non-Native builders in South Florida have often looked for construction clues from Seminole chickees and used what they learned to improve their own products.[10] Sometimes the skills were actually learned from the Seminoles themselves. As tribal members have seen an increase in financial stability in recent years due to gaming revenue, it has become more difficult for chickee builders to find willing laborers within the tribe. This has caused builders to look elsewhere for help, often leading them to hire non-Indians for the harvesting and construction processes. Even when non-Seminoles work on the construction crews, the structure created will still be considered an authentic chickee as long as the owner of the chickee building company is Seminole. Many times these non-Seminoles will later start their own separate hut building companies using the skills they learned from master chickee builders.[11] In this case, to protect the authenticity of a Native American craft, they cannot under any circumstances call their products chickees.

The anthropologist Alexander Spoehr stated in 1939 that building a chickee was a simple task: "It is relatively easy to construct a house. A man may build it himself, working part time for five or six days, or get a friend to help him and build it in two or three. Although sawed lumber is desirable for roof and floor, a house can easily be made of local materials. The attitude toward house building is rather casual, and no magical practices seem to be associated with house construction."[12] While it may be true that people around the globe have been building and thatching huts for thousands of years, Spoehr certainly oversimplified the chickee building process.

A master chickee builder can easily tell when a chickee is built by a non-Seminole or when a builder of any origin takes shortcuts in his or her work. The artisanal nature of chickee building truly sets the finished product apart. In her 1977 article in the *Miami Herald*, Kathryn Hall Proby calls Native Americans "America's original construction workers." She eloquently described thatching a roof: "In rhythmic motions, Howard handed up one frond at a time to Jimmy, the top of the frond twisted downward, forming a symmetrical design on the inside. The design rivals the intricate patchwork skirts of Indian women, while the outside thatching gives the appearance of soft hay in a stack."[13] It is very apparent, even to most outsiders, that thatching an authentic Seminole chickee is not a simple or haphazard process.

Hut building is big business in South Florida, and the competition is stiff. A quick Internet search returns countless results for "tropical hut" builders. Some of these companies offer both chickees and tiki huts, while others specialize in one type of structure or the other. The consumer may or may not really understand the difference, but Seminoles have built their reputations as the best hut builders.

Wade Osceola worked as a chickee builder for twenty years in and around the Hollywood Reservation. He said that after Hurricane Andrew, people realized that Seminoles built a superior product. The structures built by non-Natives were completely destroyed, while the authentic chickees weathered the storm much better. The materials were the same, but the quality of construction varied. According to Osceola, "Seminoles also put more passion in their construction techniques because building chickees is not only a business—it is an inherent part of Tribal culture." Fortunately, laws have been put into place to help protect the authenticity of chickees.

Codes and Laws Pertaining to Chickees

Chickees were specifically defined in, and exempted from, the 2001 Florida Building Code 553.73, Section 8, part i: "The following buildings, structures, and facilities are exempt from the Florida Building Code as provided by law, and any further exemptions shall be as determined by the Legislature and provided by law: Chickees constructed by the Miccosukee Tribe of Indians of Florida or the Seminole Tribe of Florida. As used in this paragraph, the term 'chickee' means an open-sided wooden hut that has a thatched roof of palm or palmetto or other traditional materials, and that does not incorporate any electrical, plumbing, or other nonwood features." The same exemption was noted in the updated 2010 Florida Building Code under Section 102.2 (h). This specification keeps non-Seminoles (or non-Miccosukees) from using the term *chickee* to describe their structures in order to avoid meeting the strict requirements of the Florida Building Code. It also helps support the authenticity of chickees by allowing Seminoles to continue to construct these structures in a traditional way without adhering to the Florida legislation. It is important to note here that not all chickees would be exempt from the code—only those basic structures without electricity, plumbing, or nonwood features (such as concrete flooring). Zoning laws for the area in which the chickee was built would still apply, however.

Chickees are further protected under the Indian Arts and Crafts Act of 1990: "The Indian Arts and Crafts Act of 1990 (P.L. 101-644) is a truth-in-advertising law that prohibits misrepresentation in marketing of Indian arts and crafts products within the United States." Simply put, it is illegal to sell art or crafts under the pretense that they were produced by Indians. The law carries hefty penalties—for individuals, up to a $250,000 fine or up to five years in prison for the first offense. Businesses can be prosecuted and fined up to $1 million. The law usually applies to smaller craft items such as Indian jewelry, baskets, pottery, or clothing, but chickees are also covered under the law because they are built by master artisans.

Though not a part of every American's vocabulary, people familiar with the word *chickee* automatically associate it with Seminoles. Codes and laws such as these are intended to protect the integrity of chickees and ensure that non-Native builders do not claim to be authentic chickee builders. Even the laws, however, are not foolproof, and some incidents still occur. Seminole elder and master chickee builder Bobby Henry experienced this type of misrepresentation firsthand.[14] A hut building company near Key West was advertising that it built authentic Seminole chickees, constructed by Bobby Henry. In actuality, he had no association with this company whatsoever. The hut building company wanted to use a prominent name to advertise its business but misrepresented Seminole authenticity. Bobby Henry did not divulge to me the outcome of this falsification.

As consumers begin to understand the differences between chickees and other thatched huts, they can make their own decisions about the type of structure that best meets their needs. There are builders from all backgrounds who build beautiful huts, often just as durable as authentic chickees. These huts may also be cheaper in price. As long as consumers are informed of their options and know what is what, I hope that instances of misrepresentation will cease. There is a place in the hut building world for both chickees and other structures as long as each structure is clearly marketed with its proper origin.

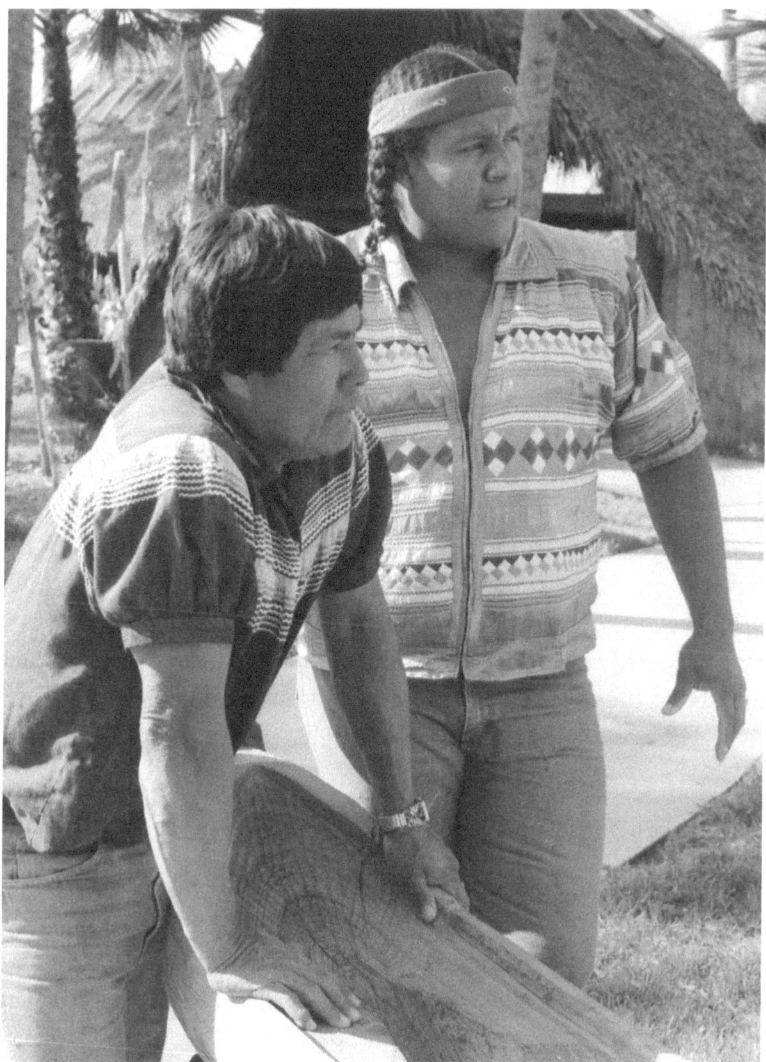

Figure 2.1. Bobby Henry (*left*) and Danny Wilcox (*right*) with a dugout canoe—Tampa, Florida. Bobby Henry, one of the most highly regarded Seminole tribal elders, was born in 1937, deep in the woods near Ochopee on the Tamiami Trail. He started building chickees at thirteen years of age, assisting his dad to "get the income coming in" and to help support his family. Bobby Henry focused his energy on building chickees for fifty-five years but is now retired. He was featured in a 1975 article in the *Miami Herald*, titled "Out-of-Work Seminole Falls Back on Heritage—It Helps to Pay Bills." In 1974, he lost his construction job and relied on his culture—building chickees—to help make ends meet. Henry also practices many woodworking crafts, including making canoes. State Archives of Florida, *Florida Memory*, http://floridamemory.com/items/show/106812.

3

The Architecture of Chickees

Two main components fit together to form the architecture of a chickee—the frame and the roof. The importance of these two building blocks cannot be overstated. With so few elements, a chickee must be constructed very carefully in order to be a success. By understanding both of these components, we can start to understand the architectural complexity of a seemingly straightforward structure.

The Chickee Structural System

The frame of the chickee provides strength. Chickee structural systems were made from either cypress or palmetto wooden members, though cypress was considered the more traditional choice. In some cases, chickees were also made from hard pine, according to Bobby Henry.[1] Seminoles used either Sabal palmetto (Arecaceae, genus *Sabal,* also known as cabbage palm) or cypress (*Taxodium spp.*), depending upon the availability of resources in the local environment. Seminoles farther south in the Everglades used cypress, while Seminoles in and around the Brighton Reservation normally used the trunks of the cabbage palm tree for the upright posts. Cypress trees, the most water-tolerant of all Florida species, are abundant in the swampy lands of the Big Cypress region but are less common around the Brighton Reservation. The Sabal palmetto or cypress trees provided all the structural components of the traditional chickees, from the upright posts to the roof framing system. In addition to being readily available (depending upon location), both cypress and cabbage palm trees are particularly good at resisting rot, making the original chickees fairly long-lasting.[2]

Modern chickees are held together by galvanized nails. Before nails became widely available, chickee components were notched and/or tied together. After the frame was constructed, the palmetto fans were thatched and tied down to the roofing frame. The upright posts had a carved-out round or V-shaped notch on top to allow the diagonal roofing members to rest securely inside. Alternately, the upright post might have been flat on top and the roofing components themselves notched. Thinner horizontal and diagonal members framed the roof. The interior framing system of the roof was traditionally composed of cypress, palm, or pine components cut to a variety of sizes. Today, some chickee builders use store-bought two-by-four (cut to a desired length) components to further simplify the construction process.

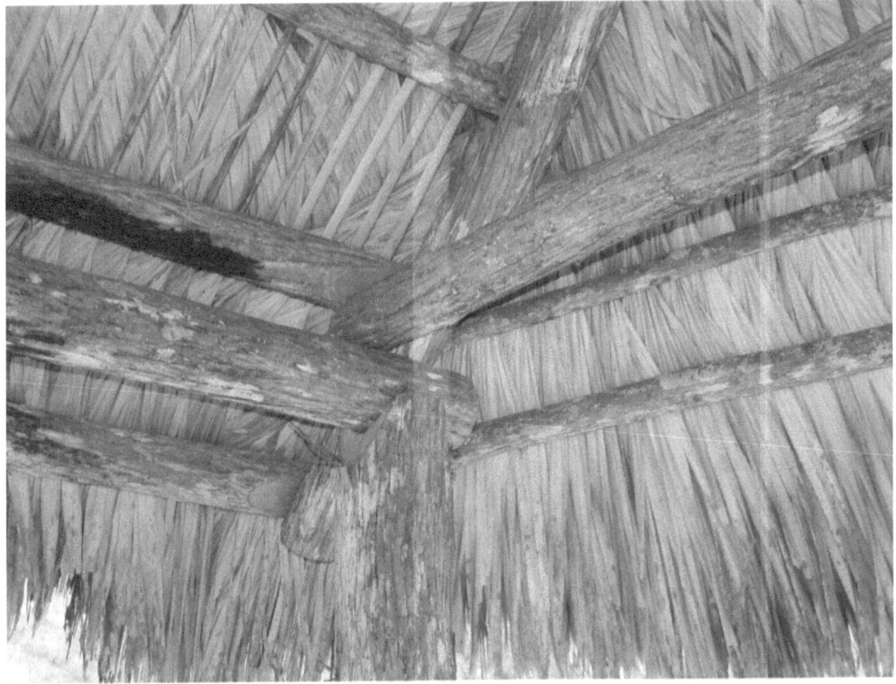

Figure 3.1. Chickee with notched upright posts. Note that the bark has been left on all the structural members in this modern example found at the Ah-Tah-Thi-Ki Museum. Photo by the author, Big Cypress Reservation, 2013.

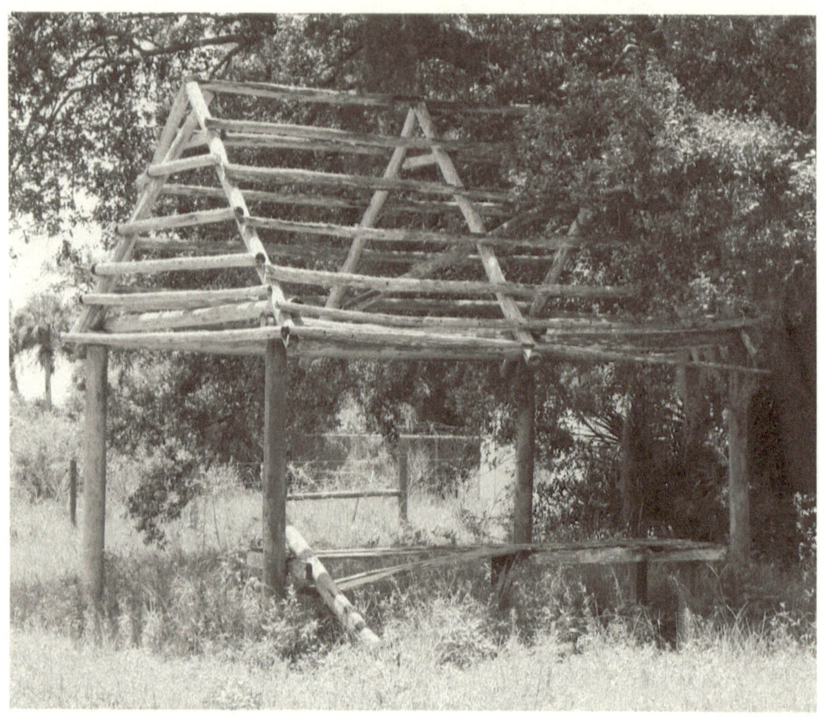

Figure 3.2. Bare chickee frame with no palmetto fronds. Photo by the author, Brighton Reservation, 2013.

Chickees traditionally had a minimum of four upright posts—one in each corner. Larger chickees, commonly seen on the reservations today, often require more uprights for stability. Chickee uprights, called "legs" by chickee builders, vary in diameter depending on the size of the structure or due to the preference of the builder or owner. Modern chickees exhibit great variety in the size of building materials, but the earlier chickees had relatively thin upright members. Because chickees were viewed more as temporary structures, it would have been a waste of resources to use extremely large cypress trees as the chickee legs. Seminoles needed to use components that were easier to harvest, which came from trees that were younger and lighter. In the 1800s, there was no access to chainsaws to cut down trees or trucks to haul them out of cypress domes. Seminoles used materials they could feasibly handle. From an architectural standpoint, small structures would need smaller uprights to support the roof and stabilize the building. In chickees today, the legs range in size from a few inches to over a foot in diameter. Keep in mind that while thicker legs may be very aesthetically pleasing, they come from larger, older trees that may not be as easy to locate and harvest.

Cypress is commonly harvested within the Big Cypress Reservation or farther south in the Big Cypress National Preserve (BCNP). Larger cypress poles are used for the legs (six to twelve inches in diameter and nine to thirty feet long), and the smaller ones (two inches in diameter) are used to create the roof rafters. The average chickee requires around twenty-five to forty cypress poles, and straighter trees produce superior raw building materials.

Chickee legs are usually set three feet into the ground to add overall stability to the structure. Today the posts are dug out with a posthole digger or shovel, and in the past they were dug with a shovel. Florida's sandy soil can be quite unstable, so it is imperative that the legs are set deep below the water table. The base of the legs was traditionally covered with dirt, while many chickees today are further reinforced by the addition of concrete at the base. Poured concrete adds much more stability for larger, heavier chickees. This is a modern practice, as the original chickees relied solely on the stability of the ground in which they were placed.

Today, the bark is usually stripped from the surface of the legs and other structural components. It was typically left intact on the traditional chickees. Stripping the bark, though tedious, helps prolong the life of the structure. According to chickee builder Matt Gopher, "The poles last longer if they are debarked. . . . It gets rid of the termites and other bugs that will eat into the wood."[3] The most common tool used to peel the bark from the poles today is the freshly sharpened draw blade. In the past, when draw blades were not commonly accessible, many Seminoles would use butcher knives for this process. A new method that has emerged over the past ten years is what some people call the "lazy man's way," or the pressure washer. This technique, though rapid, is dangerous because the pressure washer is so powerful it can easily remove the sprayer's toenails.[4] In some cases the stripped posts may be painted or stained to change the appearance of the structure.

Cypress is a highly prized, durable building material, but the population of these trees would be in jeopardy if there were not measures in place to prevent overharvesting. When the National Park Service conducted a study of the BCNP in 1981, it concluded that cypress might

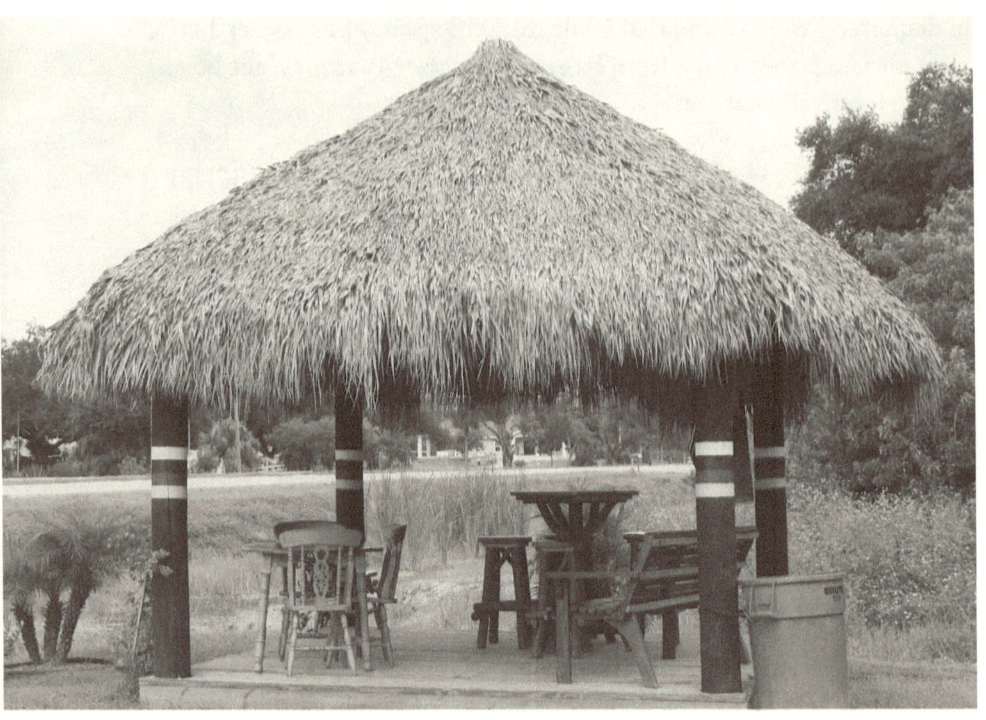

Figure 3.3. Chickee with upright posts painted with the Seminole medicine colors (white, black, red, and yellow). Photo by the author, Big Cypress Reservation, 2009.

eventually become overharvested due to the commercial chickee building industry:

> We could not identify any areas of the preserve as primary sources of cypress poles; generally in the BCNP they are harvested near villages or along secondary roadways, wherever the trees are readily accessible. We saw Indians cutting cypress near the intersection of US 41 and Loop Road. Cypress suitable for chickee construction is an abundant resource in the BCNP, and the number necessary for resident Indian home construction is insignificant. Commercial demand could eventually result in overharvest, however, since cypress normally grows quite slowly in South Florida. Damage due to cutting in inappropriate places seems to be a more serious problem, particularly since the areas near roads where the trees are most commonly harvested are also the places most visible to visitors.[5]

Today, more than thirty years later, when commercial chickee building is more popular than ever, the BCNP has not encountered any problems with overharvesting of cypress trees. Seminole and Miccosukee tribal members, as well as independent Seminoles, have unlimited access to harvesting cypress and palmetto in the BCNP as long as it falls under "Usual and Customary Use." As part of the BCNP's enabling legislation (October 1974), these groups are allowed to use the preserve for traditional purposes such as harvesting materials to build chickees, collecting plants for medicine, hunting animals for personal use, and even occupancy. The Seminole and Miccosukee people have been using that land since long before it was established as a preserve. They respect the land and know not to overharvest certain areas.

As cypress has become more difficult to obtain and since builders now have a plethora of options at their local lumberyards, chickee builders have started to implement different materials into their structures. It is a little surprising that the older builders have grown accustomed to this practice as well, as the older generations within the tribe are often viewed as more traditional. Pressure-treated pine, one of the most popular choices, can be easily cut to the builder's specifications. In some cases, chickee builders use precut utility poles for uprights. Pressure-treated wood has several advantages over untreated lumber. It is often more durable, longer lasting, and less susceptible to damage from insects compared to untreated lumber; it is also very accessible. Builders may simply obtain the uprights and other framing components from the lumberyard. Just as the rest of society has grown accustomed to the convenience of being able to purchase lumber in stores rather than harvest it from the wilderness, so have the Seminoles. This modern convenience does not necessarily detract from the authenticity of the finished structure and proves that Seminole culture is evolving in the modern world. On the downside, pressure-treated pine has a greenish appearance that may not be as aesthetically pleasing as fresh cypress. Additionally, because the lumber is treated with chemicals, it is not considered a sustainable material.

All the available options provide chickee builders the freedom of choice. Chickee builders have different preferences when it comes to building materials for both the legs and the rest of the frame. Some builders stick with tradition by using cypress, some primarily use pressure-treated lumber for durability and accessibility, and others use a combination of materials or base their decision upon whatever the owner wants. One builder I interviewed used only cypress to maintain a traditional appearance.[6] Bobby Henry typically used pressure-treated uprights in his designs and cypress for the rest of the frame. Joe Dan Osceola said he was the first Seminole to start using pressure-treated lumber for chickee building. He believes that using pressure-treated lumber is a good thing because termites and beetles get into the cypress, especially in the ribs and rafters. He even sometimes used landscaping timber for the ribs. Norman "Skeeter" Bowers also uses pressure-treated lumber because it lasts longer.

The Palmetto-Thatched Roof

The roof is one of the most important elements of any building—it turns a set of walls into a habitable space. Overhead coverings serve a utilitarian purpose by protecting inhabitants and their belongings from the weather and other elements. They can also reflect a specific craft or architectural style. Roofs may be made from a variety of materials, some of which—metal sheeting, wooden shingles, ceramic tile, and organic green roofs, to name a few—add to the overall character of the building. In some cases, the roof can be so significant that it defines the building. This is often the case when it comes to thatched roofs.

Thatched roofs are made from overlapping pieces of plant material that connect to form a watertight seal. Thatching dates back thousands of years, making it one of the oldest roofing techniques. When thatch is applied properly, the structure is watertight. Cutting corners or not thatching tightly enough can lead to leakage shortly after the roof is applied. The wooden chickee frame will have a similar lifespan no matter who builds it, but a chickee with a properly thatched roof will survive much longer than a poorly thatched chickee. All components of the chickee are important, but the thatched roof is what really elevates chickee building into such a significant art form.

Although the type of wood used to construct the chickee frame may vary, the roof is always thatched with Sabal palmetto fronds. Palmetto leaves are actually one of the most common materials used for thatching worldwide. The Sabal palmetto, or cabbage palm, is the state tree of Florida. This species of palm tree is so abundant in the Florida Ev-

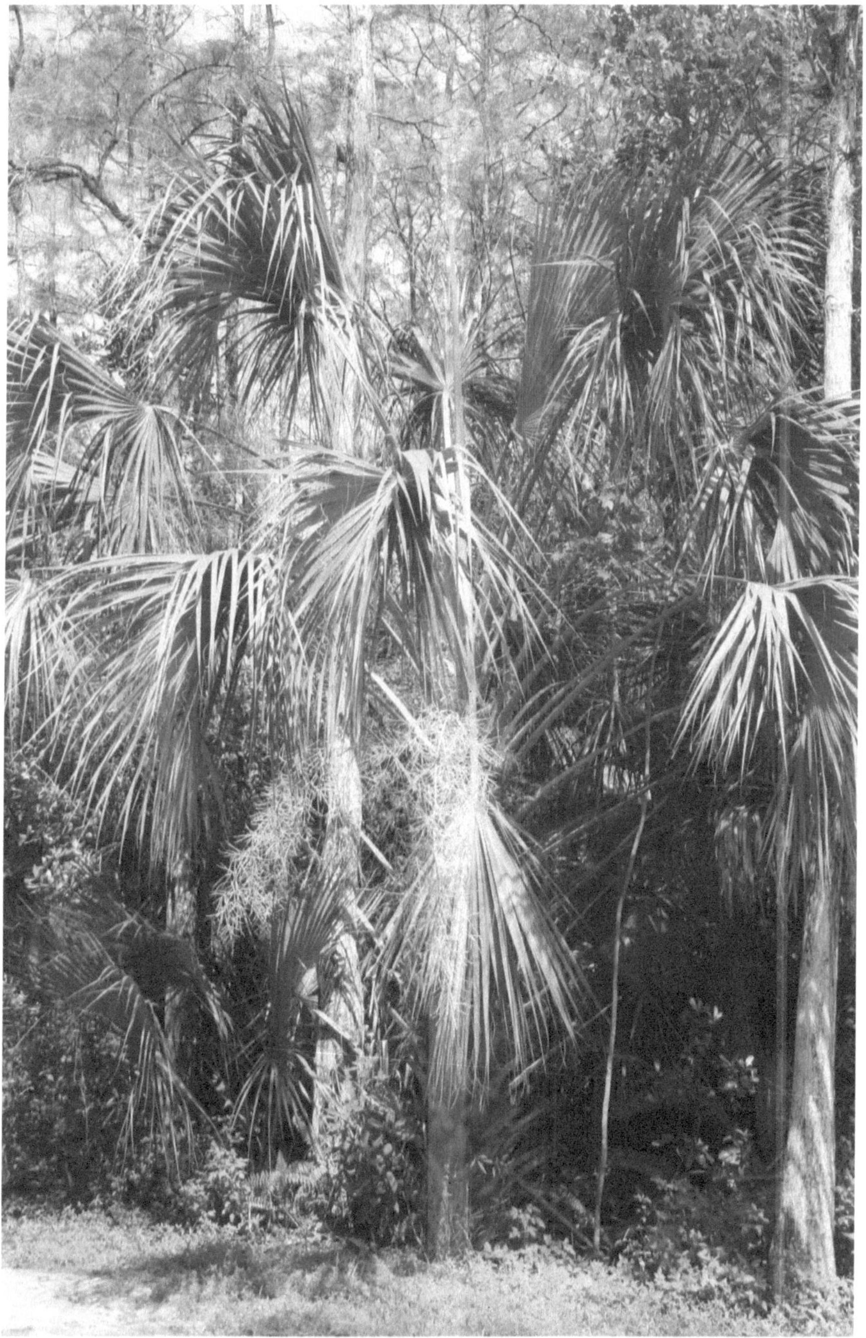

Figure 3.4. Cabbage palm trees behind the Ah-Tah-Thi-Ki Museum. Photo by the author, Big Cypress Reservation, 2013.

erglades that it seems to be the logical choice for a roofing material. In addition to providing building materials, the cabbage palm also provides a source of food—swamp cabbage, also known as hearts of palm. The Seminoles utilize other types of palm trees as well. Saw palmetto, another abundant species, is commonly used for crafts such as Seminole dolls or as the base of sweetgrass baskets.

A large number of cabbage palm trees grow along the roadside in southern Florida, and visitors may often notice harvesting crews cutting the fronds along the smaller roads of the state's interior. Harvesting palm fronds is not harmful to the environment. In fact, it helps regulate the growth of the cabbage palms themselves. Seminoles only remove

Sustainability

Sustainability, *eco-friendly*, and *green* are hot terms in the field of architecture and design today. Even before environmentally conscious design hit the mainstream, thatched-roof "architects" were incorporating sustainable techniques and materials into their dwellings.

The materials used for thatching may vary, but the architecture has a common thread—people use the materials around them to create buildings completely suited to their environment. The fact that thatched roofs are typically made from readily available materials means that supplies do not need to be brought in from other places. This process expends less energy and places less strain on the environment. Additionally, thatched roofs are often made from materials that are abundant and can be composted back into the earth when they have outlived their useful life. Builders are also careful not to overharvest their thatching materials so that the supply still exists for future rethatching needs and so that the health of the trees is not compromised. Thatched roofs are eco-friendly—without even trying!

Florida International University (FIU) professor Sarah Sherman created a sustainable interior design project based upon the Seminole chickee in 2009. Her students came up with different approaches to the chickee by incorporating new materials and building techniques and presented their designs to a panel of Seminoles as well as their professors and other students. Sherman summarized the results of the project and discussed how the Seminoles connect to the environment:

> To appreciate the Seminoles' connection with the environment, and specifically the chickee's original role within the village contrasted with its role in Tribal living today, we must first understand the term "sustainability."
>
> The commonly accepted meaning of sustainability provided by the United States Environmental Protection Agency is based on a simple principle: Everything that we need for our survival and well-being depends, either directly or indirectly, on our natural environment. Sustainability creates and maintains the conditions under which humans and nature can exist in productive harmony, which permits fulfilling the social, economic and other requirements of present and future generations. In general, sustainable building practices promote resource conservation including energy efficiency, renewable power, and water conservation features, while also considering environmental impact and waste minimization to create a healthy and comfortable environment and address issues such as historic preservation, access to public transportation and other community infrastructure needs. Builders and designers consider the entire life cycle of the building and its components as well as the economic, social and environmental impact.
>
> Understanding sustainability (or the capacity to endure), in this context, we can reflect on the many roles the chickee has served and grasp its importance to the Tribe as well as its consideration of Florida's natural systems. In a way, sustainability is the modern interpretation of the Seminole traditional belief that man has connection to his environment.
>
> If we view the chickee through the lens of sustainability it is clear that its origins sprang from land and the Seminoles' adaptations to Florida's sub-tropical environment. The building process, the materials and the location in the village site plan used environmental considerations and were the precursor to sustainable practices. The way of life and building techniques derived from the Seminoles' habitation at a time when Tribal survival was the primary focus. However, the chickee and its utility evolved over the Tribe's history.[1]

1. Sherman, "Sustainability and the Seminole Chickee."

some of the fronds of the trees, a practice that does not threaten the overall health of the trees. The fronds grow back within a year or less.

According to Sandy Billie Jr., when you collect the leaves, it is important to leave four or five fronds on the tree to ensure regrowth. "Rooster-tail" fans are young, and they curve around; they are not suitable for use in chickee roofs.[7] The palm leaves are attached when they are still a little green. This makes them easier to work with and allows the builder to thatch them into the appropriate pattern. One cannot wait too long before applying the thatching. Wade Osceola said that the longest you want to wait is about four or five days from the time the materials are harvested.[8] Otherwise, the leaves will become too brittle and will break when you weave them together. The leaves turn from a bright tan color to a dull tan when they have completely dried out.

Thatching is an inherently creative craft that allows for personality and creativity among builders, but it can also reflect familial influence. Thatching techniques are often passed down from generation to generation, a practice that helps build family ties and promotes community togetherness and bonding. For the Seminoles, thatching skills are transmitted through cultural systems and are the result of clan members coming together to build the structures for their camps. Within the camps, the skills are traditionally passed down from uncle to nephew or from father to son (or from mother/aunt to children in the cases when there were no men in the camps).

An effectively thatched roof provides a completely watertight system that keeps inhabitants and their belongings dry and protected from the elements. According to Chairman Billie, traditional chickees were built with a 6'-tall base roofline or lower, but Seminoles eventually raised the average height to 6½' to appear more inviting or accessible to outside visitors. The average height of a door is 6'8", so the 6' entrance of older chickees would feel substantially lower. This low roofline (or even lower ones, which were more common in the past) helped keep rain from blowing into the open-sided structure. The thatching extended beyond the bottom edge of the roof frame to provide a drip edge. Rainwater that ran down the roof of the chickee was collected and used for cleaning, according to the late Betty Mae Jumper: "And, another thing about the rain, we would use the water for washing. The rain would come off the corner of the chickee. We

Family Ties

Joe Dan Osceola was born in the Everglades. He moved to the Brighton Reservation at ten years old with his mother and siblings when his father died. He attended public school in Okeechobee and then went to Georgetown College in Kentucky. He grew up in a chickee and remembers that it became quite uncomfortable during the rainy season and during winter when they only had a sheet of canvas to block the wind.

Although Joe Dan is a tribal senior, he has only been building chickees for the last thirty years. He did not learn chickee building as a child like most other builders, and in fact he did not learn it at all until he married his second wife, Virginia, who came from a very traditional background. He learned his chickee building techniques through his in-laws.[1] Joe Dan commented that he was a very creative builder in his prime. "I'm always looking for ways to build a new variation of a hut," he said. "Everything is hand fitted. No two trees grow alike and no two chickees will ever be alike."[2] This is certainly a fact I confirmed during the chickee survey, where each chickee had at least subtle differences.

Joe Dan Osceola was the president of the Seminole Tribe of Florida, Inc., from 1967 to 1971. The Seminole Tribe is divided into two governing bodies—the Seminole Tribe of Florida (the government side), and the Seminole Tribe of Florida, Inc. (the financial side). He was the youngest person across Indian Country to be elected as his tribe's leader. He engaged in numerous entrepreneurial activities in addition to chickee building, including running a tobacco shop (First American Tobacco Shop) and a gift shop. He and his wife still operate the gift shop today, but Joe Dan has not built any chickees for years. He told me that he misses that part of his life and remembers it fondly.

Wade Osceola, Joe Dan's son, is also a chickee builder. Wade was born and raised on the Hollywood Reservation. He started building chickees in 1987 when he was seventeen years old; it was his primary occupation for twenty years. He and his two brothers helped his father with the chickee building business. Wade learned chickee building from his father. "He was a drill sergeant," he laughed, "but he instilled in me a strong work ethic." At first he did it because he had to, but he soon came to en-

(*Continued*)

joy it. He does not build chickees as a business anymore, but going back to the ceremonial ground chickees once or twice a year at the Green Corn Dance helps remind him of his culture. It helps put him in the right frame of mind. He had been helping rebuild the ceremonial chickees at the time of the interview.

Sandy Billie Jr. also learned chickee building from his father, the late Sandy Billie Sr. (1925–2003). Sandy Jr. started building chickees when he was six years old, being the "handyman" who nailed down the fans. Sandy never had an official chickee building business but instead owned a lawn service. Nevertheless, he has constructed five chickees by himself, and he assisted his father in building several others. The late Sandy Billie Sr. built what was once the largest chickee on the Brighton Reservation. It was about 80'×40', with a concrete floor, and was about three stories high. "People admired it," Sandy remembered. Like many other builders, his father built chickees to provide money for his family. Sandy Jr. was not always eager to help in the chickee building process. "When I was younger," he said, "I was a party animal, I took my time collecting the leaves. When you are mature and you have a family to provide for, you gather the leaves faster."

1. Joe Dan Osceola, interview by author, Hollywood Reservation, Fla., July 5, 2013.
2. Rex, "Building Business Indians Pass on Chickee Tradition."

would shampoo and use soap and take a shower under the rainwater. We also would put out big pails to catch the rainwater for washing clothes."[9]

Thatched leaves were traditionally tied to the roof support system. During the Seminole Wars (1816–1859), fleeing Indians did not have access to nails. All components of the chickee had to be connected by other means. In a 1979 interview, Milton D. Thompson recalled his observations of chickees before the widespread availability of nails: "I have seen some of them in the early twenties where all the thatching and timbers were tied with deer hide—with strings and so on.

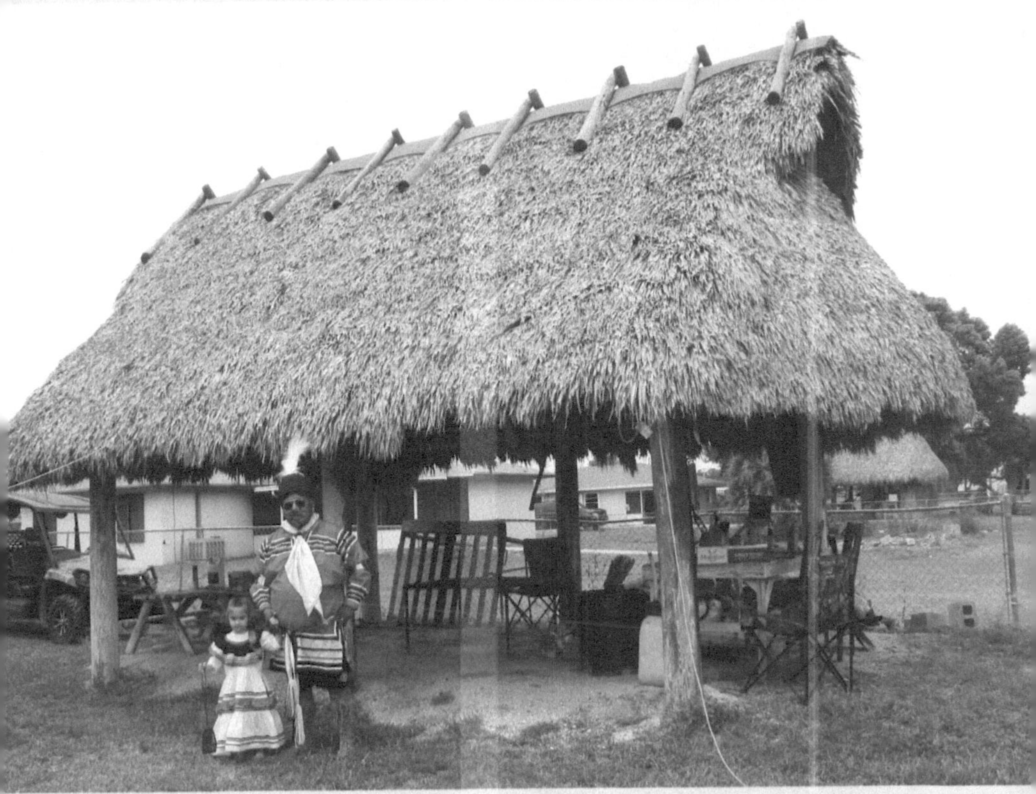

Figure 3.5. Chickee builder Sandy Billie Jr. with his granddaughter in front of the cook chickee behind his house. Sandy only uses the cook chickee a few times a year, particularly to celebrate July 4th. Although it is a national holiday, it is also the day his father was born and the day he died. Sandy likes to honor his father every year under that chickee. Photo by the author, Brighton Reservation, 2013.

Now, of course, they use nails, but in the early days they would tie the timbers together and tie the fans on the timbers. They were all tied, not nailed on."[10] Galvanized nails made their way to the reservations shortly after. Roy Nash reported in 1930 that, at that time, the nails were quite affordable and accessible, and most chickees he encountered had thatch attached with nails.[11] The use of nails greatly sped up the chickee building process. Commercial chickee building would be nearly unimaginable without such modern conveniences.

The roof ridge is the horizontal line where the sloping sides of the roof intersect at the top. This critical and often vulnerable connection

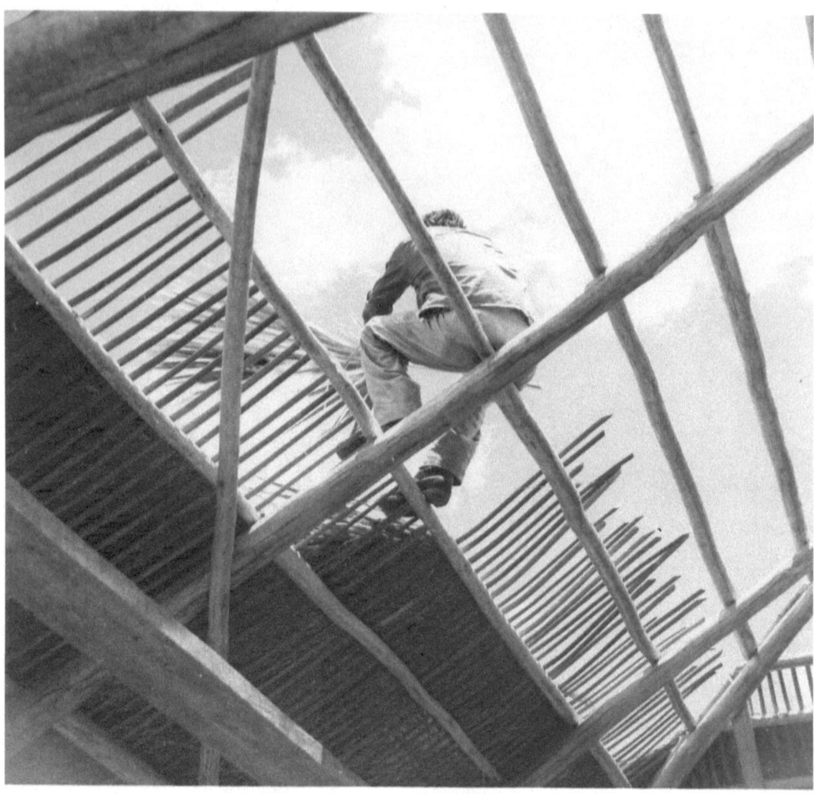

Figure 3.6. Unidentified man attaching palm fronds to the cypress frame of a chickee roof. Ah-Tah-Thi-Ki Museum, Boehmer Collection, 1961 (ATTK catalog no. 2009.34.390).

requires special attention for weatherproofing. As the highest point of the roof, the ridge is a prime target for inclement weather. Protection is critical. Various materials can be used as a ridge cap for chickees, and among the materials of choice are tar paper, asphalt, or metal (such as tin). The ridge cap reinforces the top of the roof where water could penetrate the thatching. Small wooden members called roof weights crisscross slightly to keep the ridge cap in place. The roof weights on chickees are usually round logs with a small diameter and a few feet in length. The bark is either left on the members for a natural look or stripped off. In some cases, 2"×4" wooden boards are used to hold the ridge cap in place. Chickees feature several sets of roof weights, spaced at varying distances, depending on the span of the roof.

All roofs require maintenance and eventual replacement. Most

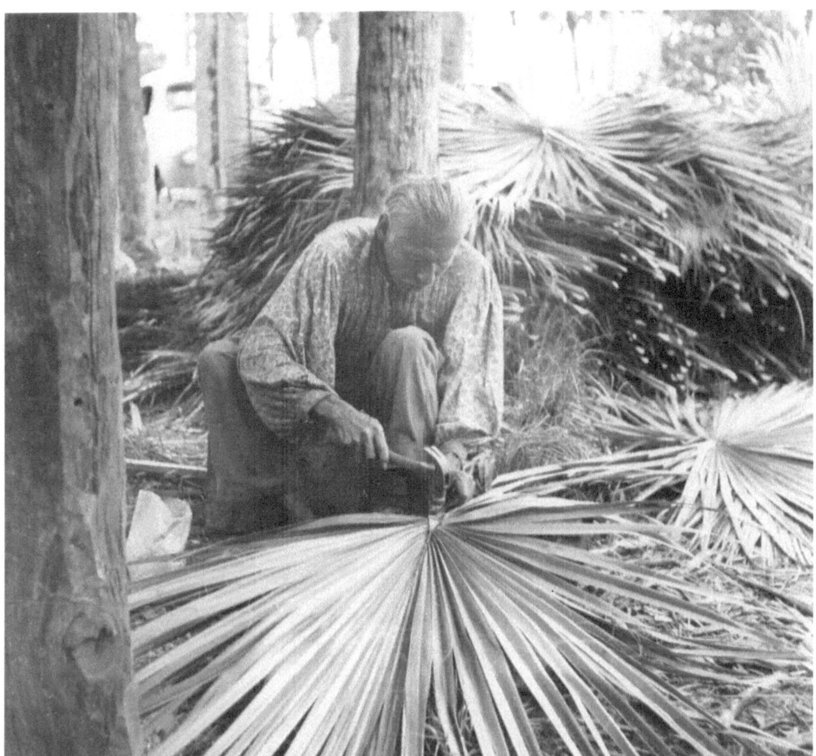

Figure 3.7. Seminole Ben Wells hammering a nail into a palm frond. After the nails are inserted, the palm fronds are handed to the person installing them on the roof frame. Ah-Tah-Thi-Ki Museum, Boehmer Collection, c. 1960 (ATTK catalog no. 2009.34.1460).

chickee roofs last only five to seven years before they need rethatching. By that time, they usually begin to develop holes that eventually cause the roof to fail. In some cases, a chickee roof could last longer, depending upon how tightly the thatch was applied. Once the roof is rethatched, the structure should be stable for another five to seven years. The upright posts usually last twenty years, or potentially longer when using nontraditional materials such as pressure-treated pine.

The roof is where a chickee builder's skills will truly shine. A chickee roof thatched by Bobby Henry, for example, was so tightly woven that it would last nearly fifteen years—more than twice the lifespan of the average roof. He would also add a large overhang from the corner of the uprights, a minimum of thirty-six inches and sometimes up to eight feet, for additional rain protection.

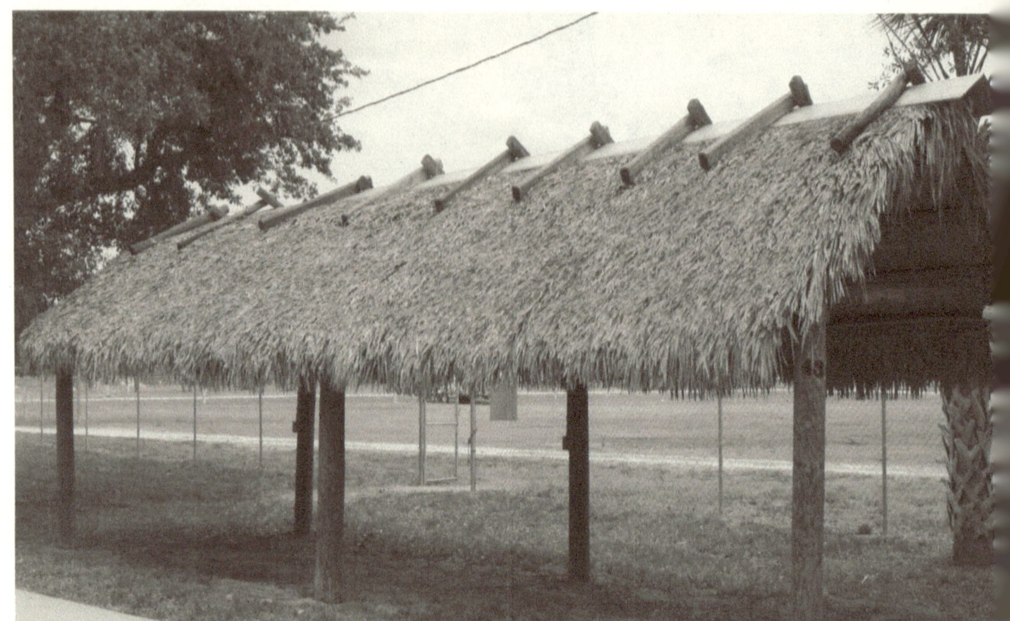

Figure 3.8. Chickee featuring a metal ridge cap and 2″×4″ roof weights. Photo by the author, Brigh
Reservation, 2011.

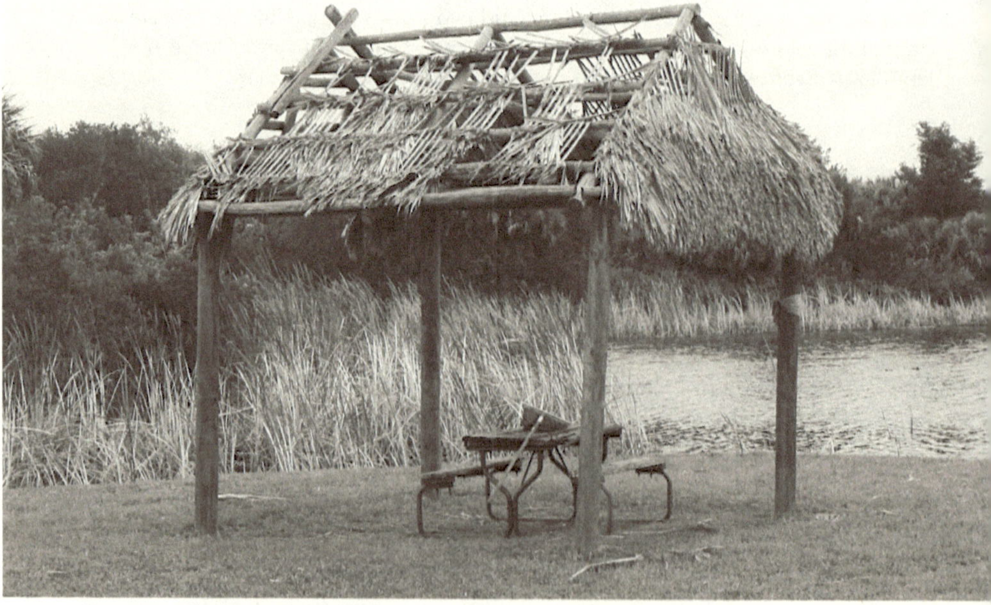

Figure 3.9. Chickee with roof in poor condition. The roof needs to be rethatched. Photo by the auth
Brighton Reservation, 2011.

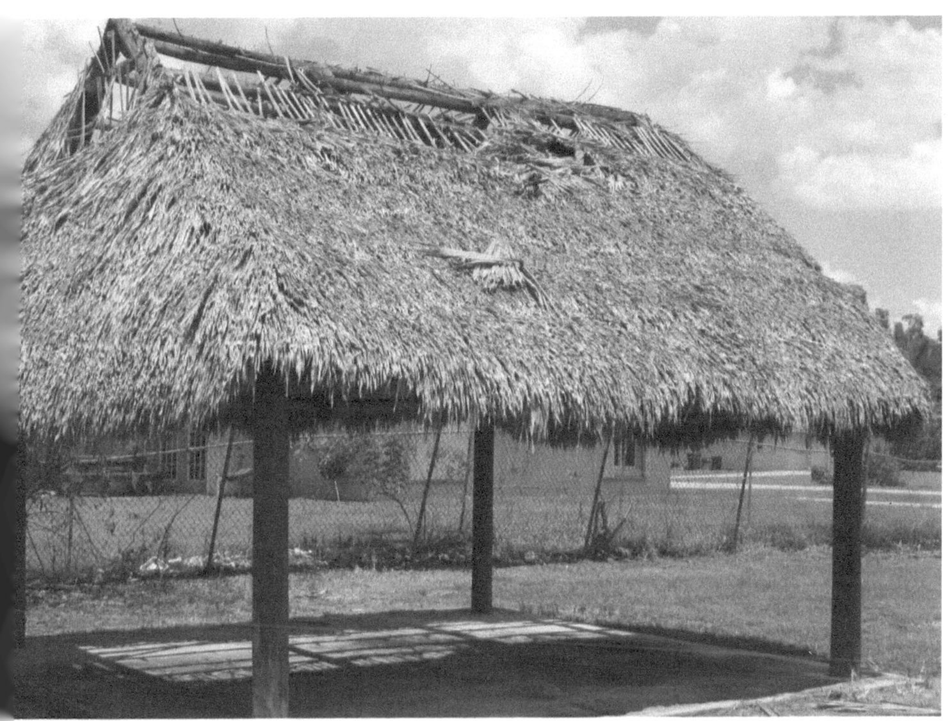

Figure 3.10. Chickee at Big Cypress with numerous holes in the roof. Photo by the author, 2009.

Clay MacCauley, a retired missionary employed by the federal government to report on the living conditions of Indians, was sent to study the Seminoles by the Smithsonian Institution in the late 1800s. He gave a detailed description of the artistic nature of the chickee roof in his 1880 account: "The thatching of the roof is quite a work of art: inside, the regularity and compactness of the laying of the leaves display much skill and taste on the part of the builder; outside—with the outer layers there seems to have been less care taken than with those within—the mass of leaves of which the roof is composed is held in place and made firm by heavy logs, which, bound together in pairs, are laid upon it astride the ridge. The covering is, I was informed, water tight and durable and will resist even a violent wind."[12] The view from underneath a chickee is still artistic to this day. Some chickee builders apply the thatch in one direction, while others use the zigzag method, also called the "right hand left hand method," in which the underside of the roof shows the fronds going in opposite directions in alternate rows.[13]

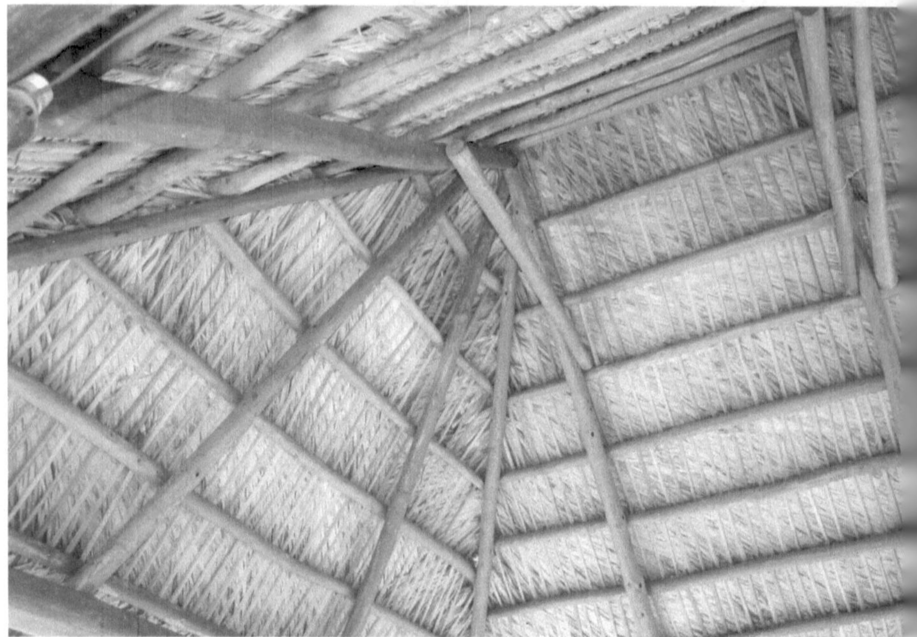

Figure 3.11. Underside of a chickee roof thatched in one direction. Photo by the author, Brighton
ervation, 2013.

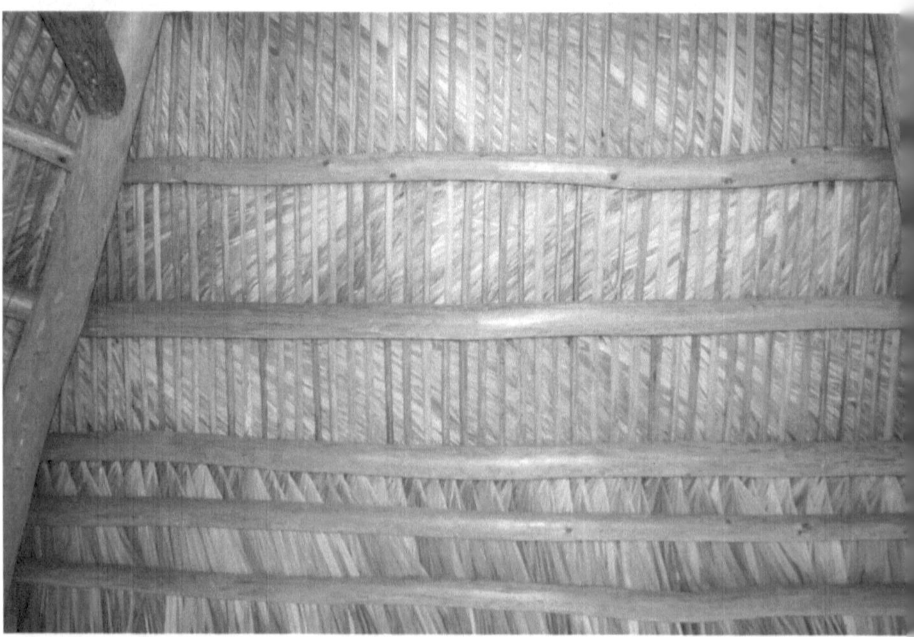

Figure 3.12. Underside of a chickee roof featuring zigzag thatching. Photo by the author, Big Cyp
Reservation, 2013.

Bobby Henry shared with me some other tips for building long-lasting chickees: The roof ridge is a very vulnerable part of a chickee; if you thatch the top of the roof three times on itself, you will eliminate the need for a ridge cap underneath the roof weights. Chickees built at the beach wear out faster, so it is best to double up on the thatching in the corners. If you thatch in a zigzag method, the water will not trickle straight down and make holes in the roof. Several other builders also mentioned the importance of the zigzag method. Not only is it aesthetically pleasing, but it also creates a more watertight structure. Ronnie Billie, on the other hand, always thatches from the left (instead of from the right or zigzagged) due to his clan's (Wind Clan) dancing traditions at the Green Corn Dance Ceremony.

Chairman Billie pointed out that the chickees in Big Cypress and along the Tamiami Trail historically had steeper roofs than those in Brighton. The steeper pitch allowed the structure to shed rain more

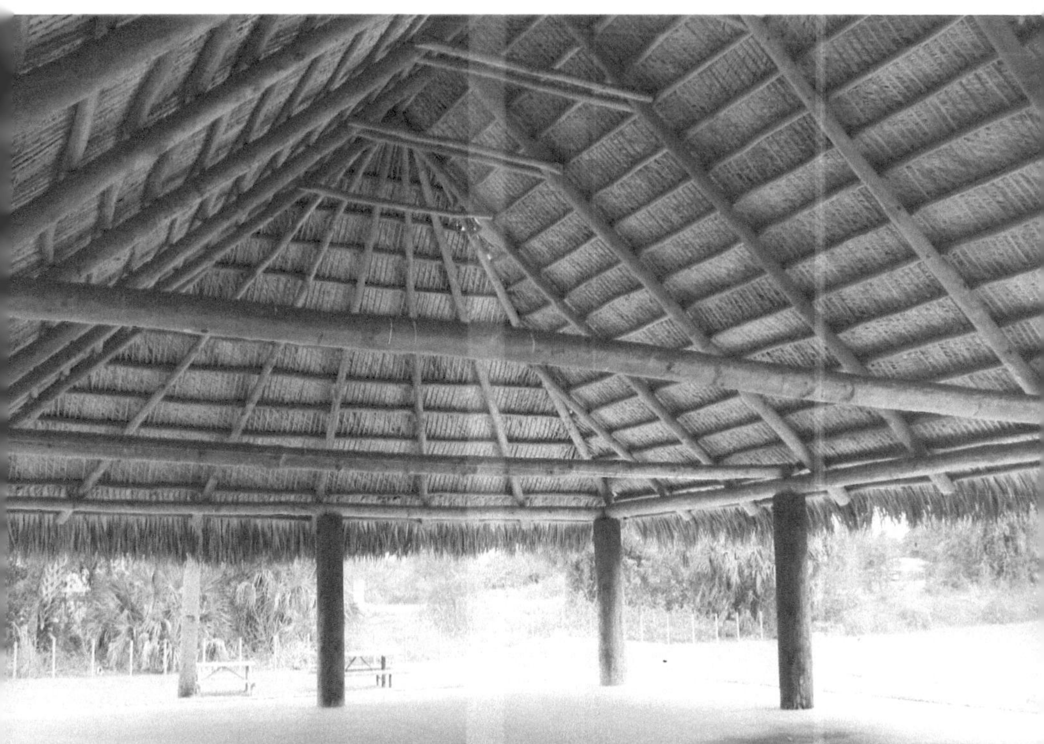

Figure 3.13. Interior of the chickee built by James Billie at the preschool on the Brighton Reservation. Not a single palm frond is out of place. Photo by the author, 2013.

easily, which was particularly important in the Big Cypress area, with its long rainy season. Chickees in Big Cypress were built with a 12:12 roof pitch (45° angle), while the chickees in Brighton typically had a 6:12 pitch (26.57° angle). Chairman Billie increases the lifespan of the chickees he builds by thatching the palm fronds at a distance of approximately two inches, or three finger-widths, apart. This method is more expensive because it requires more palm fronds and labor, but it ultimately results in the highest-quality roofs. In a 1977 article, James Billie states: "Building a good chickee is an art, and they are paying for the art itself, too."[14] He made a substantial living off those artistic chickees and has always refused to reveal his specific thatching techniques.

Thatched Roofs around the Globe

The organic materials used for thatching are widely available. In some areas around the world, few other options for roofing materials exist.[1] Thatching materials vary from location to location based on climate, but they typically fall into three main categories: soft-stemmed grasses; stiff-stemmed, reedlike grasses; and leaves such as palm.[2] Thatching materials typically either occur naturally or are a by-product of an agricultural process such as food harvest.[3] Not quite as common are plants grown specifically for the purpose of becoming thatch.[4]

Vernacular architecture (architecture indigenous to a particular region or period of time, created to meet specific needs and reflect cultural values) around the globe commonly exhibits the use of thatched roofs. Indigenous peoples such as the Mayas in the Yucatan Peninsula and the Incas in the Andes of South America used thatched roofs on some of their housing. The tukul, a circular hut made with wattle-and-daub construction topped with a thatched roof made from sumbalit grass, is the most common house type in the Ethiopian highland villages in Africa.[5] In Galicia, Spain, the palloza house with a rye thatched roof is very common. In Singapore, attap palm is a common roof covering. In Indonesia, roofs are commonly made from alang alang thatch—a type of grass. In Papua

New Guinea in the South Pacific, the Raun Haus (or roundhouse) features a thatched roof made from kunai grass. Large cottages and homes throughout the United Kingdom feature sophisticated thatched roofs made from thick layers of reed and straw. Back in Florida, thatched roofs can be found on the reconstructed council house and church at Mission San Luis in Tallahassee. This site was the main village of the Apalachees in the mid- to late 1600s and was the Spaniards' westernmost capital in Florida.

Thatched roofs have many advantages, as described by master thatcher Nicolas Hall in his thatching handbook. Hall writes that thatched roofs fare extremely well in both hot and cold temperatures because of their insulating properties (which also create excellent sound control). They are also very versatile, allowing builders to apply them to a variety of different roof shapes where other, more rigid materials would be hard to apply. Applying a thatched roof does not require the use of sophisticated machines or tools. In fact, a thatched roof can be installed with something as simple as a hammer and nails. Thatched roofs are also relatively inexpensive to maintain. They can often be patched instead of replaced in their entirety. Many of the materials used for thatching grow rather quickly—grass and palm leaves both regrow in a short amount of time.[6] Robert West, another master thatcher, notes that construction costs are often lower for thatched roofs because there is no need for gutters, downspouts, and soffits to remove rainwater like there is with other roofing types.[7] Thatched roofs naturally drain themselves when installed properly. Hall mentions that thatching can also boost the local economy by providing opportunities for small businesses that specialize in applying thatched roofs.[8]

Like any building element, thatched roofs also have their share of disadvantages. Thatch comes from organic material, which makes it susceptible to decay. Thatched roofs, thick or thin, often become a haven for animals and insects that ultimately destroy the roof and make for an uncomfortable living environment for the inhabitants beneath. Thatched roofs are more combustible than other roofs, and insuring a house made with a thatched roof can often be quite expensive. Seminole chickees have been known to burn down in a matter of minutes. Lewis Gopher,

(*Continued*)

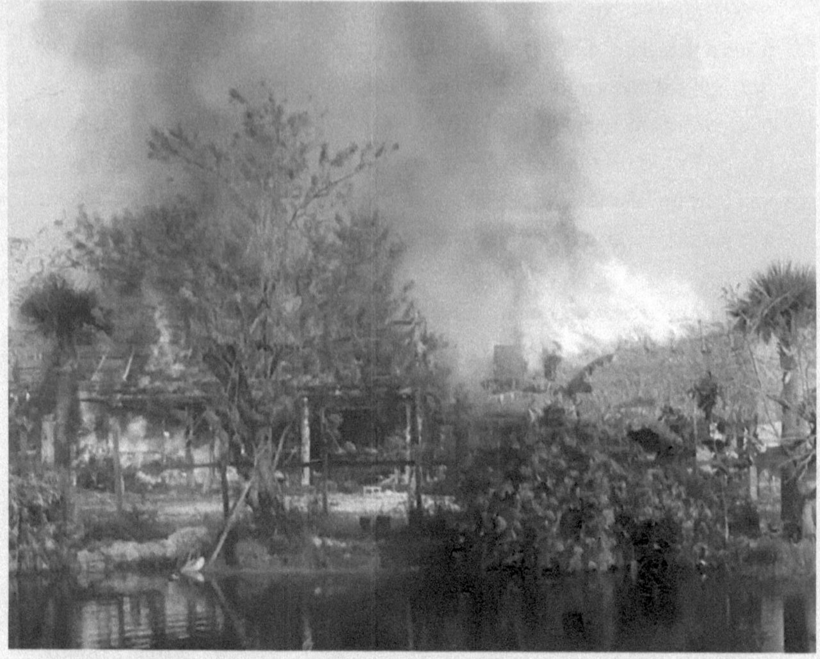

Figure 3.14. *Chickee fire.* When chickees catch fire, they burn down quickly. Peter Gallagher, *Seminole Tribune*, c. 1980s.

tribal member from the Brighton Reservation, distinctly remembers only seeing one chickee burn down, at the Green Corn Dance when he was eight years old. He remembers people passing water buckets in a line to get water to the flame-engulfed structure. He does not recall just how quickly it burned but knows it happened almost instantly.[9]

Proper roof pitch is critical for thatched roofs—it must be steep enough to allow adequate water run-off (usually 45°); otherwise, water can collect and deteriorate the roof at a rapid rate.[10] Furthermore, thatching is also quite labor intensive.[11] Despite these drawbacks, thatched-roof structures are durable, versatile spaces that have a personality second to none.

Although the lifespan of certain types of thatch is relatively short (especially palm, with a typical lifespan of less than ten years), other thatching materials can outlive inorganic roofs. As with most building crafts, the quality of the roof will depend mostly on the skill of the thatcher and the quality of materials used, but the materials themselves do have a limited lifespan. Long straw lasts fifteen to twenty-five years, combed wheat reed can last thirty to forty years, and water reed—one of the most common thatching materials in Europe—can last fifty to eighty years.[12] According to a study of the life expectancy of home components conducted by the National Association of Homebuilders and Bank of America Home Equity,[13] asphalt shingle roofs (the most common roofing type in the United States) last around twenty years or less. Wooden shakes and shingles last in the twenty-to-thirty-year range. The most durable roofing materials—slate, copper, and clay/concrete—last the longest, at fifty years or more. Thatched roofs stack up quite well when compared to other roofing types in terms of life expectancy in general, but chickee roofs typically only last five to seven years (more, if thatched tightly and if weather conditions are favorable).

While thatch is still primarily used in traditional applications, it should not be viewed as an old-fashioned building material. "Living on the edge," a structure by Arjen Reas, mixes a contemporary house with a traditional Dutch farmhouse and features thatching not only on the roof but also on parts of the exterior walls. Het Entreehuis, by Bureau B+B in the Netherlands, resembles a barn or vernacular Dutch structure but

(*Continued*)

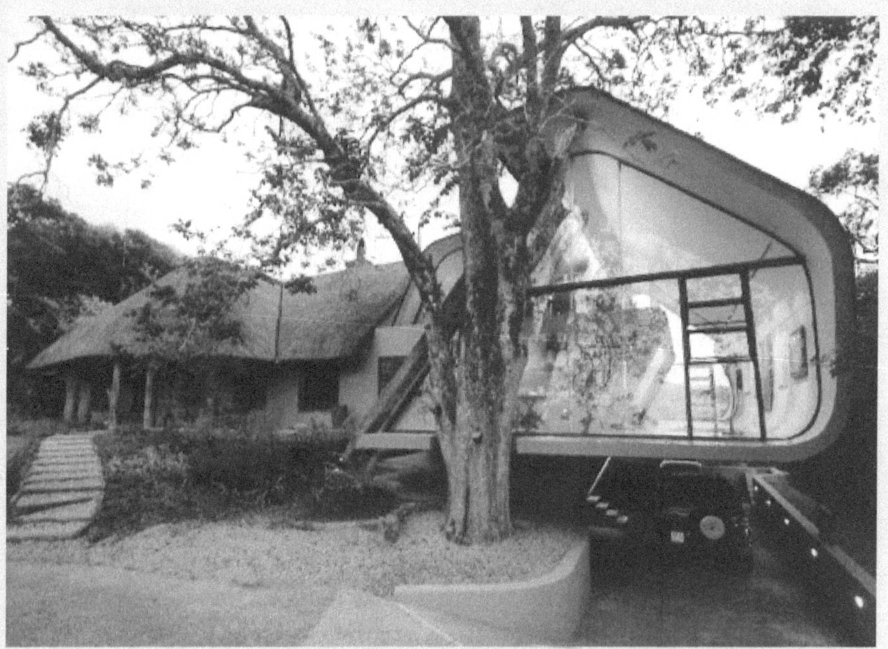

Figure 3.15. Exterior view of the Wright House by Elmo Swart Architects. Photo by Swart Architecture + Photography.

features a thatched roof that completely stops at the junction of the roof and exterior wall rather than overlapping like the traditional structures would. This subtle change creates a much more contemporary appearance. The Wright House in Durban, South Africa, by Elmo Swart Architects, is perhaps a perfect example of juxtaposing old and new techniques in contemporary architecture. The Wright House features an ultra-modern curved feature attached to a traditional thatched roof structure. The C-shaped metal and glass addition mimics the curves and lines of the thatched area so that the overall structure remains quite unimposing in the midst of the modestly sized thatched-roof houses so common in South Africa.

1. Hall, *Thatching*, 1.
2. Ibid., 3.
3. Robert West, *Thatch*, 9.
4. Hall, *Thatching*, 3.
5. Kahn and Easton, *Shelter*, 8.
6. Hall, *Thatching*, 1–2.
7. West, *Thatch*, 10.
8. Hall, *Thatching*, 2.
9. Lewis Gopher, interview by author, Brighton Reservation, Fla., June 20, 2013.
10. Hall, *Thatching*, 9.
11. Ibid., 2.
12. West, *Thatch*, 42.
13. National Association of Home Builders/Bank of America Home Equity, "Study of Life Expectancy of Home Components," 8.

Floors and Walls

Traditional chickees used for cooking, storage, and entertaining had a dirt floor. Former Tribal Historic Preservation Office (THPO) cultural adviser Tony Billie explained to tribal archaeologist Maureen Mahoney that closer to the Tamiami Trail, clay was sometimes built up as flooring material in the wet season to keep inhabitants dry. Sleeping chickees, however, had a raised platform made from wooden logs or planks. The platforms were traditionally supported by a set of posts separate from the uprights that held up the roof.[15] Today, chickees have a variety of flooring options. Some have a traditional dirt floor, while others feature poured concrete, gravel, tile, brick, or wooden decking. The decision whether or not to apply a flooring material rests with the owner.

Most traditional chickees were completely open-sided, featuring no walls. Mosquitoes thrive in damp environments such as the Everglades. They can make life unbearable, and the Seminoles devised methods of protecting themselves from mosquitoes inside chickees. Seminoles would commonly use a mosquito net made from thin cloth or calico or animal hides to cover the sides of the sleeping chickee when necessary.[16]

Big Cypress resident and chickee builder Lonnie Billie recalls using plywood as a wall covering in the winter. In warmer weather, the plywood was used to make tables or was simply turned into firewood.[17] Many photographs from the transitional period discussed in chapter 7 also show chickees with walls. Most chickees on the reservations today are left open-sided, but some are completely enclosed, with walls made from brick or wood, or fully or partially enclosed by particleboard or mesh screen.

Shapes

Traditional chickees were generally rectangular or square in plan with gabled roofs. Later chickees evolved to feature hipped roofs as well. Hipped roofs require more palm fronds and are more labor intensive, but they better protect inhabitants. As chickees have become less intended for year-round habitation, builders exercise more creative freedom, and the structure can take on any shape that the owner wants. One main advantage of thatching is that it is very flexible and can cover any shape of structure effectively. Although the rectangle and square are still the most common chickee shapes today, builders also experiment with hexagons, octagons, and irregular shapes. Even decorative "umbrella"-type chickees with only a central upright post can be found throughout the reservations (see chapter 8 for more information about the umbrella chickee).

Harvesting Materials

Prior to chickee construction, the builder must harvest the necessary materials. Within the camp setting, the entire family often pitched in

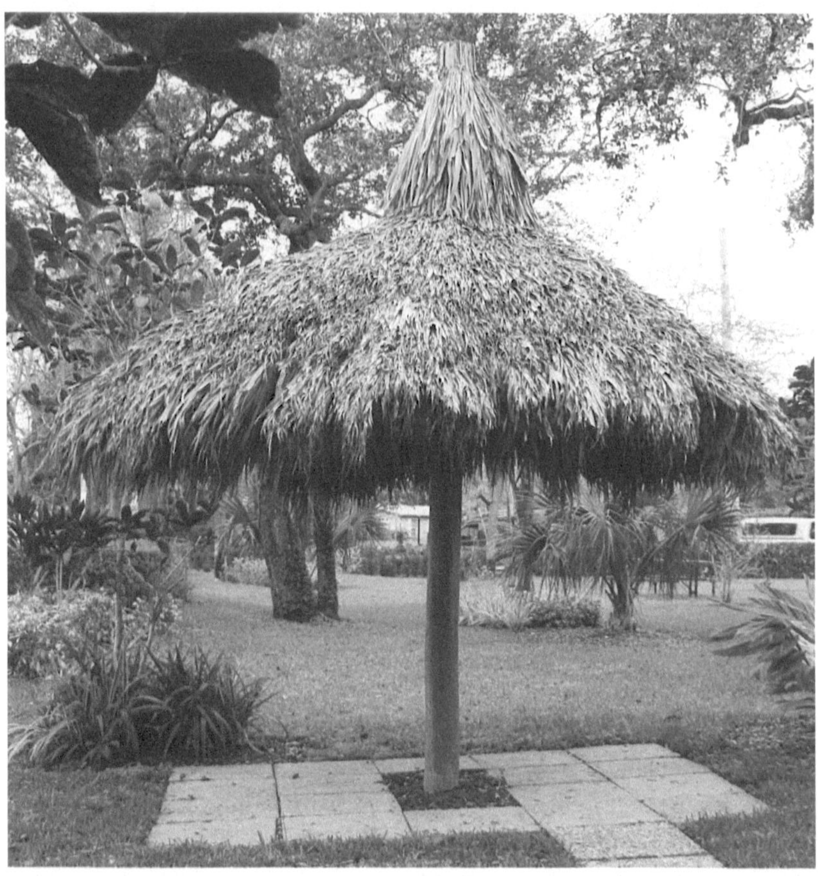

Figure 3.16. Decorative umbrella chickee. Photo by the author, Hollywood Reservation, 2012.

to help gather materials. For the average-size chickee, it will actually take longer to harvest building materials than to put the chickee together.

Seminoles would historically gather materials wherever possible, but today it can be a more complicated process, especially when collecting enough materials to sustain a commercial chickee building business. The "Usual and Customary Use" legislation covers materials harvested for personal chickees as well as those built for commercial purposes within the BCNP. As previously mentioned, many modern chickee builders employ non-Seminoles for labor. The non-Native employees are not allowed to harvest in the preserve unless a Seminole, Miccosukee, or independent Seminole is also present. The Seminole

Tribe of Florida (STOF) enacted its own legislation in 2011 regarding the harvesting of chickee building materials on reservation land. The Forest Product Ordinance requires chickee builders to contact the Forestry Department of the STOF prior to harvesting any materials. This type of notification allows the Forestry Department to communicate with the pasture owners or lease owners to inform them there will be people on their property. Additionally, it helps the Forestry Department keep a check on cypress harvesting on the reservations in order to understand how it impacts tree growth. Since Seminoles harvest in a sensitive way passed down through tradition, the Forestry Department has not encountered any problems with overharvesting by tribal members. As outlined in the ordinance, there is no charge for harvesting materials for use on the reservations. If the cypress is harvested to be used for business purposes, however, the builder will receive an invoice for materials. The same policy also applies to harvesting palm fronds, although they are more abundant and have a quick growth cycle, so the ordinance is less strictly enforced. If a non-Seminole is caught harvesting materials unsupervised on the reservations, his or her materials will be confiscated, and the offender will be fined for trespassing.[18]

Chickee builders often travel outside of their reservation or home area to gather all the necessary construction materials. Pressure-treated pine is easily accessible since it is purchased from lumberyards rather than harvested by builders. Palm fronds may be gathered in small quantities on the Big Cypress Reservation or the BCNP, or more abundantly on the Brighton Reservation; they are also commonly gathered along the property lines of the minor roads between the interior reservation areas, particularly between Big Cypress and Immokalee.

Tools

Most builders use a combination of both traditional and modern tools—including machetes, hammers, and chainsaws—to construct chickees. Bobby Henry stated that his preferred tools were hatchets, small and large axes, machetes, and the "white man's tomahawk," or chainsaw. When Ronnie Billie first started building chickees he primarily used an ax to cut the wood instead of a chainsaw or bow saw. He thought using an ax actually made the harvesting process faster. Years later he made a small business out of cutting cypress for other builders and then started his own chickee building business. Back when his primary job was harvesting cypress, he did not have a four-wheel-drive truck to make the process simpler. He had to drag the cypress out of the woods and now suffers from back problems due to years of hard labor.

Norman "Skeeter" Bowers likes to use a machete with a hooked end to harvest the fans: "That type of machete helps you grab onto the fronds before you cut them." He has also used landscaping snips to cut the palm fronds. Though the snips were quite efficient, many other Seminoles mocked him for using such an unconventional tool. Today, however, chickee builders use a plethora of nontraditional tools including drills, posthole diggers, and jackhammers to break up the rocks in the ground, and they use scaffolding to reach tall heights.

Types of Chickees

Traditional Seminole camps were comprised of different types of chickees based upon the various requirements of camp life. During the latter half of the nineteenth and for much of the twentieth century, camps usually contained four or five chickees,[19] with larger families having more chickees in their camp.[20] The cook chickee was the heart of the camp, and at the center of the cook chickee was the "star" fire. The fire was made of "four or more extremely long logs that met at the cooking hearth and extended like rays beyond the building. As they burned, the logs were nudged toward the center to feed the flame."[21] Chairman Billie explained that the purpose of this starlike arrangement was utilitarian more than aesthetic or cultural. It simply helped keep the fire lit throughout the night so that it would still be burning and available for cooking in the morning. The underside of the cook chickee was marked by a layer of black discoloration.

Most traditional cook chickees were A-frame in shape, with the sides of the structures extending nearly to the ground to allow for adequate smoke ventilation. There was no thatching at all on the open ends. Some of the modern cook chickees I encountered had the same shape or a similar shape with slightly shorter sides, but most just featured open pockets in the triangular ends of the gables. The different styles of cook chickees are explained in more detail in later chapters.

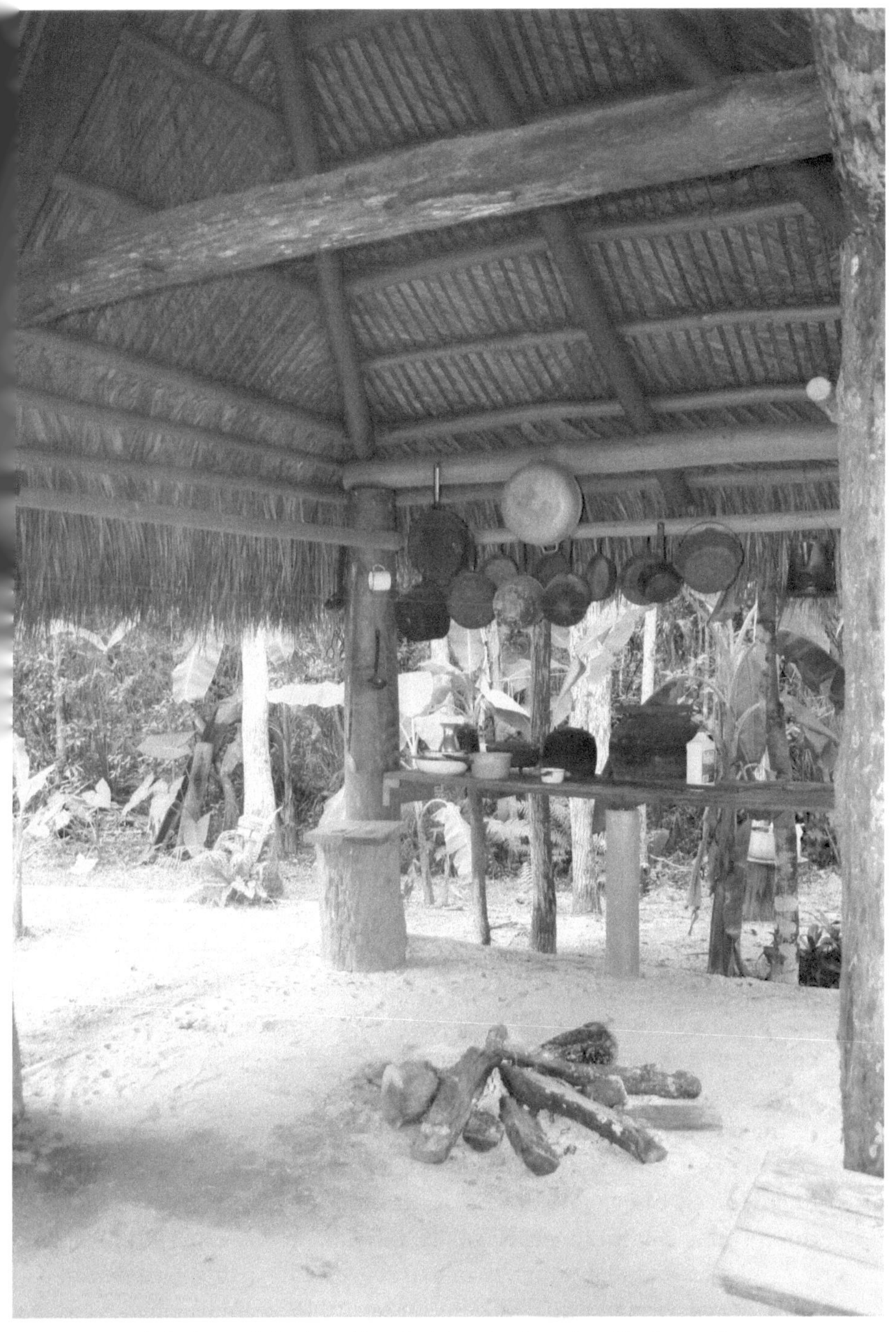

Figure 3.17. Cook chickee with blackened interior. Photo by the author, Big Cypress Reservation, 2013.

Another critical component of the chickee camp was the sleeping chickee. Sleeping chickees had a flat wooden platform raised about three feet off the ground. This type of floor helped protect sleeping inhabitants from water and Everglades wildlife. Being elevated off the ground also made cleaning simple; crumbs and dirt were swept away with ease.[22] The platform was typically made from split palmetto logs, flat side up, and covered with mats for sleeping. More evolved sleeping chickees had a platform made from sawed boards.[23] Since few people have lived in a camp setting on the reservations since the 1980s, sleeping chickees are not as common today. Other types of chickees found within Seminole camps included structures for storage, entertaining, and dining. In chapter 6, I provide an in-depth discussion of camps.

Most Seminoles no longer live in a camp fashion on-reservation today. This shift in lifestyle dynamic has caused chickees to change and adapt to meet the needs of the individual or the immediate family rather than the overall needs of a larger camp unit. As a result, chickee design has become more a matter of personal preference.

How Chickees Suit the Environment

Many people believe that living comfortably in the Florida Everglades is no easy feat. The environment is damp, incredibly hot and humid, and infested with all sorts of creatures—from bugs and snakes to alligators and panthers. Seminoles found a way to make life in the Everglades more than just "bearable." They did not arbitrarily use the materials around them to make their dwellings. They perfectly constructed them to suit the environment they call home. According to Nabokov and Easton, "To understand the factors that form Indian architecture, one must look for what environment and culture made possible, not inevitable."[24]

The open sides of the chickee allowed cross-ventilation to naturally cool the structure. Sleeping chickees with raised platforms allowed air to flow freely both above and below the floor to provide an even more comfortable environment. Nabokov and Easton describe the chickee as "an ingenious adaptation to an extreme climate, using local materials and basic design principles."[25] Chickee camps were usually located in tree islands, or "hammocks," which had the added advantage of providing shade and cool breezes.

William Arnett further expands on this idea in his paper for the *Florida Anthropologist* in 1953. He describes the advantages of chickees: "The typical Seminole Indian House takes full advantage of the outdoor living qualities of the Florida climate and provides a living space completely open to the breeze. The raised platform places the occupants above dampness and permits free circulation of air above the floor and beneath it as well; the wide sheltering roof of palmetto thatch protects the interior from the summer sun and from the drenching rain; the completely open sides admit the breeze and make maximum summer comfort possible."[26] Arnett further compares the modernist houses built by Florida architects in the 1950s to the Seminole chickees:

> There is remarkable similarity in concept between some of the forward-looking houses of Florida architects and the traditional houses of the Seminole Indian. The floor, like that of the Indian house, has been raised above the dampness, and space has been provided under the house for the breeze to blow through. Since the necessities of urban living generally require a house to be more than one room deep, the roof has been pitched upward so as to provide clerestory ventilation in all of the principal rooms. By orienting the house toward the prevailing wind, the breeze enters at the right and blows through the high openings at the left, inducing a free flow of air through the building.[27]

Chickees are a prime example of architecture perfectly suited to a less-than-ideal environment. Although the times have changed and most people are accustomed to air conditioning (compared to, say, fifty years ago), a chickee is still a very pleasant place to be when the weather is warm. I have found relief from the beating Florida sun under a chickee on many occasions.

Chickee Building Difficulties

There are four major problems as noted by chickee builders—weather, insects, material supply, and poor-quality work. Weather has always been a concern for chickee builders, and methods for strengthening a chickee to withstand hurricanes will be discussed in later chapters. According to Chairman Billie, chickees must be built with Mother Nature in mind from the beginning. The chickee cannot be too rigid or the whole thing, rather than just some palm fronds, will blow away. He stated, "It's gotta move a little, with nature." If you see palm fronds hanging all over the place in a disorderly fashion, that is a tell-tale sign that the chickee has encountered strong wind. The chairman rode out several tropical storms in the past in the chickees he constructed. His chickees also withstood Hurricane Wilma in 2005. The ability of a chickee to weather storms also depends on how stable the ground is where the uprights are located and the overall quality of the builder's work.

Insects can pose a serious problem for chickees. According to Lonnie Billie, smoking the cypress before installing it will help keep insects at bay (they smoke the cypress for all chickees not just the cooking ones, which are naturally smoked). Norman Huggins likes to use shaved-down pressure-treated lumber for the uprights, which proves to be more insect resistant. Ronnie Billie built a chickee in early 2013, and at the request of the owner he left the bark on the cypress posts. Although the owner wanted a chickee with a traditional appearance, Billie warned him that termites would likely destroy the poles quickly. He also mentioned to me that the chickee roofs he built used to last ten to thirteen years, but now they typically last only three or four years due to storms, acid rain, and bugs. He commented that if you do not spray for bugs, you must patch the roof more often. Another builder ran into a problem with insects eating only the stalks of the palm fronds.[28]

Availability of materials is a huge topic for chickee builders. Though efforts are in place to prevent overharvesting, many builders perceive a shortage of materials or other challenges to procuring them. This topic has concerned chickee builders for many years. In a 1974 interview, Bobby Henry mentioned that cypress poles and palm fronds were becoming a hassle to harvest: "Ten years ago it was easy. . . . Now, you can't hardly take anything without asking."[29] Ronnie Billie also noted that harvesting materials, even on the reservations, had become stressful: "You now have to call in and tell people when and where you are harvesting," he said. "It is just wiser these days to use pressure-treated lumber because cypress rots much more quickly and it is harder to obtain." Wade Osceola made mention of this: "Cattle owners and wildlife people don't want you collecting it. Plus you need to preserve the lands."

Lonnie Billie thinks that using modern materials such as pressure-treated lumber helps prevent shortage issues. Norman Huggins took note of this process as well: "Instead of walking in the water, they are going to the lumberyard." He did not like the look of the pressure-treated pine when it first became popular, but with time it grew on him.

Although the STOF Forestry Department did not know of any overharvested areas on the reservations, Bobby Henry recalled in our 2013 interview one particular spot in Big Cypress where the cypress trees have been overharvested. He also mentioned that people could once harvest the materials for the Green Corn Dance ceremonial chickees on site at the dance grounds (off-reservation), but now they must go elsewhere to get the materials. He said that nontribal members came in and depleted the supply. Henry warns that "you have to respect the land." When people respect the land, there will not likely be an issue with shortage of materials.

Seminoles often looked to chickee building during hard financial times, and now they have to look for other jobs because they can no longer rely on chickee building to stay afloat. This issue is definitely not due to a lack of available work because thatched huts are going up all over the reservations and South Florida. Instead, non-Seminoles are thriving in the hut building business because they often price their structures lower. One of the builders I interviewed was quite upset about people undercutting and driving away his business. He has been in the business for about fifteen years but had been out of work as a chickee builder for the past several months. The problem lies not in the fact that other builders charge less but that the builder may create an inferior product. Ronnie Billie mentioned that outside builders often do a poor job thatching the roofs, and then the owners call the Seminoles to fix the thatching. Sandy Billie Jr. has also observed that today the focus is on earning a "quick buck" where builders just put the chickee together haphazardly and do not stand behind their work. Their focus is more about making money instead of building a solid structure. According to Norman Huggins, "some of the builders do not put their heart and soul into it. The result is the structures are just not built right to begin with." So while the overall hut building industry in South Florida has not slowed, authentic chickee builders are often getting less work. Seminoles consider the chickee their key piece of architectural history and strive to maintain their culture despite the competition from outsiders.

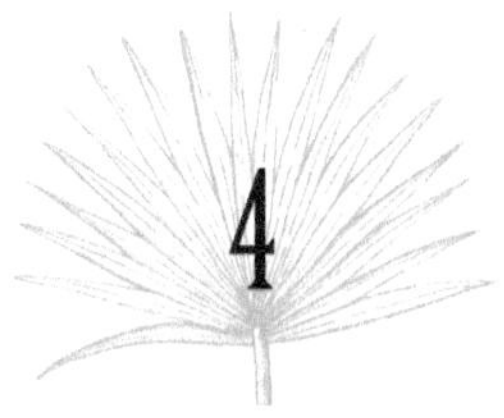

4

Seminole Architectural Roots

The chickee does not have a clear and distinct origin. Exactly when the chickee style of house came into use by the Seminoles is a topic of debate among historians, chickee builders, and Seminole tribal members in general. It is not a point of contention, however, that during the Seminole Wars (1816–1859) the Seminoles needed structures that could be built quickly (in a few days) from readily available materials and abandoned if necessary. One belief expressed by many tribal members (which is explained on the tribe's website) is that the chickee naturally evolved during this period simply because Seminoles were creative with their use of the materials—palm and cypress—that were around them. Chickees, however, have been around since long before the Seminole Wars. We might see this as a simple answer as to when chickees were used en masse by the Seminoles.

Seminole history is complex. The collective groups of people who became known as "Seminoles" were a combination of the Lower Creeks, Upper Creeks who migrated to Florida sometime later, members of other indigenous Florida populations, and sometimes even escaped and freed black slaves. It was not an immediate amalgamation and occurred slowly over the course of nearly four centuries.[1] Within this collective "Seminole" group we also see a division among the Miccosukee and the Creek Seminoles based on location and language (and later political differences). Despite recorded American histories that indicate otherwise, it is critical to point out that some Seminoles believe that they originated from where they are now and have always been here, and that the chickee has always been a part of their specific cultural heritage.[2]

A popular hypothesis favored among many historians is that the chickee was a modified version of the open-sided Creek summer houses noted by William Bartram in the late 1700s. Bartram, a naturalist who studied the flora and fauna of southeastern Indian tribes from 1773 to 1777, focused his studies on Indians in North and South Carolina, Georgia, and West and East Florida. He also visited a Seminole town at Cuscowilla, near present-day Micanopy in Alachua County, located within modern-day Paynes Prairie. Cuscowilla is considered the first "Seminole" settlement established sometime during the late 1760s and early 1770s.

Bartram describes the Creek Indian camps in depth, noting both the winter and summer houses, which were located around the square ground/council house. Of particular relevance here is the summer house:

> It is divided transversely, as the other, but the end next to the dwelling house is open on three sides, supported by posts or pillars. It has an open loft or platform, the ascent to which is by a portable stair or ladder: this is a pleasant, cool, airy situation, and here the master or chief of the family retires to repose in the hot seasons, and receives his guests or visitors. The other half of this building is closed on all sides by notched logs; the lowest or ground part is a potatoe [*sic*] house, and the upper story over it a granary for corn and other provisions.[3]

Though Cuscowilla is considered a Seminole settlement, the influence of strong Creek architecture is still ever-present in Bartram's description. Within the description, however, we can begin to extract elements that may have been modified as needed to later form the chickee. The chickee itself is certainly more similar to the Creek summer house than the winter house. Although the Creek summer house was two stories high, we see the same openness and support posts. It was very airy due to its open sides, of course similar to the chickee. The type of house described here by Bartram for the summer seasons was suitable for year-round living in the southern regions of Florida where the Seminoles resided after the Seminole Wars. It is possible that they carried the idea of the Creek summer house with them as they retreated into the southern regions of Florida, but it is hard to clearly deduce that this was the origin of the chickee due to the major differences in architecture and materials.

One commonly held cultural belief is that the Seminoles always lived in these types of structures, continuing a way of life that goes back thousands of years. These types of huts may have been a part of Miccosukee heritage long before the Seminoles amalgamated.[4] A representative from the Independent Traditional Seminole Nation of Florida shares that belief. He stated, "We have lived that way since time immemorial. The Creator created us to live on this continent and gave us the ways to follow."[5]

The chickee also shares many similarities with one type of Timucua house. The Timucua occupied an area of southern Georgia down to northern Florida. They were one of the first indigenous groups that Spanish settlers encountered; the settlers remained in contact with the Timucua until around 1704.[6] They had a large settlement near present-day Gainesville, around the same place as the first recorded Seminole settlement of Cuscowilla. Though most Timucua houses were conical in shape, they featured a structural system made from wooden logs set into the ground and were covered with palmetto thatching.[7]

Another likely story of the origin of the chickee is that the Seminoles picked up the techniques from the groups they encountered as they retreated to South Florida, such as the remaining Calusa on the southwest coast of the state. The Calusa engaged in mound building, but they also built open-sided raised homes with palmetto thatched roofs. Other now-extinct tribes in the area built thatched-roof huts as well.

Early Seminole Architecture

Homes similar to the ones seen at Cuscowilla were common among Seminoles into the 1800s. Bartram described the way the houses were built: "Their houses are constructed of a kind of frame. In the first place, strong corner pillars are fixed in the ground, with others somewhat less, ranging on a line between; these are strengthened by cross pieces of timber, and the whole with the roof is covered close with the bark of the Cypress tree."[8] These are not quite chickees, but they are still perhaps rather hutlike with their vertical post construction. We still see strong ties to the Creek architectural roots here.

Another type of construction emerged in Seminole settlements around the turn of the nineteenth century—the log cabin. Likely a mixture of European influence and indigenous building techniques, these structures were horizontal in construction (rather than the vertical frame construction supported by cross members as seen before). Log cabins do not have vertical uprights in the corners; the corners are instead made of interlocking horizontal members. Secondary structures would sit near these cabins.[9] In her interview with Tom King as part of the Southeastern Indian Oral History Project (now part of the University of Florida Samuel Proctor Collection), Mary Frances Johns (1944–2004), from the Brighton Reservation, described the two- or three-story log cabins that the Seminoles used to inhabit. King mentioned to Mary Frances that he had been told that the Seminoles did not always live in chickees and that they used to live in log cabin houses, and she replied:

> Regular two and three story log houses. . . . I heard it from my grandparents. . . . Well, they said the Seminoles being so great in numbers, and there was a lot of people who would hex a person, you know, put a hex on a person, or well there's some vampires involved, I guess. And that house is built real sturdy, with a sort of mud type thing. It's a clay, you know, like the kind you make pottery with, I guess. They used to make pottery too and they would stick this stuff between the cracks of the logs. So that nothing would crawl through, you know. And if these people who were vampires did find a crack in the wall, then they would sneak in and kill someone. So they used to make these things pretty well built. And they say that the bottom floor of the house was sort of a living area, where they are. They probably cooked outside, but they would eat in the house and store things. Then the second level, if there were two, would be used for sleeping quarters. They built these other places high on stilts sort of logs standing upright, and then the building would be built on top. It was maybe ten, twelve feet above the ground, something like that. You had to use a ladder to get up there. Now this was used mainly for grain storage and vegetables like dried potatoes or

pumpkins, things like that, they stored up there, keep a long time. Now this was after they had settled, that they started doing this. And they built these log cabins to last them for years and years. Family after family would be living in it for a long time.[10]

Since Mary Frances Johns was from the Brighton Reservation, where her grandparents were likely Creek descendants, this type of structure makes perfect sense. The houses of the Yuchi town in Lower Creek country, described by Clay MacCauley in his report on the Seminoles in the 1880s, sound very similar to Mary Frances Johns's description. MacCauley wrote, "The walls of the houses are constructed of a wooden frame, then lathed and plastered inside and outside with a reddish well tempered clay or mortar . . . neatly covered or roofed with Cypress bark or shingles of that tree." Since many Seminoles descended from the Lower Creeks, it is likely they carried their house type with them.[11] This is not to say that all Seminoles lived in houses other than chickees, but the Creek peoples did.

The surgeon W. P. Rowles described the abandoned camps he encountered in 1836 during the Second Seminole War. He noted that the camps were composed of hut structures, but not chickees: "Within a short distance from the margin of the lagoon we encountered a town, consisting of huts made by planting forks in a quadrangular form, over these poles were laid a roof of bark . . . or boards. . . . The walls were formed by bark or boards tied with splits or poles leaned against the evebeares."[12] These houses reflect the earlier construction techniques rather than log cabins.

An 1837 lithograph created during the Seminole Wars depicts an example of a Seminole village with log cabins. The lithograph matches up perfectly with Mary Frances Johns's description of the houses. These log cabins are square or rectangular in shape, with steeply pitched gable roofs. One of the structures on the right in figure 4.1 is raised on stilts as described by Johns and was likely used as a granary. The open-sided gable roof structure off to the left in the figure was used for storage. This building looks very similar in form to a chickee but with different roofing materials. All of the structures in this camp have crisscrossed roof weights similar to those used with chickees.

James Hutchinson, a renowned Florida artist, created a painting of these log cabins simply entitled *Indian Cabins*, which was printed in

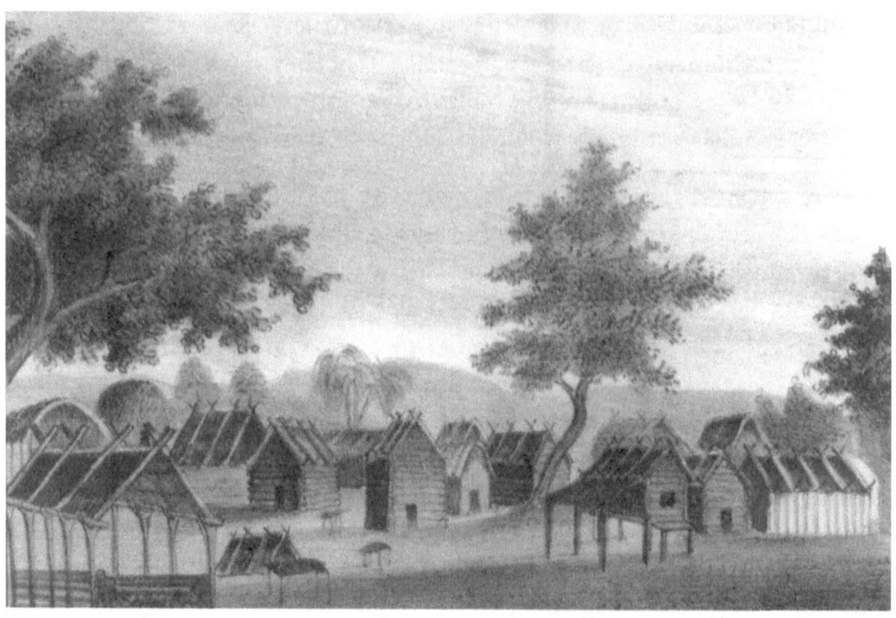

Figure 4.1. *An Indian Town, Residence of a Chief,* one of the lithographs from the events of the Seminole War in Florida in 1835. Issued by T. F. Gray and James of Charleston, South Carolina, in 1837. Library of Congress, Catalog Number cph.3b01536.

the *Florida Historical Quarterly* in 1976. He noted that the cabins were divided into two rooms, one for sleeping and one for cooking. The second story of the cabin was divided into two parts, with one part used for storage and the other open part used as a porch.[13]

Mary Frances Johns also mentioned that the Seminoles had been building chickees before the time of these wars, but they preferred to live in the log cabin structures. The chickees were the secondary structures at that time. She also stated that after the wars, she had heard of one instance where the camp contained a big log cabin. She recalled that the camp was either in Collier or Dade County. Her uncle remembered it, but in the mid-1900s very little of it was still standing.[14] Further evidence supports the fact that Seminoles sometimes had a mixture of chickees and walled-in structures in their camps, where the chickees were secondary or ancillary structures (see chapter 5).

In Richard Henry Pratt's 1879 report on the Seminoles, presented and annotated by William C. Sturtevant in the March 1956 issue of the

Florida Anthropologist, published by the Florida Anthropological Society, Pratt describes Chipco's village: "Although rude in their construction, they are quite ample for the climate, show as much mechanical skill and are quite equal in comfort to those of many of their white neighbors. The timbers for beams, rafters, posts and floors are neatly hewn; while clapboards were rived out as evenly as possible."[15] Some of the structures that Pratt sketched looked like chickees, while others looked like different styles of houses.

Sturtevant, however, thought that Pratt overstated the prevalence of such homes. According to Sturtevant, "Occasional shingled roofs on ordinary Seminole houses, such as shown by Pratt are known—there is a photograph of such a one in the Harvard Peabody Museum, taken by Alanson Skinner in the Everglades in 1910. Frame houses of various sorts, comparable to Chipco's house, have been built occasionally for a long time, but the open-sided Seminole house has repeatedly proved better adapted to the South Florida climate and the available raw materials."[16] None of these walled-in structures have been identified to still be in existence today. Though these structures undoubtedly existed, archaeological proof is hard to come by.

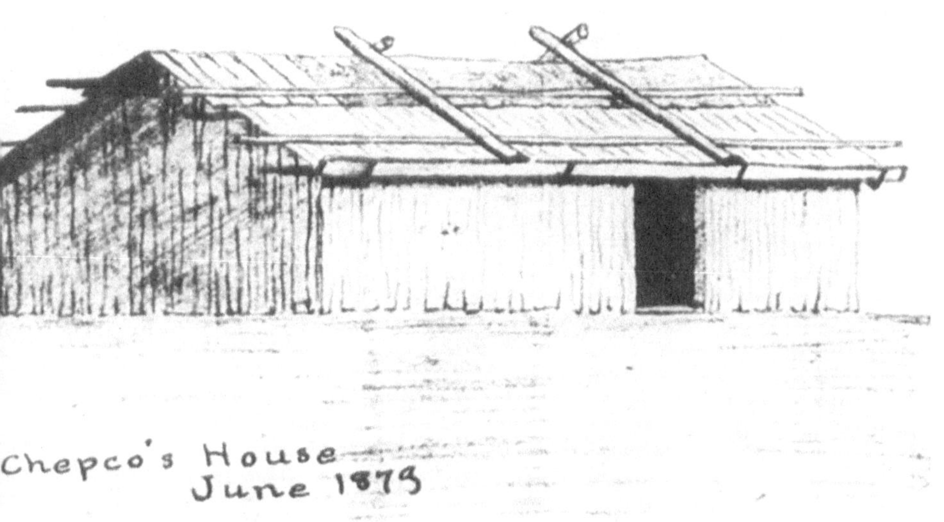

Figure 4.2. *Chepco's House* as sketched by Richard Henry Pratt in 1879. *Chepco* is also spelled *Chipco* in many documents. The Florida Anthropological Society.

Jane Anne Blakney-Bailey makes this point in her doctoral dissertation about Seminole and Creek settlement patterns: "Archaeological evidence of log cabins is rare. Historic writings and illustrations of Creek and Seminole log cabins suggest that the walls, which were composed of unhewn, notched logs, were set directly upon the earth, and there is no historic or archaeological evidence to suggest that wall trenches were used. The structures may have been partially covered with plaster, which could leave traces in the archaeological record. It is also possible that if the logs were left in place when the house was abandoned and were not reused by the occupants or scavenged by other opportunists, then rotting logs could have left stains on the earth."[17] She goes on to say: "The best archaeological evidence of vertical post structures is the presence of postholes, although very few have been documented at Seminole sites. When present, vertical posts are not necessarily indicative of houses, but could represent many types of structures including granaries, sheds, stables, or fences."[18] Seminoles also did not use nails at the time, which makes archaeological support even more difficult. We must rely more heavily on historical accounts or oral histories for the details of Seminole architecture.

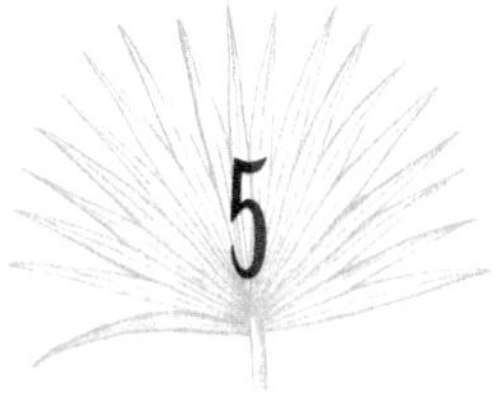

5

A Century of Evolution, 1840–1940

As the distinct groups came together and formed their "Seminole" identity, we begin to see more continuity of architecture. During the late 1800s and early 1900s, army colonels, artists, government agents, ethnologists, reverends, anthropologists, and tourists began to take note of the Seminoles and their way of life. The historic accounts described in this chapter, and other accounts like them, serve as invaluable records, as they contain specific details about Seminole houses. Since chickees were built as temporary structures with a relatively short lifespan, we do not have remnants of any "historic" chickees still standing today to examine for architectural details. And since Seminole culture and history are passed down through oral traditions by a system of familial and clan tutelage, the Seminoles themselves did not keep detailed written records of their architecture. There are no historic measured floor plans, building elevations, or wall sections of chickees created by Seminole architects.

As mentioned in chapter 4, the origin of chickee building has not been clearly defined. With that in mind, the following passages are not intended to put a "start date" on chickee building. They are instead meant to show how non-Indians viewed and recorded the Seminole structures over a one-hundred-year period of time (1840–1940). These notes additionally serve as a useful comparison for how chickees are built and used today. It is important to mention that none of these accounts actually refer to the Seminole homes as "chickees." They call them huts, lodges, buildings of rude construction, houses, or palmetto thatches. Nevertheless, these accounts help us define Seminole architecture.

Lieutenant Colonel W. S. Harney in the Everglades

One of the early accounts of Seminole chickee-style houses was by Lieutenant Colonel W. S. Harney in December 1840. Harney was ordered to find and attack "Spanish Indians" living in the Everglades during the Second Seminole War. Harney and his men traveled to an island called Intaska (named after its owner), which contained a "large hut built of cypress bark, and under it a bed made of boards."[1] This description sounds similar to a sleeping chickee with a raised platform, and it was not uncommon at that time for chickees to occasionally be covered in slabs of cypress bark rather than palmetto thatching.[2] They later found another island near Intaska while heading out of the Everglades. Harney reported that on this island there were "a great number of palmetto huts, very well thatched."[3] Here again it appears that the lieutenant is clearly describing a chickee, while the other description sounds very similar to the "vertical post structures" we encountered in chapter 4.

The Sam Jones Chickees, by Seth Eastman

The following year we find another recorded example of Seminole architecture. Seth Eastman (1808–1875) served as a mapmaker and illustrator in the U.S. Army but is most famous as an artist known for recording Native American life. Eastman began studying Native Americans in depth in 1841. Over the course of his life, he created hundreds of pictures to accompany the Henry Rowe Schoolcraft study *Indian Tribes of the United States*, which was published in six volumes from 1851 to 1857. Schoolcraft was a geographer, geologist, and ethnologist known for his study of Native American culture. In 1841, Eastman created a watercolor painting entitled *Sam Jones' Village* (1941; Peabody Museum, Harvard University). Sam Jones (Abiaki, Abiaka, or Aripeika), a Seminole chief, was a key leader in the Second Seminole War. He deserted his village just two months after Eastman created a painting of it. The painting shows three modestly sized open-ended chickees that do not have sleeping platforms. The Sam Jones chickees also lack the roof weights and ridge protection seen in later chickees. The simple construction and lack of furnishings is evidence that they were only intended for temporary occupation. The Sam Jones chickees are perhaps the most basic form recorded and reflect in their construction the need to be easy to build and abandon.

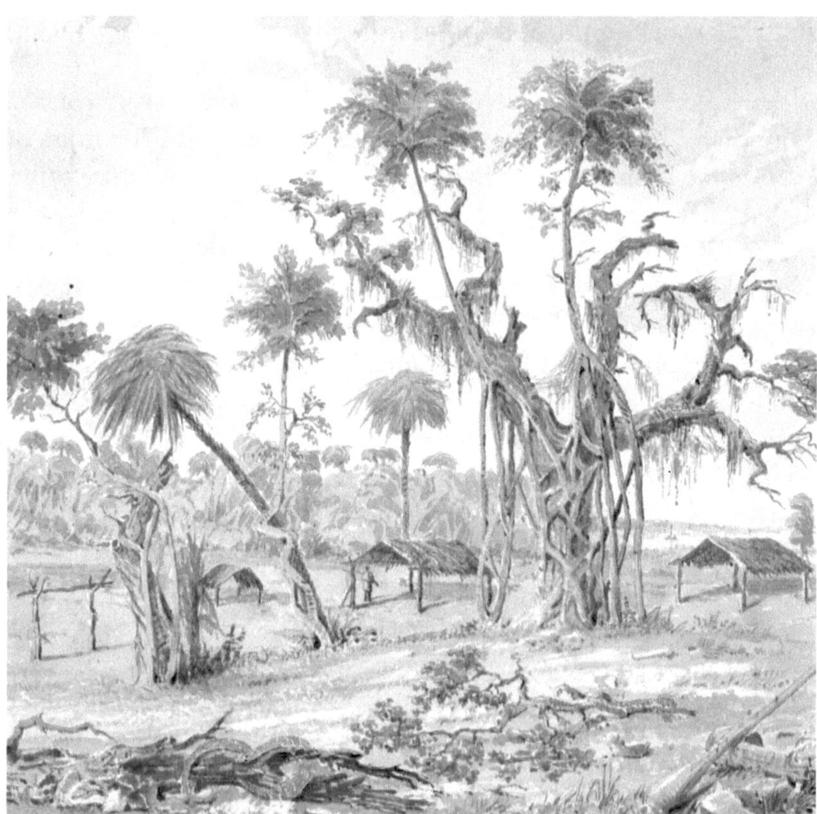

Figure 5.1. Eastman's *Sam Jones' Village.* Courtesy of the Peabody Museum of Archaeology and Ethnology, Harvard University, [41-72-10/89]. Digital File Number 99050045.

Throughout the nineteenth century, and interrupted only by the American Civil War, the Seminoles were fighting to avoid removal and to cling to their land. After the end of the Third Seminole War in 1859, little was recorded about the Seminoles. They were not building their camps out in open areas for people to see. Their homes were hidden deep within the Everglades, making them more obscure and elusive, perhaps due to a persisting distrust of outsiders. The anthropologist Brent Weisman points out that the "20-year interval of isolation between 1859 and 1879 remains the most poorly documented period of Seminole history."[4] Around 1879, things began to change. The violence of the wars was over, and people began approaching Seminoles from a different perspective—one of assimilation versus extermination or removal.

Pratt's Report on the Seminoles in 1879

Richard Henry Pratt (1840–1924) was sent on Special Order No. 122 from the War Department to investigate and report the condition of the Seminoles in 1879. Pratt was a representative of the Office of Indian Affairs and founder and superintendent of the first nonreservation federal Indian boarding school in Carlisle, Pennsylvania. Pratt had a keen interest in Native American issues and devoted much of his career to Indian education.[5]

The ethnologist and anthropologist William C. Sturtevant, who had a long-standing relationship with the Seminoles beginning in 1950, reproduced the Pratt report in the March 1956 issue of the *Florida Anthropologist*. At that point in time, Pratt's report had been vastly overlooked, but it held valuable information about the Seminoles.

Pratt thoroughly described Chipco's village—a small camp near Fort Meade, close to the central part of Florida, around eighty-five miles from the present-day Brighton Reservation. This is likely the same camp (Cat Fish Lake Indians) as described by Clay MacCauley in his 1887 report (see next section). Pratt stated: "The village is on a slight elevation in the piney woods, in the vicinity of clear beautiful lakes, in which abound black bass and other food fish. It is comprised of ten substantial buildings, similar in character, which are well represented. . . . They are located convenient to each other but without regard to order."[6] The buildings in Chipco's camp as described by Pratt were not strictly chickees. However, as depicted in his sketch of a corncrib at the camp, the structure still had a thatched roof and raised floor, and looked very much like a chickee. This could be considered a combination of the wooden hut and the chickee.

Pratt commented that "four or five years back these Indians all lived in frail houses constructed of palmetto leaves."[7] He went on to say that the Indians no longer lived in these structures, which was an inaccurate statement, as pointed out by Sturtevant. Clay MacCauley, who made contact with the Seminoles only two years later, described the chickees in much more detail and showed that the chickee remained the dominant house form for the Seminoles.

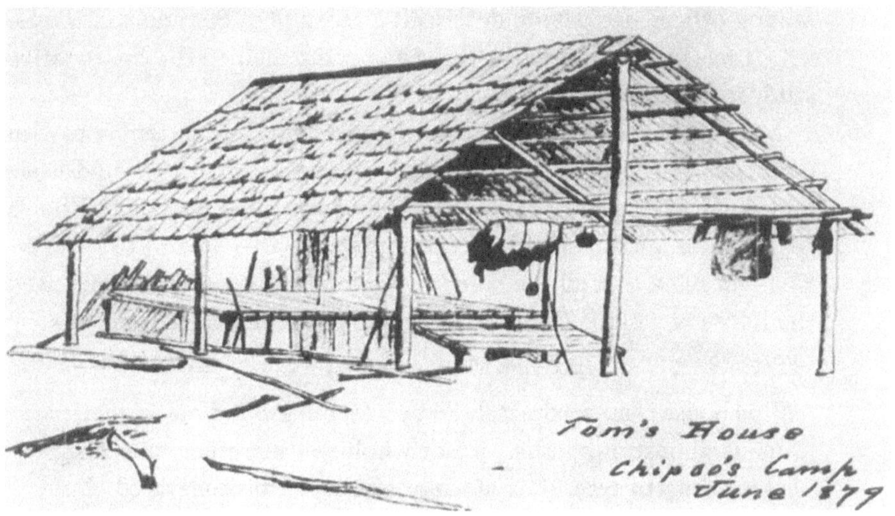

Figure 5.2. *Chipco's Camp June 1879 Corn Crib* as sketched by Richard Henry Pratt. The Florida Anthropological Society.

Clay MacCauley's 1887 Report

The Reverend Clay MacCauley (1843–1925) was asked by the Smithsonian Institution's Bureau of Ethnology to "inquire into the condition and to ascertain the number" of Seminoles living in Florida in 1881. Though MacCauley lacked formal training in ethnology, he spent three months living in South Florida and wrote detailed descriptions about Seminole life during the 1880s. His report was published in 1887 and is often considered the most definitive account of the time.

Both Pratt and MacCauley wanted to make contact with the Seminoles, learn about them, and help develop new Indian policies.[8] Finding them, however, was not easy. MacCauley noted in his 1887 report, "This invisibility of a Seminole's house from the vicinity may be taken as a marked characteristic of his home. If possible, he hides his house, placing it on an island and in a jungle."[9] People knew about the Seminoles, of course, but very few outsiders had direct contact with them until the Seminoles began to set up "tourist camps" in the early part of the twentieth century. MacCauley's report described many aspects of Seminole life, including clothing, housing, economics, and crafts, among others. He gave a descriptive account of Seminole chickees, which was unprecedented at that time and remained the comparative study for many decades.

MacCauley noted that the Seminoles lived in fixed settlements with domiciles, gardens, and fields. A few times a year they would leave and occupy temporary camps, sometimes to hunt, to secure Koonti flour, or for special spiritual ceremonies like the Green Corn Dance. He mentioned that all the homes were constructed similarly and used the house of Charlie Osceola, or I-ful-lo-ha-tco, on the edge of the Big Cypress Swamp, as an example.[10]

> This house is approximately 16 by 9 feet in ground measurement, made almost altogether, if not wholly, of materials taken from the palmetto tree. It is actually but a platform elevated about three feet from the ground and covered with a palmetto thatched roof, the roof being not more than 12 feet above the ground at the ridge pole, or 7 at the eaves. Eight upright palmetto logs, un-

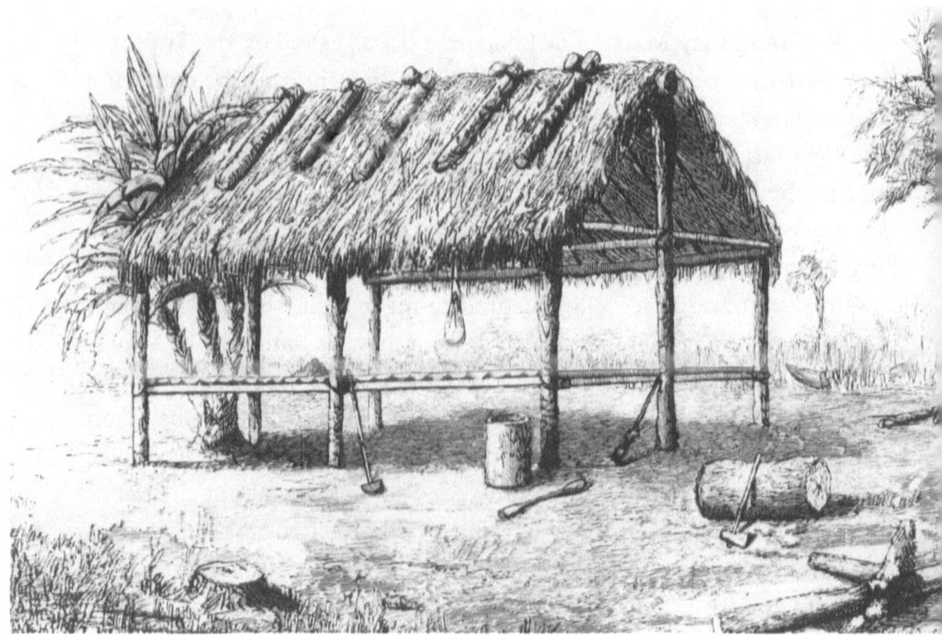

Figure 5.3. Clay MacCauley's chickee sketch. National Anthropological Archives, Smithsonian Institution (Neg. no. 1178-N-8-1).

> split and undressed, support the roof. Many rafters sustain the palmetto thatching. The platform is composed of split palmetto logs lying transversely, flat sides up, upon beams which extend the length of the building and are lashed to the uprights by palmetto ropes, thongs, or trader's ropes. This platform is peculiar, in that it fills the interior of the building like a floor and serves to furnish the family with a dry sitting or lying down place when, as often happens, the whole region is under water. The thatching of the roof is quite a work of art: inside, the regularity and compactness of the laying of the leaves display much skill and taste on the part of the builder; outside—with the outer layers there seems to have been less care taken than with those within—the mass of leaves of which the roof is composed is held in place and made firm by heavy logs, which, bound together in pairs, are laid upon it astride the ridge. The covering is, I was informed, water tight and durable and will resist even a violent wind. Only hurricanes can tear it off, and these are so infrequent in southern Florida that no attempt is made to provide against them.[11]

MacCauley noted that the houses were open-sided and had no distinct rooms. Food and household items were often kept in the space above the ceiling joists, and utensils were hung from the uprights. The way in which MacCauley described the chickee might make it sound like a poor type of dwelling, but he asserted that it was actually perfectly suited to the South Florida environment: "A shelter from the hot sun and the frequent rains and a dry floor above the damp or water covered ground are sufficient for the Florida Indian's needs."[12] He does mention, however, that these houses offered very little privacy.

McCauley stated that while Charlie's camp was the norm, some Seminoles built other types of dwellings. He knew of five enclosed houses, four of which were covered with split cypress, and the other was a log cabin. "Key West Billie," in particular, created a wooden house for his family and even installed doors, windows, and interior walls to make separate rooms. The house featured exterior stairs that led to the upper level and a balcony.[13] Although the Seminoles had not been living in these cabins for decades, perhaps Key West Billie remembered the design from his childhood or learned about it through his family members. Here we see the three types of houses: chickees, enclosed wooden huts, and log cabins.

Seminoles often occupied "lodges," or small, temporary structures, when they left their more permanent settlements. According to MacCauley, "These lodges, placed very close together and seemingly without order, were almost all made of white cotton cloths, which were each stretched over ridge poles and tied to four corner posts. The lodges were in shape like the fly of a wall tent, simply a sheet stretched for a cover."[14] These types of temporary structures had been in use for some time, and we can assume that the V-shaped trees with a rod across them as seen in Eastman's painting depicted the same type of structural framework. In other instances, the lodges were "covered above and around with palmetto leaves and in being shaped some like wall tents and others like single-roofed sheds." Palmetto leaf–covered platforms three or four feet in height connected the lodges. These areas were used for storage.[15] MacCauley's description of camp life is covered in the following chapter.

During the late 1800s, chickees started to become more refined. Their raised platforms provided substantial ventilation and protection from water.[16] When MacCauley visited the Seminoles, they were much more "settled" than during the Sam Jones era. The wars were over. The chickees were beginning to be adapted to meet the needs of the Seminoles as their settlements became less transitory.

The Ingraham Everglades Exploration of 1892

While some people, like Pratt or MacCauley, were sent to "study" the Seminoles, others stumbled across settlements around the same time period by mere accident. James Edmunson Ingraham, president of the South Florida Railroad Company of the Plant System, set out to explore the Everglades on foot in 1892 with twenty-one of his companions. They focused on the area south of Lake Okeechobee. Ingraham and his crew wanted to assess the viability of putting a rail system through this area.[17] Ingraham took brief notes about Seminole housing. He discovered remnants of a camp in a hammock that contained "a lean-to-roof that had once been thatched with palmetto, a few poles stuck into the ground and half burned logs, end to end, some small lemon trees and pumpkin vine indicated the absence of frost."[18] Lean-to structures such as this were indicative of temporary occupation.

Ingraham also described two other camps he encountered. Billy Harney's camp, located within a hammock, had one building covered with "rive board," or split wood, and "four palmetto thatches," or chickees.[19] He further makes mention of John Jumper's residence, which contained two chickees and a garden where he grew corn, potatoes, and pumpkins.[20] Again, we see a mix of structures in the camps, not strictly chickees.

H. A. Ernst in Pine Island

Prior to the 1900s, there was little pictorial evidence of chickees. Although MacCauley, Pratt, and Eastman all sketched Seminole houses, H. A. Ernst took what was likely the first photograph of chickees at the Pine Island Settlement in present-day Broward County around 1897.[21]

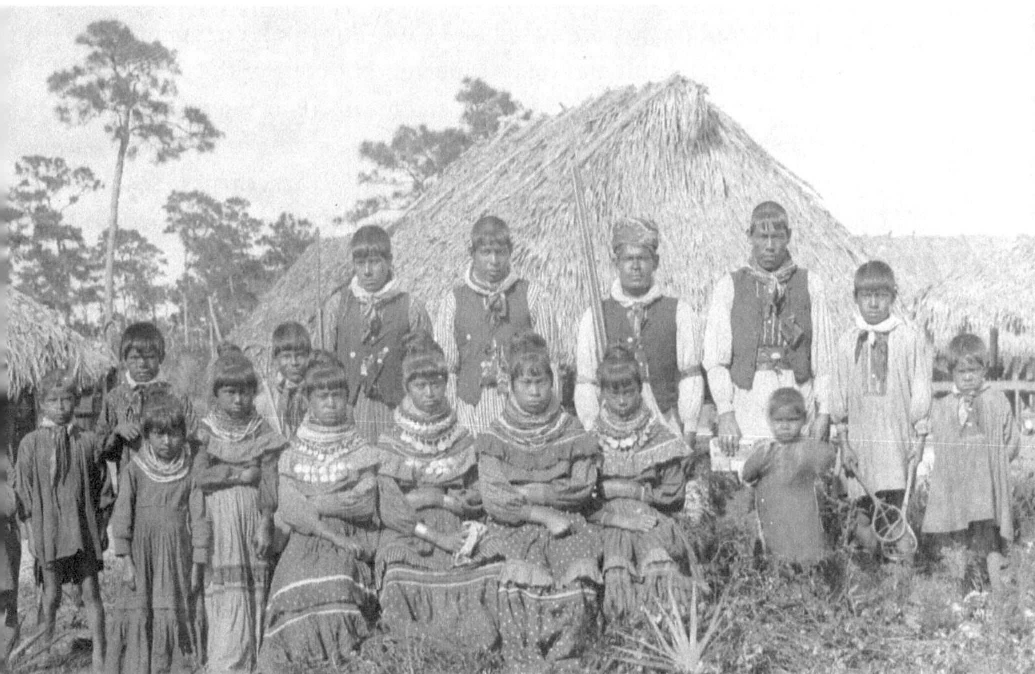

Figure 5.4. *Seminole Indians, first photograph on record taken at Pine Island FL,* photographed by H. A. Ernst. National Anthropological Archives, Smithsonian Institution (BAE GN 13187).

The photograph of the chickees in the Pine Island settlement shows roof thatching that extends to the raised floors. Some of the chickees in this camp also have hipped roofs (rather than just gable) and seem more evolved than the chickees of MacCauley's report. This settlement was more permanent, and we can sense that more effort was put into the construction.

A. W. Dimock and Julian Dimock, 1905–1907

Photos like those taken by Ernst are few and far between. Less than a decade after the Pine Island photos, however, a father and son duo created a great photographic record of the Seminoles. A. W. Dimock and his son, Julian, or "camera-man," became some of the first outsiders to thoroughly photograph Seminole life in the early 1900s. A. W. authored several journal articles and books about natural history, while Julian was the master photographer. The father and son team visited the Seminoles numerous times, but their first encounter was likely in 1905, when they made a trip from Marco Island down to Storter's store and trading post in Everglades City. They took ten general photographs of the Seminoles on this journey but none of their houses.[22]

The pair crossed the Everglades many times during the next few years in a small powerboat, documenting the Seminoles along the way. In his 1907 article for *Harper's Monthly*, A. W. described a Seminole settlement he encountered. The camp consisted of thatched-roof structures with raised platform floors.[23] The glass plate photographs Julian took in 1907 clearly show the chickees of that time. A photograph of an abandoned chickee depicts the architectural framework, an interior image shows the pattern of the thatching, and several others show entire chickees or bits and pieces of the interior and exterior of the structures. The Dimocks did not go back to the Everglades in 1908 or 1909.

Alanson Skinner's Expedition in 1910

Alanson Buck Skinner (1886–1925) developed a fascination with ethnology at a young age. He worked for both the American Museum of Natural History in New York and the Museum of the American Indian and had an interest in tribes in North and Central America. In late summer of 1910, Skinner traveled to Florida on behalf of the

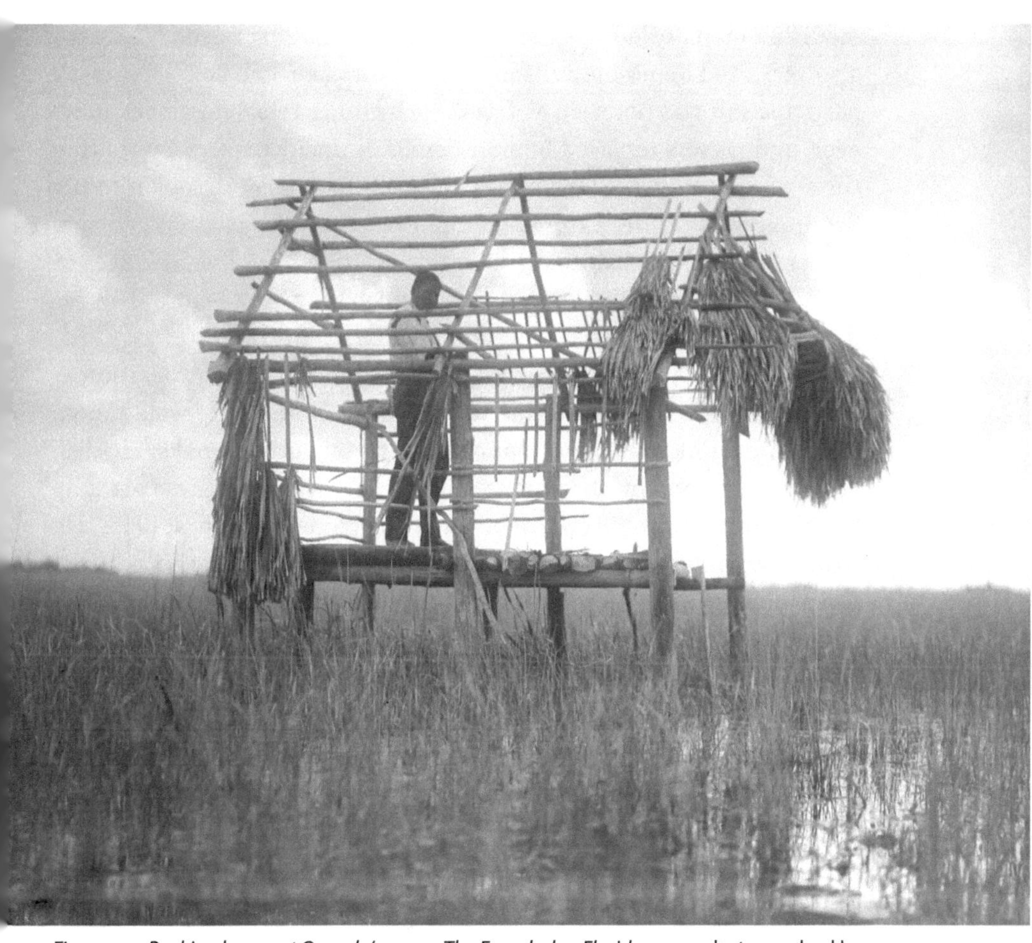

Figure 5.5. *Packing house at Osceola's camp, The Everglades, Florida, 1907*, photographed by Julian Dimock. This photograph shows the architectural framework of a chickee. Interestingly, this photo shows what appears to be thatching on at least one side of the chickee, not just the roof. Image #48162, American Museum of Natural History Library.

American Museum of Natural History to obtain specimens relating to Seminole ethnology. He visited several Seminole villages, only one of which had ever been visited before by a non-Seminole. Frank Brown, son of Bill Brown (owner of Bill Brown's Boat Landing and Trading Post, today part of the Big Cypress Reservation), was his tour guide. The Brown family had built an exceptionally strong relationship with the Seminoles around the Big Cypress area from the late 1880s to the early 1900s. Frank Brown was similar in age to prominent Seminole medicine man Josie Billie, and the two were lifelong friends.[24] Brown also recruited Seminole Wilson Cypress for their journey.[25] Cypress's participation was not seen as favorable by other tribal members, however, and he was replaced by non-Seminole Joel Knight.[26] By visiting the area with Brown, Skinner was able to get an insider's look into the Seminole way of life. Skinner commented that "they are exceedingly conservative, dress habitually in native costume, and live in lodges of approximately the same type as those which they built before their exile from their homes in Georgia and northern Florida."[27]

Another key player also accompanied Skinner on this expedition—Julian Dimock. Julian and his father had become quite well known for their documentation of Seminole life through their books, articles, and photographs by that point in time. A. W. Dimock was actually the reason that Brown got involved as the guide in the first place. He wrote to Bill Brown to ask if his son Frank could join the expedition; A. W. also helped plan much of this trip himself.[28]

Skinner took notes on the clothing, hairstyles, camp life, crafts, houses, religion, and social organization of the Seminoles. He described the typical Seminole camp in this passage: "As we traveled through the cypress . . . we came upon a well-marked trail, about three feet broad, and here dug out for easier passage of canoes. After a short journey we saw the yellow glint of the palmetto-thatched lodges of an Indian village. As we drew near, the effect was charming. On a little 'hammock,' or meadow island, surrounded by dark cypress trees that stood in the glass-clear water, were clustered eight or ten Seminole lodges. The palmetto fans with which they were thatched had faded from green to old gold in color, and above them the sky formed a soft background."[29] Skinner additionally gave an excellent description of the chickee: "The typical Seminole lodge is a pent roof of palmetto thatch raised over several platforms on which the occupants sit or recline. There are no sides, since the Everglades and the Big Cypress are so far below the frost-line that the atmosphere is rarely cold, and the protection from the rain afforded by the closely thatched roofs with their wide projecting eaves is all that is necessary. The lodges average fifteen feet by twelve, but they vary greatly in size. They are made of cypress logs nailed or lashed together. A few houses have a raised floor throughout, giving the appearance of a pile-dwelling."[30] Skinner not only painted a picture of

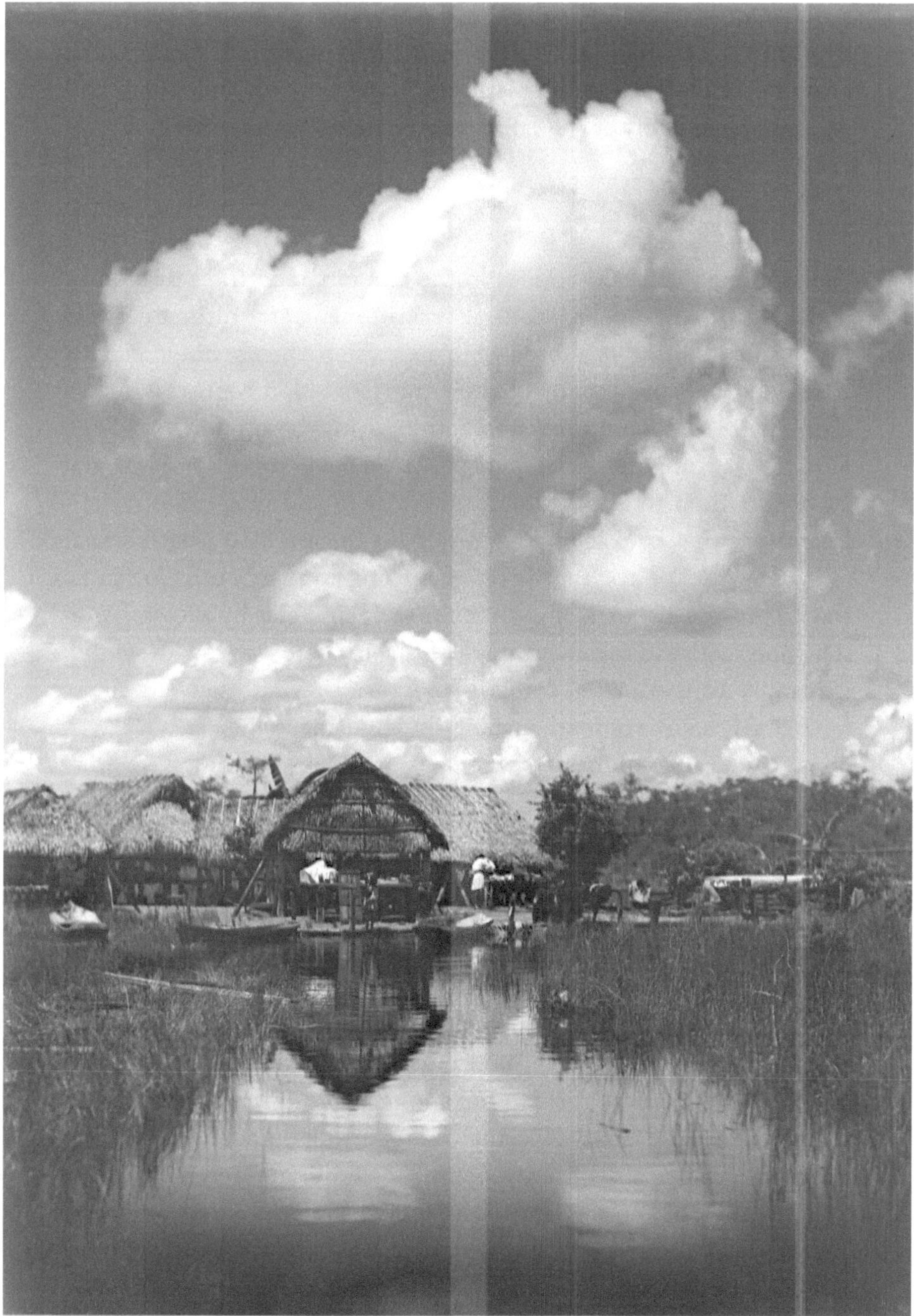

Figure 5.6. *Little Billy's camp, The Everglades, Florida, 1910*, photographed by Julian Dimock. This image illustrates the camp structure. Image #48152, American Museum of Natural History Library.

the Seminole structure, but he also described the houses in the context of their setting. He collected several ethnographic objects for the museum, while Julian took pictures of these objects and additionally photographed many of the camps they visited.[31]

The Tourist Camp Era

The draining of the Everglades in the late nineteenth century deeply impacted the Seminoles' natural environment and ultimately their financial stability.[32] It altered their hunting patterns, hindered their trade, and destroyed many of their transportation routes. While the economy of the Seminoles was going down, the economy of South Florida was going up, due in part to Miami being touted as a hot tourist destination. In 1915, several newspapers and magazines claimed Miami was the "land of opportunity."[33] In the interwar period shortly following World War I, tourist camps sprung up over South Florida as a way to provide a source of income for the Seminoles by allowing them the opportunity to take advantage of this tourism market. These tourist camps were enticing, primarily because they afforded the chance for a steady source of food, income, and housing.[34] They catered to the increased number of tourists who had a fascination with Native American culture.

These camps exhibited to outsiders, for the first time, how Seminoles lived, ate, and worked. Seminoles were very private and often did not welcome outsiders into their camps. The atmosphere of the tourist camps changed that in a way, though the attitude outside of this tourist market remained static. The inhabitants did not just come to the camps as if it were their job; they actually lived in them. Chickees were an integral part of these tourist camps. A few Seminole families lived in one of these camps prior to the end of World War I in 1917, but the number greatly increased during the following decade. The two largest tourist camps emerged at Coppinger's Tropical Garden on the Miami River and Musa Isle Grove. Coppinger's Tropical Garden opened in 1914 and closed briefly from 1926 to 1928 due to hurricane damage.[35] Other camps similar to Coppinger's and Musa Isle were established throughout Florida.

In 1929, there were thirty-five people living at the Musa Isle camp and around twenty-five at Tropical Garden.[36] These statistics were taken at a critical time considering the major project that had been in the works for several years—the Tamiami Trail. The Tamiami Trail, which opened in 1928 to connect Tampa to Miami, was a huge engineering feat with both positive and negative impacts on the Seminoles. It further disrupted their transportation patterns and ecology, leaving few options other than joining the tourist camps.[37] On the other hand, this new road helped bring many more tourists to South Florida and may explain why so many families were living the tourist camp life in 1929. Even the Seminoles not living directly in the established camps brought their isolated homes out closer to the trail.[38] Ethel Cutler Freeman noted there were thirteen camps along the trail in 1939.[39]

The Seminoles who lived at these tourist camps still followed their

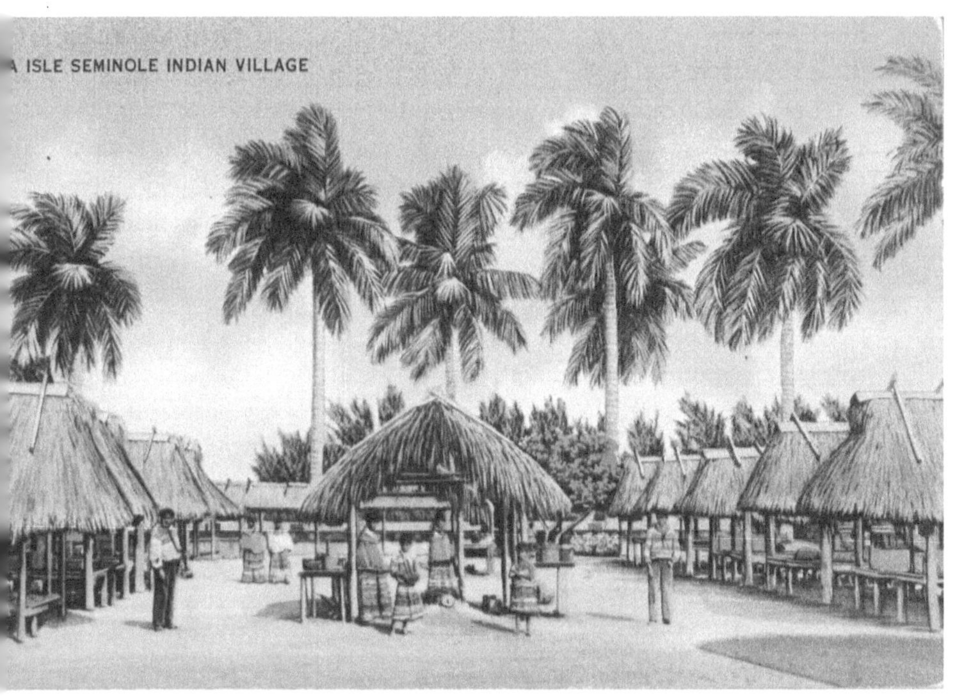

Figure 5.7. Postcard from the Musa Isle Seminole Indian Village. Note the two cook chickees in the center of the camp here—the second is hard to see, but it is directly behind the first. Also note the linear arrangement of the tourist camp (most camps were arranged around the cook chickee in a nonlinear fashion). Ah-Tah-Thi-Ki Museum, Doubleday Collection, c. 1950s (ATTK catalog no. 2001.74.4).

traditional customs for courtship, births, deaths, and tribal council.[40] They built and maintained their chickees and sold crafts from them. The historian Harry A. Kersey Jr. described the activities at the camps: "The Indians who lived within these villages were not on static display; rather, they engaged in activities typical of Seminole camp life such as cooking, sewing patchwork garments, or carving canoes and the like."[41] Tourists paid to see Seminoles perform everyday tasks, and alligator wrestling became a huge attraction at these villages. The historian Patsy West further described the Musa Isle camp: "Musa Isle had seven house sites and normally five of these chickees were utilized by the Seminole families hired by the tourist camp" and "two designated cooking chickees were erected in the center of the Musa Isle village."[42] It is interesting to note the number of cook chickees in the tourist camps, as we see in the next chapter that camps typically only had one central cook chickee. This was due to the mix of different clans in these tourist camps and the fact that different clans could not cook under the same chickee.

These tourist camps were a huge South Florida attraction from the 1920s to the 1940s.[43] As West described, "the Seminole villages became some of Florida's most popular and longest running pre-Disney attractions."[44] After this time period, many Seminoles began to settle on the established reservations and had a greater ability to seek other employment opportunities.

During the heyday of the tourist camps, the average person could witness an account of Seminole camp life for the first time and discover the types of housing where the Seminoles lived. Many postcards from this era prominently feature chickees, particularly postcards from Musa Isle. It is likely that many Americans who could not vacation in South Florida themselves received postcards from friends and family members that depicted the Seminole chickees.

Although these camps brought financial security to the Seminoles who occupied them, they were also a subject of controversy. Some people believed that the Seminoles were "on display" and treated as an attraction, not as humans.[45] Despite the controversial aspect, tourist camps brought attention to the Seminoles and helped give exposure to Native American architecture that reached beyond tipis, wigwams, and igloos. The tourist camp postcards from the post–World War I era brought the image of Seminole architecture to the mainstream. Many of the activities that got their start in these tourist camps (such as alligator wrestling and basket making) have helped shape the cultural identity of the tribe today.

Bobby Henry ran a modern-day tourist camp in Tampa from 1982 to 2002. Chairman Billie created a Seminole village in Tampa in the early 1980s and wanted Henry to run it. At first there were only about sixteen to twenty Seminoles in Tampa; now the number tops one hundred. The village contained several chickees, much like the original tourist camps, and in 1987 Henry constructed a sixty-foot-tall chickee that perfectly demonstrated his skills as a master chickee builder. When I asked him how he reached the top, he told me that he used scaffolding—a common practice when constructing large chickees. The

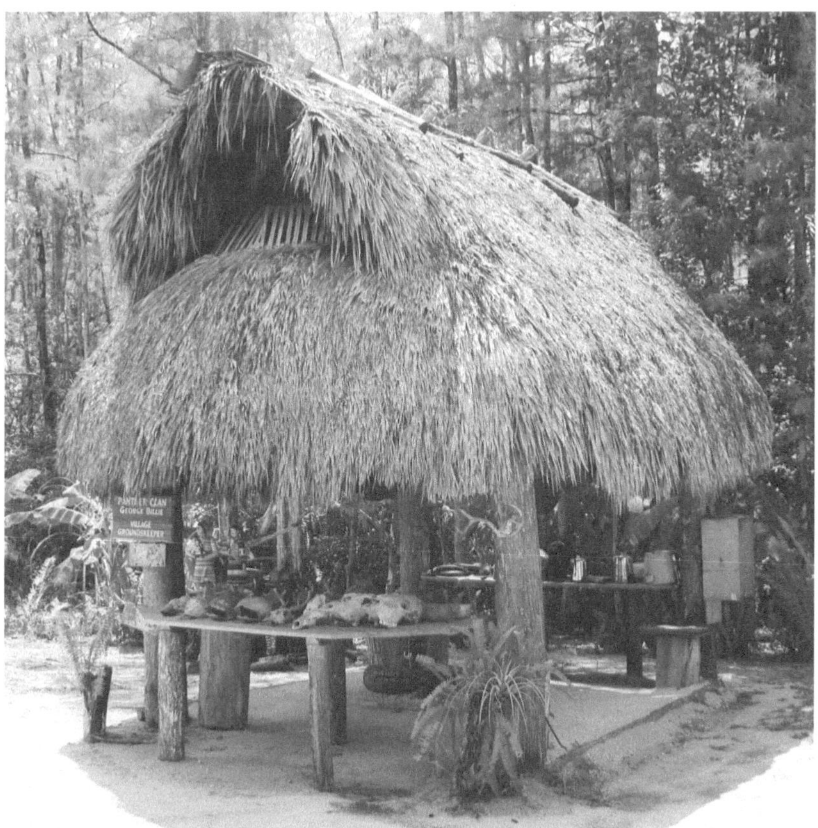

Figure 5.8. Photograph of the cook chickee at the Seminole Village of the Ah-Tah-Thi-Ki Museum. Photo by the author, Big Cypress Reservation, 2013.

thatched roof on this supersized chickee required 40,000 palm fronds, compared to approximately 1,200 for a standard chickee. Bobby Henry enjoyed building tall roofs such as this because he thought that made the chickee look beautiful and churchlike.

There is another modern version of one of these tourist camps in use today at the Ah-Tah-Thi-Ki Museum. Many tribal members who work at these modern tourist camps grew up in the tourist industry and have a different idea about what is appropriate in such settings. They cater to the interests of the tourists while also presenting an accurate display of many aspects of Seminole culture. The tourist camps have remained successful today because they strike a balance between allowing the workers to make money and display aspects of their culture while not revealing too many private details to outsiders.

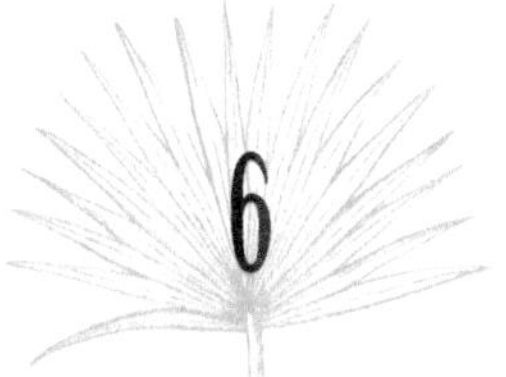

6

Seminole Camps

Architecture scholar Amos Rapoport stated that "it also follows that one cannot merely consider a particular building because people do not live in, or act exclusively in, single buildings; they use various buildings, a variety of outdoor spaces, settlements, and whole regions: they inhabit cultural landscapes. One cannot, therefore, look only at 'architecture.' Any given building exists in a wider context to which it is linked through the activity system of its occupants. The nature and extent of this context, its relation to culture, and activity systems, is not self-evident."[1]

Up until this point, I have primarily focused on the chickee as an individual structure, but the chickee should not be studied in isolation. One of the most significant aspects of the chickee lies in its role within the camp, or *estehvpo* (*istihapo*). Spiro Kostof stated: "No building is an isolated object, sufficient unto itself. It belongs to a larger setting within a bit of nature or a neighborhood of other buildings, or both, and derives much of its character from its natural or manufactured environment that embraces it."[2] Native Americans typically arranged their structures into larger groups—camps, homesteads, villages, and towns—and the Seminoles were no exception to this ritual.

Following retreat into South Florida after the wars, the camp became the central focus of Seminole life as opposed to the towns or settlements occupied previously. The camp was not merely a cluster of chickees; it was a highly organized residential unit. Towns were more broadly focused, while the camps were more intimate and featured a smaller number of structures. The main focus of the camp was the family instead of society as a whole.

Seminoles follow a matrilineal social system. When a child is born of a Seminole mother, that child becomes a part of her "clan" or family unit. The Seminole Tribe currently has eight different clans: Panther, Bird, Bear, Deer, Wind, Bigtown, Snake, and Otter, though many more existed in the past. When the matriarch of the clan dies, the clan becomes extinct. Clan association is hugely important to the Seminoles, and symbology is seen throughout the reservations and in other aspects of culture. These nonhuman entities represent strength, courage, and endurance, and clan laws help guide all aspects of Seminole life.

Camp composition is based upon this matrilineal kinship. Members of the camps usually included a woman and her husband, their daughters and the husbands and children of their married daughters, and their unmarried sons. Many of the later camps also contained any individuals related to the matriarch (sisters, fathers, and older related individuals). Young men traditionally lived with their mothers/sisters until they married into a new family. At that point, the newlywed moved into his new wife's camp. His clan would not change at this point, only his camp. Most members of a camp will belong to the same clan (except for husbands). It is considered taboo to marry within the same clan, even if the couple are not related by blood.

Both the clan and camp can be considered basic familial units for the Seminoles. The anthropologist Alexander Spoehr studied the structure of the Seminole community, particularly clan camps and kinship, as part of his dissertation on social change among southeastern Indians in the 1930s. Spoehr believed the camp was even more of a binding unit than the clan itself, noting that "it is a local as well as a kinship group, with its members living in one spot, and with the houses, cooking utensils, pigs, chickens, and other material appurtenances giving it solidarity of appearance and tangibility that the clan lacks."[3] Spoehr focused on the Cow Creek Seminoles on the Brighton Reservation and observed that the camps he encountered were relatively permanent in nature.[4] There were, however, certain reasons for a family to abandon a camp, especially cultural or environmental reasons. Prior to government aid, the Seminoles still mostly sustained themselves with gardens and by hunting, fishing, and so forth, so if resources dwindled, they would need to relocate. Many people would consider the camps "mobile and flexible" according to Jessica Cattelino, author of "Florida Seminole Housing and the Social Meanings of Sovereignty": "when garden soil became less productive, nearby game was depleted, or camp conditions became unsanitary, all residents picked up and relocated."[5]

Every member of the camp participated in making it a smoothly functioning unit, and in most cases the camps had clearly defined gender roles. This was common in such societies as the Seminoles. As noted by Jane Anne Blakney-Bailey: "The close proximity to family members facilitated the orchestrating of common goals and the sharing of tasks, which were typically divided along gender lines. Women were responsible for domestic activities, including raising children, cooking, and pottery and basket manufacturing, as well as tending agricultural fields. The men, in turn, were responsible for warring, hunting, maintaining tools, guns, and other equipment and the construction and up-keep of structures, canoes, and ritual objects."[6] Men and women typically had specific roles within the camp, but they all pitched in when it came to certain tasks, including building chickees, whenever the need arose. Everyone, regardless of age or sex, was able to contribute to building chickees in the camp. The tasks were divided by skill level, and the younger or more novice members would complete the basic tasks. Harvesting materials and assembling the frame were the more difficult tasks, while putting nails in the fans and handing them up to the roofer were considered much easier. One person would put a nail in the fan, then hand the fan to the person on the roof, and that person would nail it to the framework.[7]

Most Seminoles today have likely helped at some stage in the chickee building process—from gathering palm fronds, handing up fans, or nailing members together, to the more complex tasks of harvesting or debarking cypress, digging holes for the uprights, or assembling the structural framework. Additionally, during the Green Corn Dance Ceremony, everyone (young or old, male or female) pitches in to build or rethatch chickees. Chickee building is certainly an inherent part of Seminole culture, but only a handful of Seminoles have made a full-time business out of practicing this particular Native craft.

In some camps, few if any men were present. In those cases, the women built the chickees in their entirety. Women were, of course, the matriarchs in Seminole society. As mentioned before, they mostly cooked and tended the camps, but in some cases they had to build chickees out of necessity.

Components of the Camp

It should be clear by this point that chickees are not large enclosed and subdivided spaces like most people would consider a "house." Instead, we can envision the camp unit as a whole more akin to a "house," because within each camp there were different chickees for different uses. In any home you would expect to find, at minimum, spaces for living, dining, cooking, and sleeping. In modern homes, you would also expect, of course, to find at least one bathroom. Within a Seminole camp, there were separate chickees or structures/areas that met all of these needs—sleeping, living/dining, cooking, and "bathrooms" in the form of outhouses or a spot in the woods.

Camps were highly organized spaces, oftentimes in spite of their outward appearance. Nabokov and Easton commented: "What appears random or haphazard in old photographs of Indian camps and villages often represents a pattern. . . . Indians were deeply attached to their architectural patterns, found them practical and enjoyable, and resisted the white man's attempt to change them."[8] The chickees within a camp were all arranged in a particular way based upon "various implicit and explicit rules governing position and movement."[9] No matter what exact rules outlined the camp organization, it seems all Seminole camps were arranged around the cook (or cooking) chickee or the central cooking area. Although chickees changed slightly as settlements became more permanent, camp life itself remained fairly static.

Spoehr noted the camp configuration, consistent with earlier documentation and confirmed by oral histories: "The houses face toward the center of the clearing and fan out in all directions from the cook house."[10] The cook chickee was constructed similarly to the other chickees in the camp, but it did not feature a raised platform. While many chickees in the camps had been adapted by the early 1900s to feature a hipped roof, the cook chickee continued to be built in the gabled roof style. The roof of the cook chickee had open ends or open pockets to allow smoke from the central fire to escape. It was not uncommon to hang pots, pans, and drying meats from the roof rafters of the cook chickee.[11] Everything was easily accessible and off the ground, away from water and wild animals. According to Spoehr: "Here the culinary art of the Seminole housewife is practiced. Hung on the rafters of the smoke-blackened interior are her pots and pans, with other small necessities stuck in various nooks and crannies within handy reach for seasoning the pots simmering on the fire."[12] At the campsite, the logs of the fire pointed in the four cardinal directions—east, north, west, and south. The chickee placement was also strategic, never haphazard. The beds in the sleeping chickees always faced east since the dead are buried with their heads to the west. According to former Brighton representative Johnnie Jones, chickee huts typically faced the north-

"Star" Fire

The fire is the heart of the Seminole camp, and it burns continuously. Just as people around the world gather around their dinner tables as a family for nightly dinner, the Seminoles congregated around the cook chickee. Visitors to the Seminoles often documented the importance of the fire. MacCauley noted, "One observes that the center about which it gathers is the camp fire. This is never large except on a cool night, but it is one of unceasing interest to the household. It is the place where the food is prepared, and where, by day, it is always preparing. It is the place where the social intercourse of the family, and of the family with friends, is enjoyed. There the story is told."[1]

Skinner described the fire as well. "In the center of this space is the cook-house, in which a fire is constantly burning. It is kept up in a curious way. Large cypress logs are cut and laid under the cook-house, radiating from a common center like the spokes of a wheel. At the 'hub' the fire is lighted, and as the wood burns it is constantly shoved inward and hence never needs to be cut into short lengths. At this fire, the only one in the camp, the women cook for the entire village."[2] Skinner took an excellent photograph of a cook chickee in 1910. This chickee features a prominent star fire in the center.

Roy Nash remarked that the Seminoles make the best camp fire he

(Continued)

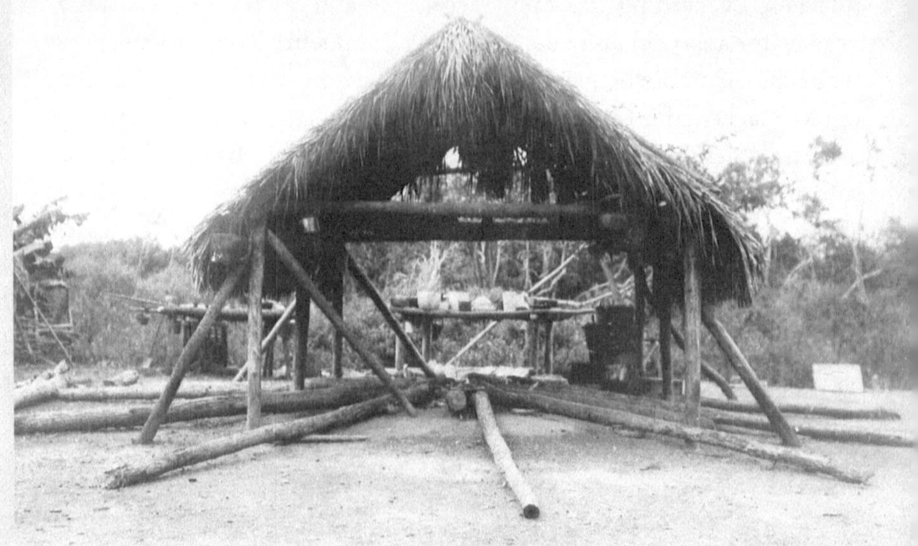

Figure 6.1. Alanson Skinner's *Seminole Cook House*. Photograph from 1910. Courtesy of the Braun Research Library Collection, Autry National Center, Los Angeles; Photo #A.63.44.

had ever seen, and he had traveled the world. "He [a Seminole] takes 8 or 10 dry logs, of any length that a man can conveniently carry and any diameter he can conveniently cut, and arranges them as the spokes of a wheel. At the hub he kindles his fire. To brighten it, he pushes in a couple of logs; when it grows too hot he pulls them apart. Three points to support [a] pan or kettle may be arranged by the merest touch. The elements of the fire themselves furnish a seat for whomever stirs the pot, let the wind blow whither it will. Dogs, chickens, pigs, lie between the logs at night sheltered from the wind and warmed by the embers."[3]

According to Nabokov and Easton, Creek summer towns also featured the buildings all arranged around a "sacred star fire."[4] "The spiritual focus of these buildings was the sacred star fire, which was tended with the utmost respect."[5]

Seminoles still consider the fire in the center the of the cook chickee the heart of the camp today.

1. MacCauley, *Seminole Indians of Florida*, 51.
2. Skinner, "Notes on the Florida Seminole," 70.
3. Nash, *Survey of the Seminole Indians of Florida*, 4.
4. Nabokov and Easton, *Native American Architecture*, 110–111.
5. Ibid., 108.

south direction around the central cook chickee. "It's built like that so everyone knows who is in that particular camp," Jones said. "Everybody's accounted for that way."[13] The cook chickee, with its star fire, was certainly the heart of the camp.

In addition to buildings and structures, gardens also played a key role in the camps. Seminoles grew beans, sweet potatoes, pumpkins, melons, and other produce within the camps themselves; corn and sugarcane grew outside of the camp in other hammocks. Corn was especially important for the Seminoles. According to James Goss, author of *Usual and Customary Use and Occupancy by the Miccosukee and Seminole Indians in Big Cypress National Preserve, Florida*: "Corn is important not only for food, but for the sacred tradition of the Green Corn Dance."[14] The Green Corn Dance is still an important part of traditional Seminole culture today. The ceremony takes place at the beginning of the corn harvesting season and helps ensure the success of the harvest and the well-being of the community. Many purification rituals are performed during the Green Corn Dance. Corn is also a main ingredient of sofkee, a traditional Seminole beverage.

Roy Nash, special agent of the Indian Office, described a typical camp in his 1931 survey of the Seminoles.[15] "Guava Camp" was located thirty-five miles southeast of Immokalee, in the western margin of the Everglades, about fifty miles northwest of Miami. Eight people lived in Guava Camp. The cook fire was the center of the camp, and a fifty-foot radius of dry land surrounded the fire. Nash recorded that four structures were grouped around the central fire. The closest structure was about fifteen feet from the fire, and the farthest was at the edge of the clearing. The largest chickee in the camp was 12'×20'. He noted that this house had three sections of platform—one for eating and two for sleeping. Two of the other structures were slightly smaller than the first and had undivided platforms. The fourth structure had a chickee frame but no roof and was used to dry skins and cut up meat. The camp also featured a platform for washing dishes, a stockade around banana plants, a pig or alligator pen, a distant water hole and place for washing clothes, and a garden. He found that the chickees in the camps were as MacCauley had described, except the palm fronds were nailed together rather than tied.

Throughout Seminole history, temporary camps for hunting and trade were quite common (see the discussion of MacCauley's observations in chapter 5). It took a long time to travel to the hunting and trading areas, so it made sense to stay on-site to make the trips more worth their time. These temporary camps declined in popularity once the Seminoles began to regularly use motor vehicles, as transportation by canoe or horse had been very time-consuming. The use of temporary camps also began to decline when Seminoles started to obtain other sources of food. Garbarino described one type of temporary camp setup still in use in the 1960s: "During the vegetable growing season, some people leave their Big Cypress camps and go to Immokalee to work. There is a camp area in Immokalee where Indians have built chickees in which they live when working on the ranches or at the shipping depots. A few Indian women live in Immokalee permanently with their non-Indian husbands because these men are not allowed to live at Big Cypress."[16] The use of temporary camps is an infrequent practice today except for the Green Corn Dance, which has remained a critical part of Seminole culture. The location of the ceremony mostly remains the same, while the occupancy of the camp itself is temporary.

Camp Locations

Seminole camps were typically established within hammocks, or expansive "tree islands." Hammocks are elevated areas (the term *elevated* is used very loosely here) surrounded by wetlands. Hammocks were considered the driest places in the area. Camps themselves were modest in size, and the homes were often built close to a water source to meet cooking, cleaning, and other subsistence needs.[17] They were rather undetectable from outside the hammock unless the onlooker could spot parts of the roof thatching or see smoke coming from the cook chickees.[18] Camps were usually spread far apart, not near each other like houses in a subdivision.[19] The location of the camps often followed food and plant cycles and weather. In particularly wet years, camps were established on even higher ground.[20]

Pine Island, once the highest point in Broward County and the largest settlement in southeastern Florida, was occupied by the Seminoles as early as 1828. It was abandoned at the turn of the twentieth century, however, with the impending draining of the Everglades.[21] The Pine Island settlement was a very tight-knit area, such as what one would expect to find in a camp setup. It contained around twenty-five houses, ceremonial grounds, and nearby fields. Around eight to ten families occupied Pine Island.[22] This number is quite large compared to typical camps on the Big Cypress Reservation, which in 1964 contained one to thirteen members.[23]

As mentioned in the previous chapter, the draining of the Everglades hugely impacted the Seminoles. Not only were the Seminoles pushed out of their Fort Lauderdale–area settlements, including Pine Island, but they had no choice but to abandon their Miami-area settlements as well. That circumstance, coupled with the opening of the Tamiami Trail, drove many Seminoles to set up camp on the government-established reservations. Others joined the popular tourist camps or established homes along the Tamiami Trail near the new service stations constructed on the remote stretch of road. These six stations (Belle Meade, Royal Palm Hammock, Big Cypress Bend [Weaver's Station], Turner's River, Monroe Station, and Paolita) provided a place for weary travelers to stop and take a quick rest. They were also enticing to visitors who could walk across the street to visit the Seminole camps and purchase handmade crafts and other souvenirs. Additional camps were set up near Copeland, Miles City, Deep Lake, and Ochopee.[24]

Roy Nash included a map of permanent camps in his 1930 report. Although Seminole elders helped him record the location of these twenty-four camps, it is likely that he missed some of the remote or well-hidden camps. All the camps he recorded were similar to the Guava Camp described earlier in this chapter.[25]

James Goss pointed out in his report that ten years later, the location of camps recorded by Nash had changed. Most of the camps established near the interior of the Big Cypress Swamp had been left behind as people relocated to the newly established Big Cypress Reservation or to the Tamiami Trail. A 1940 map of camps listed nine in the Big Cypress Preserve and sixteen along the trail.[26]

Alexander Spoehr's work focused on the Brighton community, and he listed twenty Cow Creek camps in 1939.[27] Louis Capron also studied Cow Creek Seminole camps in 1950. He noted the Cow Creeks occupied the area north and northeast of Lake Okeechobee and comprised one-third of the entire Seminole population. Most of the Cow Creeks established camps on the Brighton Reservation, and a few established their camps on private lands near ranches to find easy employment opportunities.[28]

Billy Bowlegs III Camp

One of the camps recorded by Roy Nash was the Billy Bowlegs III Camp on the Brighton Reservation. Tribal archaeologist Maureen Mahoney conducted a thorough investigation of the Bowlegs camp for her nomination of the camp to the Tribal Register of Historic Places. The Tribal Register is a list of cultural resource properties that are considered of particular importance to the Seminole Tribe of Florida and are therefore worthy of preservation. Types of properties include historic camps, buildings, structures, archaeological sites, and places where significant activities or cultural practices and beliefs are recorded or known through oral tradition. Such traditional places may include dance grounds and medicinal plant gathering areas. The Tribal Register of Historic Places is administered by the Seminole Tribe of Florida's Tribal Historic Preservation Office. Nominations of properties to the register can be made by anyone, and each application is reviewed for significance by a board of tribal representatives and officials. The Tribal Register was created as a way to recognize highly significant places for the Seminoles that, for a variety of reasons, might be ineligible for the National Register of Historic Places.

As part of her research, Mahoney spoke with three tribal members who grew up in the Billy Bowlegs III Camp in the late 1940s/early 1950s. They were granddaughters of Billy Bowlegs III who joined the camp after their parents died. They moved to the camp with their other siblings. Before they occupied the camp, it consisted of a central fire place, a sleeping chickee, a storage chickee, a dining chickee, and a *tofto*, or barnlike structure used to dry corn and other vegetables and as a place to store valuables. The camp also featured a hog pen, a sugarcane processing unit, and a garden. The Bowlegs camp had one of the largest gardens on the Brighton Reservation.

The buildings at the Bowlegs Camp had some interesting characteristics. The tofto was covered on all sides with palm fronds instead of being left open-sided. It was the only building of its kind on the reservation, however, at the time when they joined the camp. The sleeping chickee featured a metal roof instead of a thatched roof. Members of the camp would hang canvas on the open sides of the chickee to block the wind.[1] The Brighton camps often deviated away from straightforward chickees more than did the camps at Big Cypress.

1. Tribal Register of Historic Places Nomination, "Billy Bowlegs III," Seminole Tribe of Florida Tribal Historic Preservation Office, 2012.

Capron also noted that the "Miccosuki" Seminoles lived south of the lake. Many families established camps on the Dania (Hollywood) reservation, some at commercial camps in Miami and along the trail (ten there), and many at the Big Cypress Reservation and throughout the Big Cypress Swamp.[29]

Although the external events of the draining of the Everglades and the opening of the Tamiami Trail had deep impacts on the Seminoles and even camp life, internal events affected their settlement patterns over the next few decades as well. Many Seminoles who resided on the reservations (and some who lived off-reservation) came together to form a federally recognized tribe in 1957—the Seminole Tribe of Florida. Public housing initiatives started on the reservations, and more Seminoles began to move onto these reservations and soon into "modern" houses and out of chickees.

Not all Seminoles were on board with these changes, however. During that time and even to this day, there are families who chose never to officially join the Seminole Tribe (or the Miccosukee Tribe, which formed in 1962) and instead live off the reservations in the Big Cypress Preserve or elsewhere on private lands throughout Florida. These Seminoles are considered independent Seminoles and do not ascribe to a federally recognized tribe. In a survey of the Big Cypress National Preserve (BCNP) conducted by the Ecosystem Research Unit of the National Audubon Society between 1977 and 1979, eight camps were counted in the preserve along US 41. Each camp contained between six and ten chickees and was less than one acre in size. Several families lived in each individual camp. Four of the eight camps were commercial tourist camps.[30] In 1995, as surveyed by Goss, that number increased to twelve active camps in the BCNP along the Tamiami Trail.[31] Half of these camps had mobile homes in addition to chickees. Many of the chickees used as family dwellings had walls or other modernizations. Each camp was situated on an acre or less, with two to ten structures. These camps were arranged in a traditional manner and often featured a small garden, fruit trees, chickens, and hog pens.[32] There are still many camps set up in the preserve along the trail and on private lands today, with a mixture of chickees, houses, trailers, and other structures. The camp life found here is often much more structured than on the reservations due to the way the individual homes are set up.

Rituals—Birth, Marriage, Death

Camp life often changed dramatically during critical times throughout life—particularly for birth, marriage, and death. Chickees or other structures were built for these events within, or outside of, the traditional camp setting. At the other end of the pendulum, the camps might be abandoned all together (particularly for deaths).

Spoehr detailed what he called the "baby" house. He mentioned that it was a smaller version of the living house built for a mother and her newborn. The woman gave birth away from the camp and stayed offsite for four days. Upon her return to the camp, she and the newborn stayed in the baby house for up to four months. Although the house was constructed by the husband, men were not allowed to touch the woman for months following childbirth in order to avoid becoming ill.[33] Cultural beliefs such as this dictated Seminole daily life. Another woman in the camp, usually an aunt, would visit the birthing chickee to help out the new mother and bring her food.[34] A similar chickee was built for menstruating women as well. Women went to a small chickee outside of the camp for four days during their menstrual cycle to avoid making the men and boys in the camp sick.[35] These types of chickees were no longer present in the Big Cypress camps when Merwyn Garbarino conducted her fieldwork on the Seminoles in 1964–1965. She noted, "Babies today are born in the hospital and menstruating women are no longer segregated."[36] Gender separation such as this is actually quite common throughout various societies: "It should be noted that all societies use both gender-specific and nongender-specific areas as well as function-restricted and multipurpose areas."[37] These cultural beliefs, however, still shape Seminole life today, though maybe in a less extreme manner.

As previously mentioned, when a couple marries, the husband joins the wife's camp. Within that camp, the husband is expected to build a new chickee for the couple, though at first they would sleep in the wife's chickee.[38] If the marriage did not work out, mentioned Spoehr, the husband simply gathered his belongings and left the camp. If the couple had children, they stayed with their mother in her camp. The father at that point was no longer responsible for caring for the children.[39] If they remained married, the couple lived with the wife's family indefinitely or until they could afford to establish a camp of their own. Garbarino noted that by the 1960s, many young couples, though not all, hoped to be able to afford a house rather than continuing to live in chickee camps.[40]

The star fire held special symbolism for newlyweds. According to Patsy West: "The camp's fire was laid in the cooking chickee. Logs were laid in the traditional Seminole manner radiating out like the spokes of a wheel. At the time of the marriage, a ceremony took place at the cook chickee. The new husband would cut four large logs (four was a ceremonial number) and add them to the existing logs. He would also cut a pile of firewood for the camp fire."[41]

When a member of the family died, the camp was either temporarily or permanently abandoned. Seminoles believe that when a person dies, evil spirits occupy the camp, so the family must leave.[42] Another way that death impacted camp life was in the orientation of the sleeping chickee, as previously mentioned.

Camp Life

Eating and preparing food played an enormous role in camp life. Spoehr noted that "everywhere the offering of food is the mark of the courteous host, and the guest is bound to partake in the offering or else offend. . . . The offering of food is thus a much-used social mechanism for maintaining friendly relations among the Indians."[43] Men typically provided the food via hunting and fishing, and women cooked.[44] Meals within the camp were prepared in common, and the woman would take the food to her family to eat under the chickee.[45] Men and boys usually ate first, followed by the women.[46] People were allowed to eat meals prepared by other families within the camp, and all families pitched in when financial times were tough. Nobody in the camp went hungry.[47] The same hospitality regarding food was also extended to guests.[48]

Furnishings at the camp were minimal, particularly during the early years. During MacCauley's visit, he noticed that the beds did not have pillows, and an optional thin blanket or sheet was used as covering.[49] Nash noted that the Seminoles laid on a blanket or buckskin on the platform, and in winter months they covered up with a blanket as well. During rain, a muslin sheet provided protection from wind on the sides of the chickee.[50] As decades passed, however, chickees became quite cozy and featured many modern conveniences, as discussed in detail in the next chapter. The sleeping chickees were used as living rooms during the day and were the place people gathered to hang out. Spoehr's words paint a quaint picture of camp life:

> Lounging on the smooth-worn floors of the houses, the people retail gossip and news, and the camp becomes the market place for the exchange of ideas and opinions. It is where the Indian relaxes, whether merely to lie in the shade of a thatch roof and contemplate the contrast of the green sword-like fans of the surrounding palms against the blue of the sky, or to sample a jug of liquor with some friends. It provides the *milieu* in which children play and are reared; where they are told trickster tales by their mothers and are occasionally punished by an elder; and where they gradually extend the range of their acquaintance to include their fellow tribesmen. The camp witnesses the establishment of new families and the break-up of old. It is the scene of jealousy and conflict, whether such be over a love affair or the more mundane matter of having enough corn to make safki. A place of comfortable disarray, the Seminole camp is the core of the Indian's daily life.[51]

Each camp was more or less an autonomous unit. Members of the camp generally stuck to themselves outside of the Green Corn Dance Ceremony. Community activities on the whole were fairly uncommon. Garbarino noted that people mostly focused on the goals of their camps rather than goals of the tribe as a whole.[52] This dynamic certainly changed, however, particularly once the individuals became more accustomed to being a federally recognized tribal unit (the Seminole Tribe of Florida) and as the camps dissolved as people moved into concrete block and stucco (CBS) or wooden frame houses.

Skinner also spoke about Seminole camp life: "Life in the camps is cool, clean, and pleasant. The breezes sweep through the lodges beneath the thatched roofs, and the camps are usually as neat as possible. Often in the morning the Indians may be seen raking the village square clean. Little refuse is to be seen about, for while the Seminole throw bones and scraps from their meals about promiscuously, the wandering dogs and pigs soon make away with them. It is not always pleasant, however, to have several litters of pigs lying at night beneath the sleeping platform, making indescribable noises. Even the Indians seem never to have become accustomed to it."[53] Tribal members today remember that the camps were kept scrupulously clean and raked so that the tracks of any invading creatures could be easily detected.[54]

Dr. W. A. Claxton visited a number of Seminole camps in August 1930 to determine the health conditions of the inhabitants. He commented: "I would not advocate modern housing as I think they are healthier in their native habitations."[55] At that time, his diagnosis was accurate. As people became more settled into the reservations and the tribe was federally recognized, more outsiders came to view these camps as unsuitable. Sanitation and garbage disposal became huge issues.[56] In the 1950s and beyond, there were starkly different opinions about whether it was better to live in chickees or in "modern" houses.

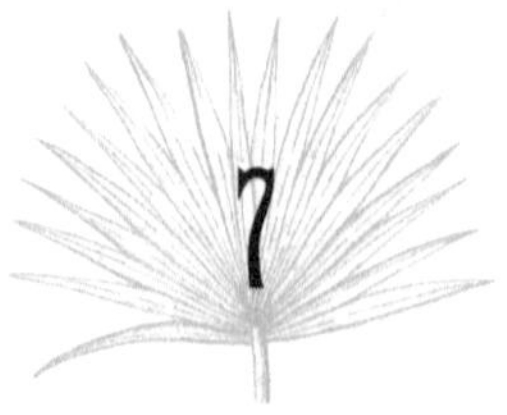

7

The Transitional Period, 1930s–1970s

Before Seminoles settled onto federal lands, the U.S. government had little control over their affairs. The Treaty of Moultrie Creek in 1823 had set out to confine the Seminoles to approximately four million acres of undesirable land created as a reservation in the middle of the state, in exchange for the twenty-four million acres they had been occupying. The Treaties of Payne's Landing in 1832 and Fort Gibson in 1834 took back the lands set aside in the Treaty of Moultrie Creek.[1] After the three Seminole Wars and Indian Removal, the remaining Seminoles who had managed to avoid relocation were living in relative obscurity, more or less freely occupying the lands they had settled in the southern part of Florida. This was not a suitable arrangement in the eyes of the state and federal government—they wanted the Seminoles contained in one specific place. Beginning in the 1890s, Congress began to appropriate monies for the purchase of land that would eventually lead to the establishment of the modern-day reservations. Initial land donations and a small land purchase began in this period, and in 1911 the U.S. government created an executive order designating a 360-acre parcel of land as the only place the Seminoles could legally settle.[2] Dania (later renamed Hollywood) became the first official reservation in 1926. Although the government appropriated this land, the Seminoles were not forced to relocate there. In fact, most were reluctant to move onto the reservation and succumb to government control. They were content to continue living in their camps spread out in the southern areas of Florida.

The Seminoles were living in economic poverty compared to the broader American public, but chickee life in those days was quite pleasant, at least compared to the other housing option at the time—ten one-room cottages built in 1926 when the Dania Reservation was established. These cottages were destroyed by a hurricane shortly after construction but were rebuilt nine months later.[3] The homes contained no electricity or running water and were first intended for sick and indigent Seminoles.[4]

Though the Dania Reservation was home to the Seminole Agency, Bureau of Indian Affairs (BIA), which administered most tribal programs, the living conditions there did little to entice others to move on-reservation. When Roy Nash conducted his survey in 1931, he concluded that the chickee was the best type of house for the Seminoles. Nash remarked: "A Seminole Family can erect a shelter in three days that will last him 30 years with an occasional renewal of thatch. There are sentimentalists infesting Florida who pity the poor Indian because he lives in an open house. Fresh air and an occasional wetting never killed anybody. The Seminole lives in an open house because he likes an open house. If a man can thatch a roof exquisitely, can he not also thatch a wall? Compare the clean, airy quarters at Guava Camp with the dog kennels provided for Indians at the Seminole Agency, and say which way is best."[5]

The Seminoles who occupied the cottages became more content once they made a few changes, however. They built and maintained cook chickees nearby and used the cottages only as sleeping quarters. The other main problem of bathing was soon resolved. At first they were not accustomed to using a bathtub or shower, since they always bathed in lakes, streams, or canals, which were absent from the vicinity of the Dania Reservation. A swimming pool was soon built near the cottages to solve this problem. Seminoles simply took a swim to satisfy their bathing needs. With time and a lot of hard work by locals, such as Seminole advocate and teacher Ivy Stranahan, more families slowly began to relocate to Dania.[6] Two other reservations, Brighton and Big Cypress, were officially established in 1935 and 1936, respectively.

President Franklin D. Roosevelt's New Deal programs, including the Civilian Conservation Corps (CCC) and particularly the Civilian Conservation Corps–Indian Division (CCC-ID), helped the Seminoles greatly improve their reservations. Government agents helped organize young crews of Seminole men to build roads, bridges, fences, and communication lines on the reservations, as well as distribute cattle and improve grazing pastures.[7] These programs first started in Dania but then moved to the larger Brighton and Big Cypress Reservations. The CCC-ID attracted many Seminoles to move onto the reservations for economic opportunities, as they were paid for working on these projects.[8] When the CCC disbanded in 1942, Seminoles remained on the reservations, where they received government aid through the BIA.

Though the reservations improved through the work of the CCC-ID, the 1930s and 1940s were filled with many internal struggles for the Seminoles. They were living as separate entities on the three different reservations and as other groups off the reservations. They were further divided upon the basis of their religious beliefs—traditionalists still participating in the Green Corn Dance and those who had converted to Christianity and given up some of their traditional customs.[9] Even the reservations themselves were not unified units. Garbarino took note of this fact at the Big Cypress Reservation even in the 1960s:

> There is very little group cohesiveness at Big Cypress. Traditionally, the people lived in isolated camps in the Big Cypress Swamp or the Everglades proper, and while there was some visiting between these camps, decisions were never made that would be binding on more than one residential unit, for there was no one who could make a decision binding on several camp groups. Communication was slow and uncertain. When the various camps were in agreement and acted in concert, it was usually because the adaptive requirements were such as to produce naturally similar responses to similar needs and situations. Households are cohesive units, but interaction among members of different camps, except for the adolescents, is between relatives more than between neighbors.[10]

Overall, the Seminoles were not making decisions as a whole. This separation nearly jeopardized their viability as a tribe altogether.

Native American "Advocacy"

Native American rights and independence were becoming hot issues across the nation throughout the 1930s, 1940s, and 1950s. Social reformer and Native American advocate John Collier helped draft the Wheeler-Howard Act of 1934, which guaranteed tribal sovereignty, promoted self-government, and encouraged tribes to start their own businesses.[11] The Seminoles living in Florida, however, did not take full advantage of the act at that time. They, and other tribes, held tightly to their culture despite the push for more government control. Over the next two decades, many non-Natives held the belief that Indian tribes would be better off if they assimilated into American society and relinquished their government supervision. Termination policies were soon imposed on many Indian tribes. The termination policies dissolved reservations, removed specific assistance by the BIA, and ultimately destroyed tribal sovereignty for those tribes affected. This was a very unfortunate situation for many of the terminated tribes who were impoverished and relied heavily upon that assistance. They were forced to assimilate into "white" society, into a life they had never known.

The Seminoles themselves faced possible termination in the early 1950s.[12] Seminole delegates traveled to Washington, D.C., in 1953 for hearings on the termination bill. They argued against termination and cited the lack of formal education, underdeveloped lands, poor health conditions, inadequate housing, and drainage issues on the Big Cypress and Brighton Reservations as the main reasons they still needed government supervision.[13] Through lots of hard work they avoided termination and eventually created their own constitution and corporate charter in August 1957. Later that year they were granted federal recognition by the U.S. government. These processes secured tribal sovereignty for the Seminoles. Reginald "Rex" W. Quinn, a Sioux, was appointed chief tribal operations officer for the BIA in 1956 and helped the Seminoles draft their constitution. By obtaining federal recognition, they continued to receive government assistance through the BIA and also became qualified for housing programs that were part of the 1949 Housing Act.[14] The act was intended to ensure that all Americans had a decent home in a safe area and to get rid of slums.

Seminole houses came under harsh scrutiny by the government, especially after the tribe received federal recognition in 1957. Chickees were seen as "primitive" and "unfit" for living.[15] Newspaper headlines throughout the state of Florida pinpointed chickees as antiquated. A January 1956 issue of the *Fort Lauderdale Daily News* reads, "Seminole Indians Are Ready to Break with Tradition and Junk Their Chickees," and an August headline that same year states, "Indian Wives Adopt White Woman's Ways: Seminoles Are Moving from 'Chickees' to Modern Homes." A 1968 headline from the *Tampa Times* even claimed: "The Chickee Isn't Chic Any More." Charitable organizations in Fort Lauderdale, such as the Friends of the Seminoles (established by Ivy Stranahan), the Florida Federated Women's Club, and others, began to raise money for Seminole homes on the Dania Reservation.[16] As long as Seminoles were living on reservations (federal land), outside agencies tried to change their living conditions. Even John F. Kennedy mentioned wanting to change substandard Indian housing in his 1960 campaign for president and implemented new housing programs during his time in office. President Johnson followed suit.

Seminoles who lived on the reservations did not usually qualify for home loans from conventional banks. Since reservation lands are held in trust by the federal government on behalf of the tribes and leased long term to tribal members, it was especially difficult at that time to put up the collateral needed to secure the loan.[17] Since individual Seminoles do not own the land on the reservations, they have nothing to offer up to the banks in case of a loan default. A bank could not buy a home on a reservation as a foreclosure and sell it to nontribal persons, for instance, and a bank often took a risk in creating such loans.

The Friends of the Seminoles allocated all of their membership dues in 1955 to a housing fund for the Seminoles.[18] They even held a public meeting in Broward County in January 1956 to discuss replacing chickees with houses—for the sake of the Seminole children who were attending white schools in the area.[19] These advocates were serious. Through local support, these charitable organizations worked with the Indian agent to construct six wooden frame houses on the reservation.[20]

South Florida has notoriously hot and humid weather, but in the winter of 1958, temperatures reached a low of 32°F on the Dania Reservation. At that time, many of the chickees were still left completely open-sided with no protection from the wind. There were seven houses on the reservation with electricity, but none of these had electric heaters. In one instance, twenty or more people huddled inside of a one-bedroom frame house to stay warm.[21] A chickee was typically quite comfortable for year-round living, but times like these made people consider the practicality of living in open-sided structures all the time.

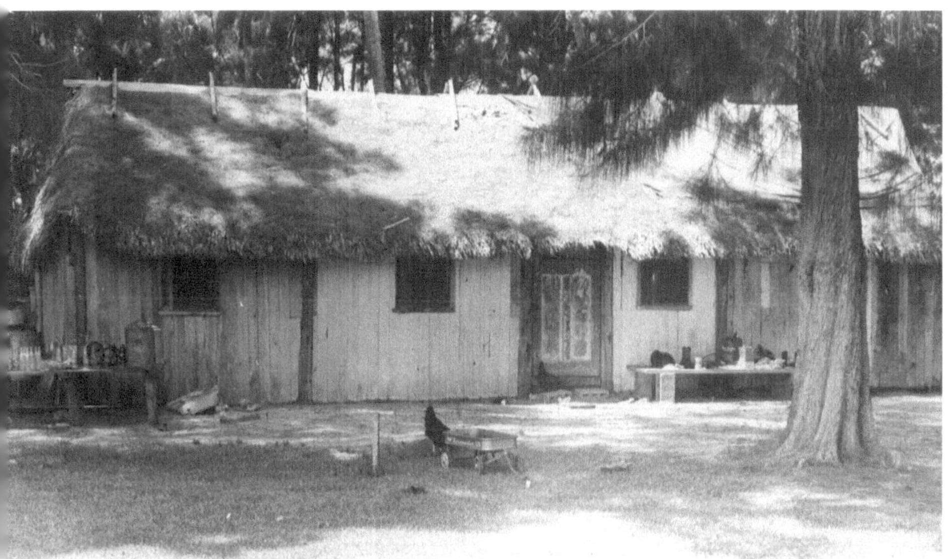

Figure 7.1. An example of what was considered substandard housing on the reservations. Note the wooden walls and the thatched roof. Photo taken to show the need for better housing, especially in Big Cypress and Brighton. Ah-Tah-Thi-Ki Museum, Boehmer Collection, c. 1960 (ATTK catalog no. 2009.34.1975).

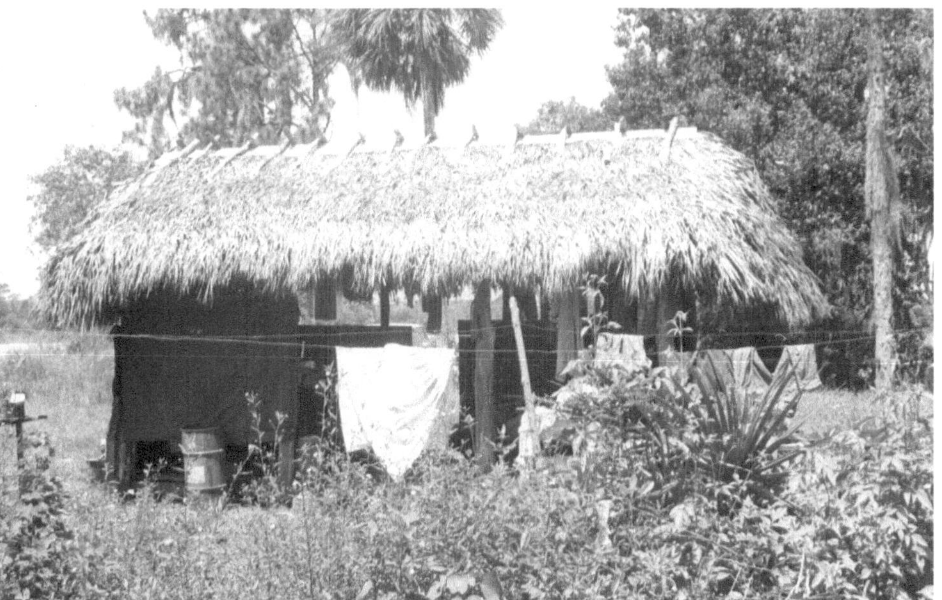

Figure 7.2. Another example of substandard housing on the reservations. Note the partial walls. Photo taken to show the need for better housing, especially in Big Cypress and Brighton. Ah-Tah-Thi-Ki Museum, Boehmer Collection, c. 1960 (ATTK catalog no. 2009.34.2008).

Chickees in the Transitional Period

Although the Seminoles who attended the termination hearing in 1953 claimed they had "inadequate housing," many others in the community did not see anything wrong with still living in chickees. Camp life was the only life most of them had ever known. Lee Tiger, spokesperson for the Miccosukee Tribe, noted in an interview in 1977, "Indians don't like houses, a lot of older people won't live in houses, some of the young people will. They can adapt to it, but the old people can't live in houses for the reason they don't like having walls around them. . . . They want to live in chickees cause that's the way they were born out here and lived in chickees all their lives and they'll probably stay like that."[22] Nabokov and Easton further emphasized this point: "Indians were deeply attached to their architectural patterns, found them practical and enjoyable, and resisted the white man's attempt to change them."[23] Many Seminoles wanted to be left to live as they pleased, while others yearned for a more modern way of life.

Most Dania Reservation houses (and some chickees) were known to have electricity during the 1950s, likely due to the more urban location of the reservation and its proximity to Fort Lauderdale. Mrs. Sam Franke became the first Seminole to have an electric range and refrigerator in her chickee on the Dania Reservation in the early 1950s. The cook chickee was partially enclosed but left open on the south side (the stove was on the north wall). Her cooking was quite popular, and at times she even had up to twenty guests eating at her table.[24] The camps in Big Cypress and Brighton during that time still lacked most modern conveniences, including electricity. Lee Tiger remembers that when he was a young boy, before his camp had electricity, they used a flashlight for lighting and an old ice box to keep their food cold.[25] By the 1960s and 1970s, however, most of the chickees were wired for electricity in one way or another. Substandard electricity was common on the reservations. Garbarino noted on Big Cypress, "much of the wiring in the chickees was potentially dangerous—overloads on the lines, and worn, exposed wires, most of which were too close to the water that was always underfoot during the wet season. Yet I have never heard of electrical fires or of anyone getting severe shocks."[26] The chickees that did not have electricity obviously did not have refrigeration or electrical appliances, and the Seminoles there still cooked over open flames and used kerosene lamps for lighting.[27]

Judie Kannon, an elementary school teacher at the Big Cypress Reservation School from 1970 to 1971, said that most of her students were still living in chickees and only one family had a concrete block and stucco (CBS) house. She noted that the chickees mostly had old-style pump sewing machines instead of electric sewing machines, and some of the chickees had televisions.[28] Most camps also had refrigerators at that time, and some tribal members even sold soft drinks and food staples in their "stores," or chickees separate from their living quarters.[29]

Willie Johns, born and raised on the Brighton Reservation, described to me the chickee camp in which he grew up. In his family's camp, they had twelve chickees. His mother and her eight sisters shared the camp, along with his fifteen first cousins. He chuckled when I asked his favorite memory about living in a chickee and replied, "You could sneak out easily." He specifically remembers escaping from the camp to watch late-night movies at the old recreation center. In Willie Johns's camp, they first received electricity in the cook chickee but then ran lines from that chickee to several of the other chickees in the camp.[30]

Many of the chickees from this era were not left open-sided like the chickees of the past. They often had complete or partial walls made from a variety of building materials. Even though chickees were changing with the times from the 1950s through the 1970s and featured many modern amenities, most of these structures still lacked one critical component: restrooms. During Gabarino's visits, she noted only one chickee with a flush toilet and septic tank. The others had either outhouses or no restroom facilities at all.[31] Even as late as 1979, the camps off the beaten path did not have indoor plumbing and relied on wells for drinking water.[32]

"Modern" Houses

Although Seminoles were accustomed to chickees and camp life, many were quite eager to move into modern housing. Evidence of early vernacular homes on the Brighton Reservation, dating back to the

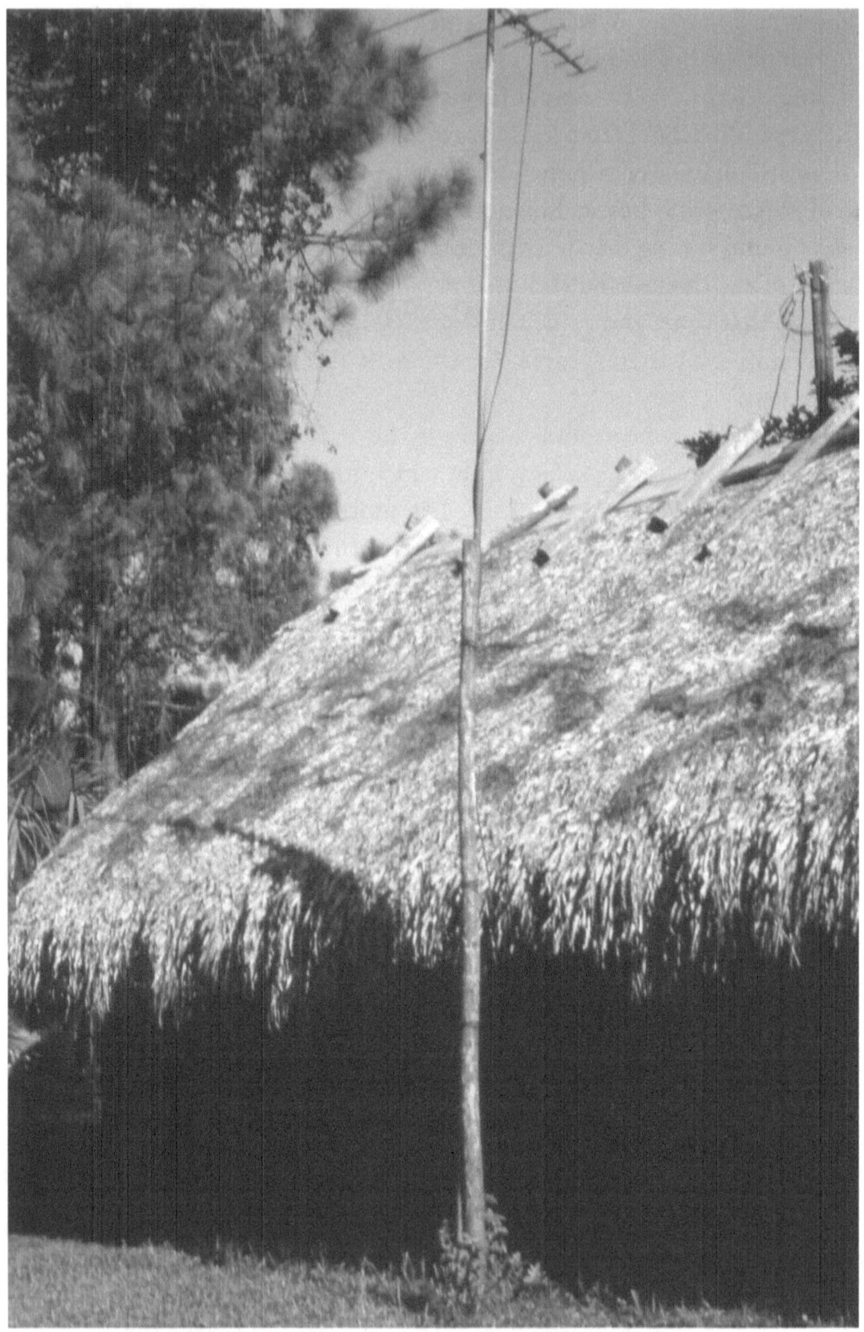

Figure 7.3. *Seminole chickee with a TV antenna—Immokalee, Florida.* An example of a chickee with modern conveniences. Photo by Peggy A. Bulger, State Archives of Florida, *Florida Memory*, http://floridamemory.com/items/show/121430.

1930s, still exists today. During an architectural survey of the reservation, I located several of these structures. The homes are very small (one room) and made from a variety of local materials. Though rudimentary, these structures show that some Seminoles desired other types of homes before the government stepped in to replace chickees. No evidence of these types of structures has been found on the Big Cypress Reservation, though it is likely similar structures existed there as well.

When Glenn L. Emmons, commissioner of Indian Affairs, consulted with the Seminoles in 1954, he said they wanted, among other things, education for their children, improvement of their land resources, democratic tribal organization, and "modern homes," which were simple frame houses instead of chickees.[33] When Jessica Cattelino conducted interviews with tribal elders for her article "Florida Seminole Housing and the Social Meanings of Sovereignty," she noted that many recalled that they longed to live in houses as children in the 1960s because it was hard to finish their schoolwork in chickees, especially in chickees that did not have electricity.[34] Chickees became very dark once the sun set. Mary Bowers, from the Dania Reservation, mentioned in her *Seminole Tribune* article that she enjoyed the changes to the reservation. She liked having homes instead of chickees, although chickees were easy to clean, and she jokingly said they "had free air conditioning." She commented in a more serious tone that chickee life had been difficult.[35] Mary Bowers lived in one of the frame houses in Dania in the 1950s and won first place in a housekeeping contest in 1956.

The Reverend Bill Osceola was the first Seminole to move into a CBS house on the Dania Reservation in 1957. Osceola hoped that the house would prove that "the Seminoles want to live like everybody else" and that they no longer wanted to live in chickees. Osceola's residence was the first "modern" home built on the reservation (the previous homes were either chickees or simple wooden frame houses). The family borrowed part of the money from the Friends of the Seminoles, and the rest came from private individuals and from personal savings.[36] In addition, since reservation land is owned by the federal government, they did not have to pay for the land itself, and the BIA served as the building contractor and inspector.[37] That helped make homes like these much more affordable.

Seminole Indians Estates, "a 40-acre paleface-style subdivision," was

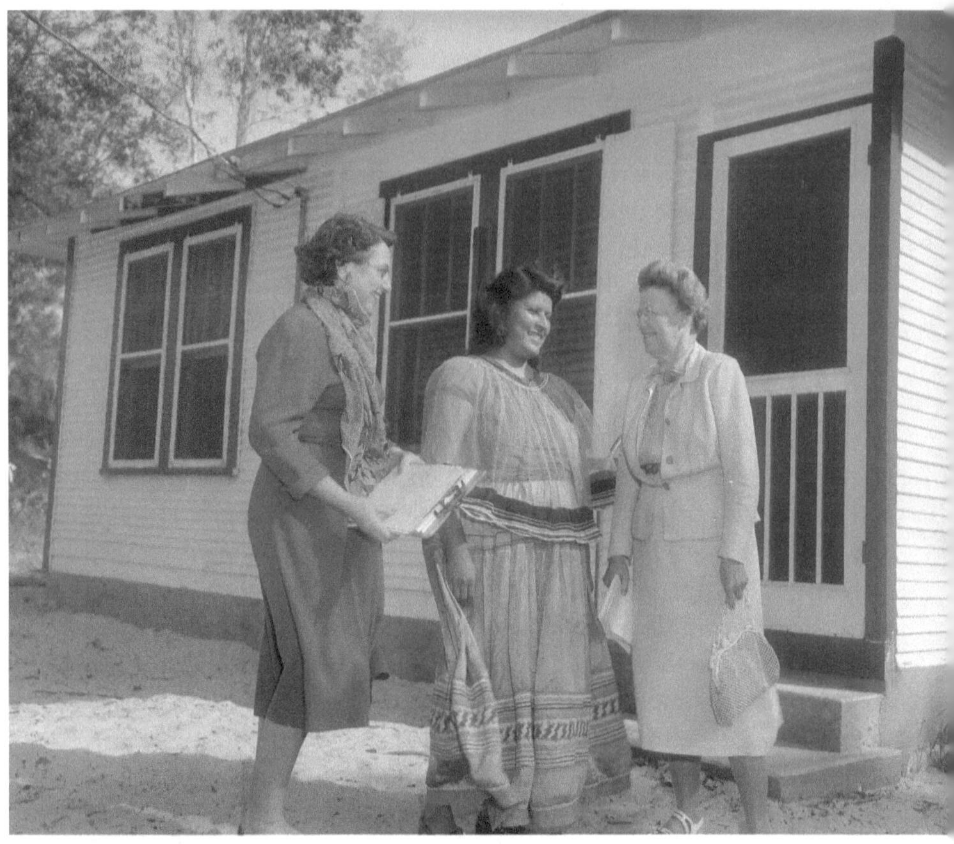

Figure 7.4. *Seminole woman, Mary Bowers, wins 1st place prize in a housekeeping contest.* Mary Bowers (*middle*) poses outside her new home with Louise Taylor (*left*), Broward County home demonstration agent, and Ivy Stranahan (*right*), president of Friends of the Seminoles. Photo by Francis P. Johnson, State Archives of Florida, *Florida Memory*, http://floridamemory.com/items/show/74042.

dedicated in 1959 on the Dania Reservation. Dania featured fourteen occupied homes (four frame dwellings and ten CBS) and four others under construction at that time.[38] Mrs. Henson Billie was featured in the *Fort Lauderdale News* when she and her family moved into this new housing community. The home was furnished through donations of the Friends of the Seminoles. She only took a few items from her chickee to her new home, including her sewing machine.[39]

One of the more popular housing initiatives on the reservations came about a decade later—the Self-Help Program of the late 1960s. The Self-Help Program provided Seminoles the opportunity to ob-

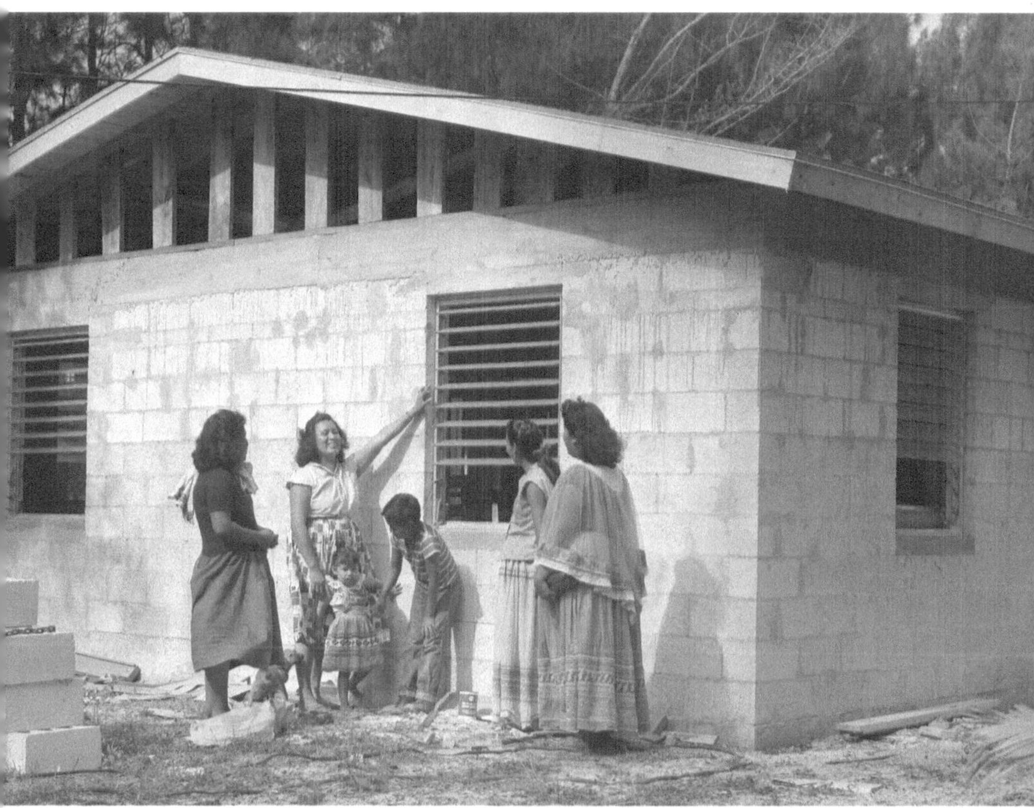

Figure 7.5. *Charlotte Osceola proudly shows off her new American style home being built by her husband.* Charlotte Osceola points out features of her new home to friends on the Dania Reservation. The home was being built by her husband, Bill, and was financed by revolving funds from the Friends of the Seminoles. Charlotte Osceola is second from the left, Mary Bower is to the far right, and Martha Osceola is second from the right. Photo by Francis P. Johnson, State Archives of Florida, *Florida Memory*, http://floridamemory.com/items/show/74036.

tain affordable housing through mutual initiatives. Seminoles had to contribute 590 hours of labor for building their own home.[40] In many cases, the women completed much of the manual labor for these houses because the men often had jobs away from the reservation.[41] A few of these Self-Help houses are still standing on the reservations today, though most remain vacant.

Rex Quinn, superintendent of the Seminole Agency in Hollywood from 1965 to 1968, worked diligently to improve the cattle program, land use, housing, education, and tribal government, among other is-

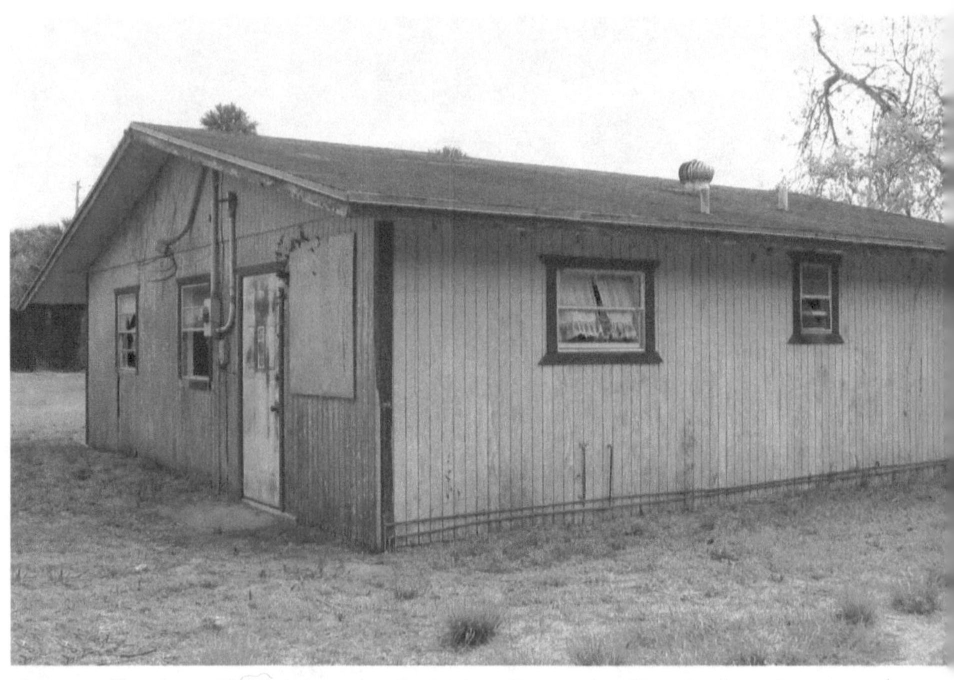

Figure 7.6. Abandoned Self-Help house on the Brighton Reservation. Photo by the author, 2008.

sues. He recorded all the camps and houses on the Big Cypress and Brighton Reservations in his 1965–1967 survey for the Housing Improvement Plan. The survey paperwork listed the name of the family; the number of occupants in the home/camp; if the home was equipped with running water, a sewer, electricity, heating, and cooking facilities; and whether the property was a "traditional Seminole camp," "traditional camp with modern equipment," "modern camp sub-standard," or "modern camp good." In Brighton, he discovered seventeen traditional camps, twenty-four modern sub-standard, and eight traditional with modern equipment. No camps were listed as "modern camp good." There were forty-nine families and 229 total residents. In Big Cypress, there were forty-three families and 169 people. On the Big Cypress Reservation, he recorded twenty-two traditional camps, three traditional with modern equipment, eighteen modern sub-standard, and zero modern good.[42]

A similar report from 1966 (located at the University of Florida Archives) showed a total of forty-two modern homes and seventy-nine camps in Hollywood, Big Cypress, and Brighton. Hollywood had twenty-three modern homes and thirteen traditional camps, Big Cypress had ten modern homes and thirty-four traditional camps, and Brighton had nine modern homes and thirty-two traditional camps. Most of these camps lacked utilities except for a "sand point well with pitcher pump." These numbers, compared to the number of residents, constituted a housing shortage.[43] Based upon these findings, the Tribal Council created the Seminole Tribal Housing Authority to promote better housing. Comprised of Seminoles appointed by the Tribal Council, the Tribal Housing Authority had a strong connection with the federal government through the BIA. They said there was an immediate need for eighty homes.[44]

For obvious historical reasons, Seminoles had a strong distrust of government, and it is very likely that neither report gives the full picture of residential camps on the reservations during the mid-twentieth century. Whether either of these two reports is entirely accurate I am not sure, but both prove that the majority of Seminoles were still living in chickees in 1966, especially in Big Cypress and Brighton. This is despite the many efforts to update the reservations.

A 1959 article from a Fort Myers newspaper, entitled "Seminoles Leaving Shacks for New Modern Houses," described the new homes on the Big Cypress Reservation. The article details how the Seminoles were adjusting quite well to their new homes. Annie Frank liked the new kitchen: "Will be much better than cooking on open fire with wind blowing and smoke getting in your eyes." Her husband enjoyed the warm running water in the bathroom.[45]

The ten CBS houses in Big Cypress recorded in the 1966 report were also mentioned by Garbarino in her study of the reservation from 1963 to 1965. She stated that they were "occupied by nuclear or extended families, one member of which owns cattle."[46] At that time, cattle owners were the most likely candidates to secure a home loan since the cattle could be used as collateral. She also mentioned that all the CBS houses had electricity but no telephones until 1967, and the new structures were set up on a sewage system with clean running water. She noted, "The CBS are sturdily built with modern conveniences, and in general the owners have enjoyed the comforts and conveniences they offer."[47] The CBS homes, however, were extremely hot in the summer and quite expensive to maintain compared to chickees. In fact, it was not uncommon for some Seminoles to knock out the windows in the original CBS homes that lacked air-conditioning to create cross-ventilation in order to make them more like a chickee. The Self-Help houses that came onto the reservations in the late 1960s were perhaps more comfortable and more affordable than the earlier CBS homes. The Self-Help houses were made with wooden walls, a cement foundation, and lots of windows that could be opened to provide adequate cross-ventilation.[48]

The newly constructed homes on the reservation featured modern bathrooms, kitchens, and often a washer and dryer. Unfortunately, many of the people who moved into these homes did not know how to properly take care of them. The BIA reports from that time indicate the houses were often dirty.[49] The women who moved into the houses had no idea how to use or clean the stove or how to use a washing machine, because those appliances were not found in chickees (except in rare cases). They did not know how to clean the floors or the windows.[50] As a result, the BIA worked with the University of Florida's Agricultural Extension Service to send in "Extension Agents" to provide home economics training for the Seminoles.[51] This program was funded through the University of Florida by the U.S. Department of Agriculture. Aurilla Birrel was sent to the Brighton Reservation in 1968 to train Seminoles on how to maintain their new houses. She spent six months working closely with Seminole women, giving them weekly training. Later reports indicate that the homes were extremely clean and orderly.

The houses built on the reservations were quite small. The Rex Quinn papers included floor plans of the original one- and two-bedroom houses from 1966. The one-bedroom units were 20'×24', and the two bedroom units were 24'×30'. That equates to 480 square feet for a one-bedroom home and 720 square feet for a two-bedroom home. (Garbarino also mentions three-bedroom homes in Big Cypress. The size is unknown, but they were likely less than 1,000 square feet.) That amount of square footage seems extremely small by today's standards following the "McMansion" trend of recent years, and it was still small compared to the average house at the time. According to the U.S. Census, the average house was 1,200 square feet in 1960 and 1,500 square feet in 1970. The size of the on-reservation homes at the time seems even smaller when you consider that multiple or extended families often occupied homes intended for single families.

Seminoles were accustomed to camp life in which the entire extended family lived together, and many tried to carry that tradition over into the new, modern structures. Mary Jene Coppedge recalled in a 1999 interview that her grandmother moved into a home when Mary Jene was thirteen in the late 1950s. Her grandmother hated it at first but adjusted to it because she continued to cook meals outside. Mary Jene's entire camp moved into the three-bedroom house—thirteen people, including the grandparents, her mother, two uncles, Mary Jene, and her seven siblings. Coppedge noted that moving the whole family into the house helped them retain their language and culture.[52] In many ways, camp life was essential to helping Seminoles retain their cultural identity.

Families did not always maintain the close relationship exhibited by the Coppedges. Moving into these new, small-scale houses often led to the break-up of the extended family. Garbarino concluded that "when an additional chickee could be raised with little effort, new units to the camp caused no stress, but the crowding of an extended family into a nonexpandable cement block building puts a strain on all the inhabitants."[53] Trying to fit an entire extended family into less than 1,000 square feet seems almost unthinkable, but some creative families made it possible by utilizing all the rooms of the house for sleeping, not just the bedrooms. Bedrooms, living rooms, and dining rooms could all be used for a nuclear family's separate sleeping spaces. Since these homes did not allow the possibility of expansion, most children ended up leaving the extended family structure when they married instead of remaining in the crowded house.[54]

Amos Rapoport mentions that this practice of space utilization was not uncommon: "In many cases of dwellings in traditional cultures, where no permanent specialized settings occur, the activities appropriate to changing situation are frequently indicated by changes in the furnishings. Frequently the presence of such cues can change the intended meaning of settings and lead to very different and 'inappropriate' activities occurring in settings an architect might label 'kitchen,' 'living room,' 'bedroom' or whatever."[55] The term *inappropriate* here means sleeping in the living room, for example.

According to a Mr. Waldrip, of the Public Housing Administration, in 1965 many Seminoles did not want CBS houses; they instead simply wanted a modern version of the chickee. He suggested creating houses with a dirt floor, cypress framing, and a palmetto thatched roof, but with the inclusion of a bathroom. He did mention additionally that it could present a problem for an architect to design such a house.[56] I do not see why this would be the case, but perhaps many people believed the structures would still be too primitive, as people wanted to see Seminoles out of chickees altogether. Chickees were indeed being modernized by the Seminoles themselves with walls and electricity in Big Cypress and Brighton, as seen in figures 7.1 and 7.2, but outsiders still considered them to be unsuitable forms of housing. Perhaps if the Seminoles had installed restrooms in their homes, the houses would have then been more acceptable to the agents who visited the reservations.

It is also interesting to note that architects began working with the Miccosukee on the Tamiami Trail in 1962 to create a modern version of the chickee. They determined that the houses should retain the appearance of the traditional chickee with a palmetto roof and a hole in the ceiling for the cooking fire. Unlike the traditional version, however, the updated chickee would include concrete blocks surrounding the base of the platform floor and walls made of screen and canvas.[57] In contrast to the unrealized idea of creating a modern chickee for the Seminoles, the Miccosukee homes were actually created. By 1965, fifteen of these modern chickees had been constructed. They featured electricity, hot water, and a few appliances such as stoves and refrigerators. They were built on stilts, raised about two feet off the ground, and had four rooms for living, plus a kitchen and bath in the center. They were left partially open-sided, with screens to allow cross-ventilation. They featured a solid roof underneath the thatch covering. The homes successfully retained much of the appearance of the chickees.[58] These homes were an agreeable compromise between traditional chickees and the "modern" homes. Even though they were not a radical departure from chickees, younger generation Miccosukees were more likely to move into these homes than the older generation.[59]

Mary Elen Bundschu, now a practicing architect, studied Seminole housing in Brighton for her architecture terminal project for a master's of architecture at the University of Florida in 1979.[60] Bundschu, a non-Seminole, felt quite strongly that the modern houses on the reservation were an atrocious theft of Seminole culture. She noted that whites were not satisfied with the way Seminoles were living, so they forced them into "poorly constructed, concrete block boxes" that destroyed their pride. She asked, "If modern conveniences are to be provided for the Indians, why not provide them in such a way which allows the Indians to continue their present existence?"[61] It is true that the homes could have been designed to better suit the tribe and their culture, but to some people (government agents and even many tribal members) they were a vast improvement over chickees.

Seminole Attitude toward Leaving Chickees

For the Seminoles, moving into "normal" homes was bittersweet—doing so garnered a sense of pride but also symbolized the breakdown of the extended family. Cattelino pointed out that the new BIA housing promoted nuclear families, with the father as head of the household.[62] Remember, Seminoles are a matrilineal society, but the BIA tried to shift the paradigm of the family to more closely resemble Anglo-American values. They wanted fathers to focus on being fathers and educating their children (which was previously done by maternal uncles and aunts). This fact was pointed out in the *Miami Herald* in 1960: "There is now in process a fundamental uprooting of the Seminole culture; change not just in external living conditions, but manifested in a slow change from a matriarchal society to a patriarchal. Change manifested in emphasis laid upon acquisition of family property—a concept once totally foreign to Seminole society."[63] While it is true that the superficial family dynamic shifted somewhat toward a patriarchal society, Seminoles have remained a matriarchal society to this day.

Moving into a modern house ushered in a whole new set of financial problems as well. First, unlike chickees, these homes needed a wide variety of furniture (not just wooden platforms for beds and tables). Second, Seminoles would now have to buy groceries rather than growing fruits and vegetables in their gardens and hunting their proteins since they did not have gardens or easy access to hunting and fishing areas. And third, perhaps the biggest expense of all was the monthly mortgage payment. Seminoles owned their homes but not the property on which the home sat. This new financial burden forced many Seminole women out of their homes and into the workforce.[64] This shifted the family dynamic even further.

Despite the popular belief that most Seminole children wanted modern homes, many were unhappy about moving out of their camps. Aurilla Birrel mentioned an unnamed teenage girl who was not happy about transitioning from a chickee into a house: "She felt that she was cooped in with all these walls around her, and she was confined. She did not like the closeness, the exposure, that she was getting. This was surprising to me coming from a teenager, who was going to school in Moore Haven, and was, I considered, a part of the outside world, shall we say. But she still had this very strong feeling for her original housing situation."[65] Mary Jene Coppedge, also a teen when she moved into a house, liked her new home but preferred the arrangement of camps:

> I enjoy my house. But if they would have asked me how I wanted my house to be built, I think I would have told them that, okay, I have lived in a camp setting all of my life, where we had my aunts and uncles in the same place, my grandparents. . . . I think if they would have just come out and asked, how would you like your house? I would have told them, put me in a camp setting. Fine, if you want to build us nice, single-family dwellings. I would much rather have had my grandmother's house here, mine here, my mother's here, my uncle's or my aunt's here, in this same location in a cluster so that I still had my extended family.[66]

Paul "Cowbone" Buster remembers chickee life fondly: "We never had any fancy possessions: no big house, no big car, no fancy clothes—but what we had was a home. Our home was a chickee made from cypress wood and palmetto fronds, but it was a home. It may be hard to live like that compared to today's lifestyle, but it seemed like life was more simple and more enjoyable in those times than it is today."[67]

Many elders who grew up in chickees think that children today are too spoiled with modern conveniences. They believe that living in the chickees kept the children closer to their families and not so caught up in worldly possessions.[68]

Garbarino also included a quote from an unidentified Seminole woman about life in a CBS house: "I didn't like the house at first. When I looked around all I could see were walls and there seemed to be no place to sit down. We didn't have a washing machine at first so we washed clothes in the bathtub. But I liked the kitchen."[69] It was certainly an adjustment from chickee life.

Willie Johns vividly remembers moving from a chickee camp to a CBS home on the Brighton Reservation when he was nineteen years old in the late 1960s. At first he felt so confined, like he was living in a box. He also mentioned how it impacted his extended family. His large familial camp split up as his aunts married and moved into houses of their own with their new husbands, and he did not see his cousins nearly as often. Johns moved into the CBS house with only his mom and his siblings. There were advantages, he recalled. He definitely enjoyed the hot showers and modern toilets. While living in a chickee, it was necessary to heat water before taking a bath. When I asked if he thought moving from the camps into the CBS home was a good or bad thing, he replied that it was a bit of both. Moving into the homes was just a sign of the times, modernization, but it came with a price. The language in particular started to become lost. After this shift, tradition and culture were taught in the classroom rather than at home in the camps.[70]

Chickee builder Ronnie Billie lived in a chickee from the time he was born until 1970. He thinks that moving out of chickees altered the Seminoles' way of life because "the government is always there. The people have to spend more money, pay taxes, and now you must jump through hoops when you want to do something on your land." As a teenager he was happy to move into a house, however. In a chickee, there was no toilet or running water. He also mentioned that leaving your clothes hanging to dry outdoors might be met with a surprise scorpion in your pants.[71]

Sandy Billie Jr. moved into a CBS house about forty-eight years ago in Brighton. He grew up with no material possessions but loved living in a chickee. "You had A/C all the time," he laughed. He mentioned that you had a mosquito net and an extra blanket when you got cold: "The first two days of winter were hell, but then you got used to it." He said they put up plywood for walls in cold weather. They used the same sheets of plywood for firewood as the weather warmed up or to make furniture such as a table. "We might not have had money, but we were still happy. We had love," he lamented. According to Billie, when people moved out of chickees they thought they were rich, and it went to their heads. "Now if someone lived in a chickee you would think they were poor. If people had stayed in camps they would have their head on straight."[72] Values have certainly changed over the years.

Bobby Henry's grandfather told him, "lots of changes are coming." Those changes became apparent when people moved out of chickees and into houses. Bobby Henry actually saw the transition as positive change because it afforded him the opportunity to attend school. On the other hand, this change also came with a downside: "Moving into a non-Indian town, you cannot just do whatever you want. You have neighbors. Government now has more control. You can't teach the language before you go to school. But going to corn dance, getting scratched, helps you hold on to your culture."[73] Going back and participating in these ceremonies year after year, living in chickees for a short period of time, puts people back into the right frame of mind.

Children were often ridiculed at public school for living in chickees,[74] so they were generally happy to move into modern homes. But the elders, unfazed by what outsiders thought, were perhaps the most hesitant to make the move. Chickees and camp life were all they had ever known, and they were sad to leave. Lee Tiger mentioned in his 1977 interview that many people were still living in chickees, including many of his aunts and uncles. He said that his uncle, an elder, would probably always live in a chickee.[75] Even when elders made the jump to home ownership, they were slow to actually fully move into them.[76]

The Buster twins on the Brighton Reservation were extremely set on residing in their chickees. Mary and Martha Buster moved from the Fort Pierce/St. Lucie area to the Brighton Reservation in the early 1950s. They first occupied the camp with their sister, her husband, and their three children (the twins' nieces and nephew).[77] The family lived in traditional chickees in the camp. After the other family members left, the Buster twins remained in the camp and continued to occupy their chickees even though they had other structures. This was likely due to their distrust of white Americans and any form of organized government. The reclusive women lived in their traditional chickees built the old-fashioned way—the chickees were tied together instead of nailed. Oral histories additionally confirm that they did not want the housing and only liked their camp.[78] The Buster twins camp contained a small house from the 1930s prior to the sisters' occupation of the site as well as two other structures from the 1960s built for the Buster twins as part of the efforts to modernize the reservations. The three homes remain, but the chickees once in the camp are long gone. Their camp is still used today as a place to teach tribal students about their history and culture.

In many cases, as seen with the Buster twins camp, the homes were built on the sites of the familial camps. In those instances, the families could still retain chickees on site for outdoor activity spaces, especially for cooking. That helped appease many of the people who did not want to leave the chickees completely.[79] Many Seminoles continued to occupy chickees through the 1970s and even up until the 1980s on the Big Cypress Reservation.

The Future, as Noted in 1979

Mary Elen Bundschu took note of how modern homes were impacting Seminole culture: "The Seminole Indians are presently in a difficult period of transition. Active measures are being taken to modern[ize] their housing facilities with plumbing and electrical provisions, but simultaneously much of the character of their environment is being lost. The chickee is being replaced by poorly constructed CBS (concrete block with stucco) housing which has proved to be unsuitable for the Everglades area and the Seminole way of life. The Seminole are faced with either changing their living patterns to adapt to new government housing, or remain[ing] in their self-made huts."[80] She even went so far as to say that "the Seminole chickee will also become an extinct construction system if it is not adapted to modern conveniences to serve a changing society."[81]

In 1979, Bundschu noted that chickees were being used to supplement CBS homes, and many home sites included a wide variety of structures.[82] I made similar observations during my chickee survey thirty years later. Maybe the exact same structures were not there, but the cultural patterns of habitation remained.

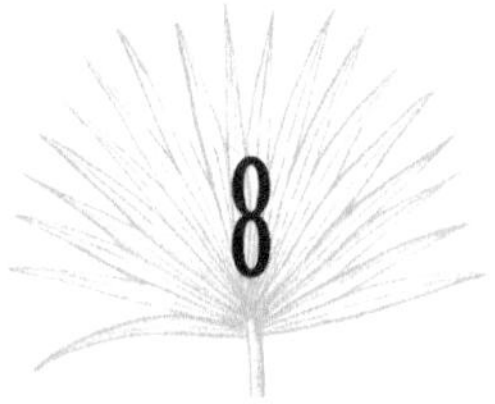

8

The Big Cypress Chickee Survey

In February 2009, I was tasked with conducting a chickee survey on each of the Seminole Tribe of Florida reservations. At first, the Big Cypress Chickee Survey was intended to be a simple inventory to see how many chickees were in existence. As the survey progressed, the goal began to change. Within the first few days of surveying we started to notice a wide range of building methods, materials, shapes, and uses. It became abundantly clear that the new goal of the survey would be to examine how the culture of the Seminole Tribe is reflected through their architecture.

The survey began on the Big Cypress Reservation (we later decided to limit the survey to this reservation due to the abundance of data we gathered). On-reservation homes and property are generally never accessed by non-Seminoles unless there is a specific need (usually pertaining to some type of tribal business). The reservations themselves have no-trespassing signs posted, and the Hollywood Reservation requires entry through a security gate. Working as an employee of the Seminole Tribe does not grant a person the authority to just walk up to people's homes. I conducted the survey with the help of the Tribal Historic Preservation Office (THPO) cultural advisers, Marty Bowers and Jacob Osceola. As Seminole tribal members who lived on the Big Cypress Reservation, they could answer many of my questions about the various chickees we encountered. They also knew many people on the reservation and were familiar with the layout of the reservation itself. And since Seminoles are still unused to outsiders in their camps,

Marty and Jacob helped to communicate the purpose of the project to the tribal members we encountered.

In conducting the survey, we drove down all the roads on the reservation—paved and unpaved. We went off-road into yards and deep into hammocks. We experienced inclement weather and encountered numerous dogs, a few alligators, lots of bugs, and plenty of the Florida heat you would expect when working in the swampy Everglades. The survey was a unique experience that went far beyond the typical architectural survey.

According to the architect Steen Rasmussen, "Understanding architecture, therefore, is not the same as being able to determine the style of a building by certain external features. It is not enough to see architecture; you must experience it. You must observe how it was designed for a special purpose and it was attuned to the entire concept and rhythm of a specific area."[1] The chickee survey was not just about observing; it was certainly about experiencing.

Methodology and Purpose of the Survey

The cultural advisers and I took approximately a year and a half (February 2009–June 2010) to complete the survey on the Big Cypress Reservation. Although we went to great lengths to make the survey as thorough as possible, we admittedly may have overlooked an obscure chickee or two. In some cases we talked to the chickee owner to gather more information than we could discern by observation, and in other cases we completed the survey based only upon what we could see. We took note of how each chickee was being utilized (cooking, dining, storage, and so forth), in addition to the shape, size, structural condition, and distinguishing architectural characteristics. We photographed, measured, and located each chickee with a GPS unit. The survey data was organized and uploaded into a geographic information system (GIS) database, ArcGis. The findings from the survey served as our data set, and most of the information in this chapter directly relates to this survey.

Throughout the survey, it was important to not cross the line from immersive to invasive. The chickees in people's yards are private structures—an extension of their homes. It would have been out of line to just walk into someone's camp without an invitation, and of course you would not just walk into someone's house without knocking. Just because these structures are almost all completely open-sided, that does not mean they are public spaces. I was carrying out the duties of my job as I had been asked, but the chickee survey went beyond what would have been required from a traditional architectural survey. Chickees (particularly on the reservations) should be respected. We believed that it was important to look at the overall facts and patterns discovered in this survey instead of drawing conclusions based upon individual chickees. I have taken caution not to mention specific private structures without the permission of the owner and instead to speak in generalities. The survey of the structures in Big Cypress helps to discern the bigger picture of how critical chickees are to the reservations today and how they are a mainstay of Seminole culture.

The Big Cypress Chickee Survey was intended to document patterns in Seminole architecture at a point in time. Since chickees are semipermanent structures of varying condition, the number may not be indicative of the exact number of chickees at present. We looked at chickees as a whole, and the sheer number we found shows how significant and relevant they still are to the tribe today. Looking around the reservation, it is obvious that there are lots of chickees, but the number we recorded far exceeded our expectations.

Big Cypress Reservation: A General Overview

Big Cypress is the largest of the six Seminole reservations in the state of Florida. It covers 81.972 square miles (over 52,000 acres) and has a population of 591 residents as reported in the 2010 U.S. Census. In 2013, there were approximately 455 buildings on the reservation—258 single-family homes, with the other 197 buildings being a mix of building types (school, gym, churches, tribal offices, health facilities, and so forth).[2]

The Big Cypress Chickee Survey yielded an astounding 479 chickees. Based upon the above numbers, there are more chickees than other buildings combined. Not every single structure is accompanied by a chickee, but on average, for every building there is a chickee. Some buildings and homes have multiple chickees, some do not have any, and some chickees are alone on the property site with no accompanying building. When you take into account the population of Big Cypress at

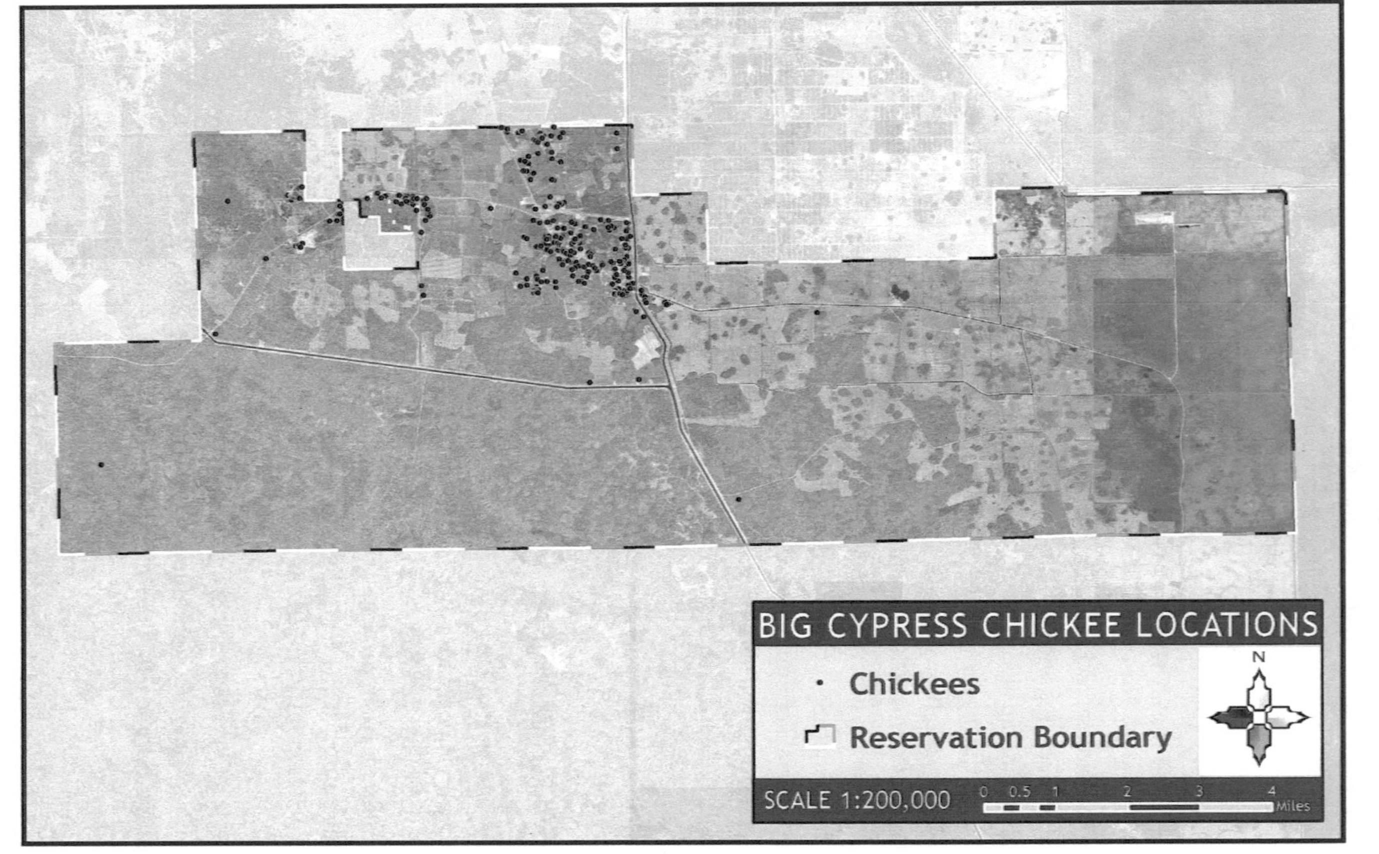

Figure 8.1. Map of chickee locations at Big Cypress, created using ArcMap by Josh Ooyman, Tribal Historic Preservation Office GIS specialist. Not only does the geodatabase feature the GPS location of each chickee, but it also contains all the attribute information gathered from the survey (chickee survey number, owner/site name, date of survey,

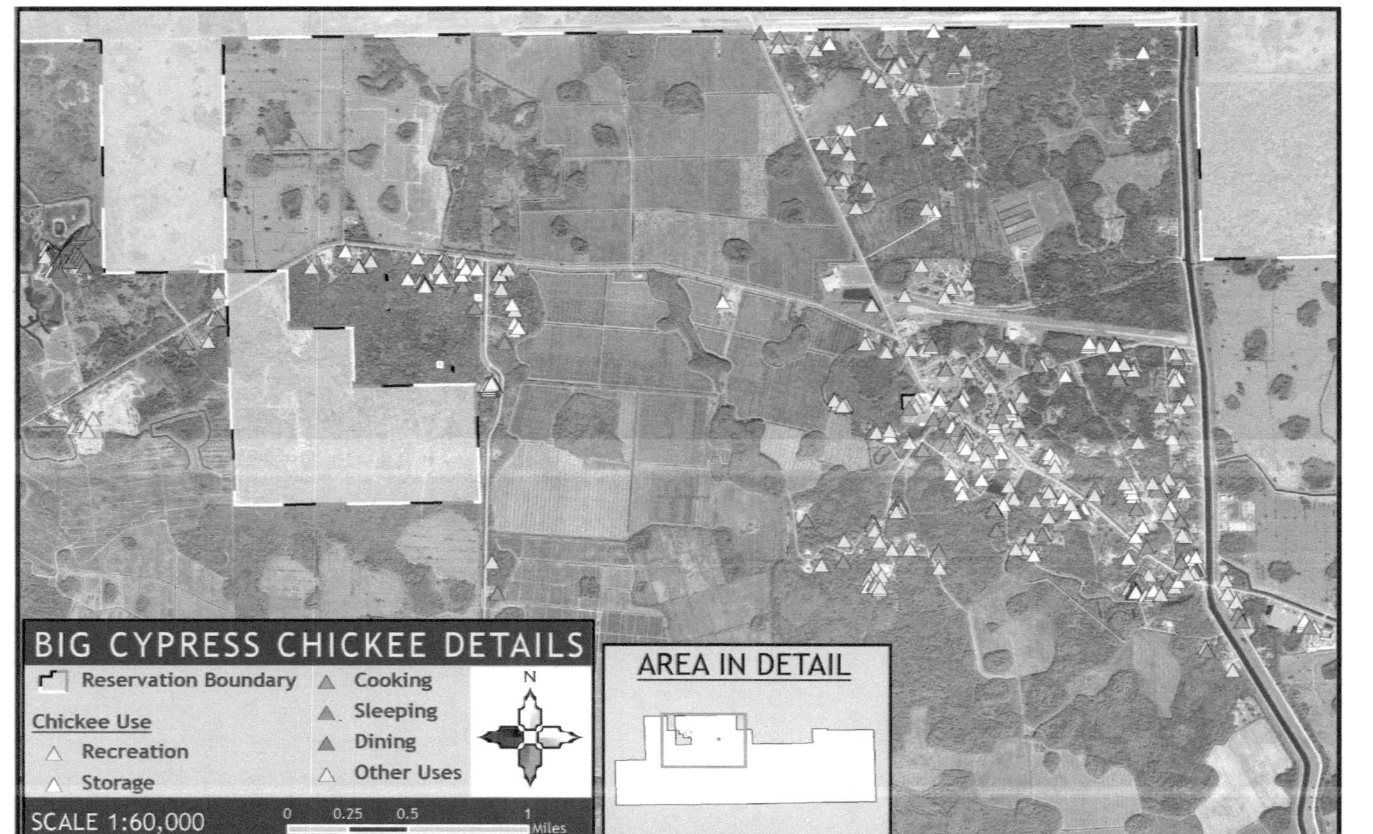

Figure 8.2. Detailed map showing how ArcMap software can be used to organize chickees by their usage. Map created by Josh Ooyman, Tribal Historic Preservation Office GIS specialist.

the time of the survey, it turns out that for every ten people there were approximately eight chickees. These chickees range in size from the tiny—a 3'×3' doghouse—to the grand—a 27'×70' recreational chickee.

The "Standard" Chickee

When conducting the survey, we looked at how, if at all, the chickee deviated from what we would consider a "standard chickee." A "standard chickee," for the sake of the survey, was a chickee with typical features. Over the years, standard chickee features changed somewhat, but still today open-sided, rectangular, modestly sized, gable- or hipped-roofed chickees with round crisscrossed roof weights and a ridge cap remain the most common type. In addition, uprights made from either cypress or pressure-treated pine would both be considered standard features today. We carefully observed each chickee for any other features that would make it stand out from the rest, such as asymmetry, unusual roofs (shape or pitch), porches, or posts in different places (such as central uprights). During the survey, we only examined the permanent attributes of the structure itself, not the contents inside (picnic tables, cars, and so forth), although what was inside clued us in on the use of the chickee. The specific information in this chapter primarily pertains to public-space chickees, while the general information, including statistics, comes from the complete survey data.

Survey Details

We began the survey at the site of the Ah-Tah-Thi-Ki Museum and THPO. There are seven standard chickees in the museum's parking lot. They are all approximately 14'×10' with hipped roofs, pressure-treated pine uprights, round roof weights, asphalt ridge coverings, and dirt floors. These chickees epitomize what is typical throughout the reservation. They are used as dining chickees for visitors to the museum or during special events.

We surveyed the rest of the chickees at the museum campus at a later date. There are two additional standard dining chickees behind the museum and a chickee behind the curatorial building that has a wooden plank floor and fenced-in half-walls that go around the sides of the structure. There are several stops along the museum's mile-long

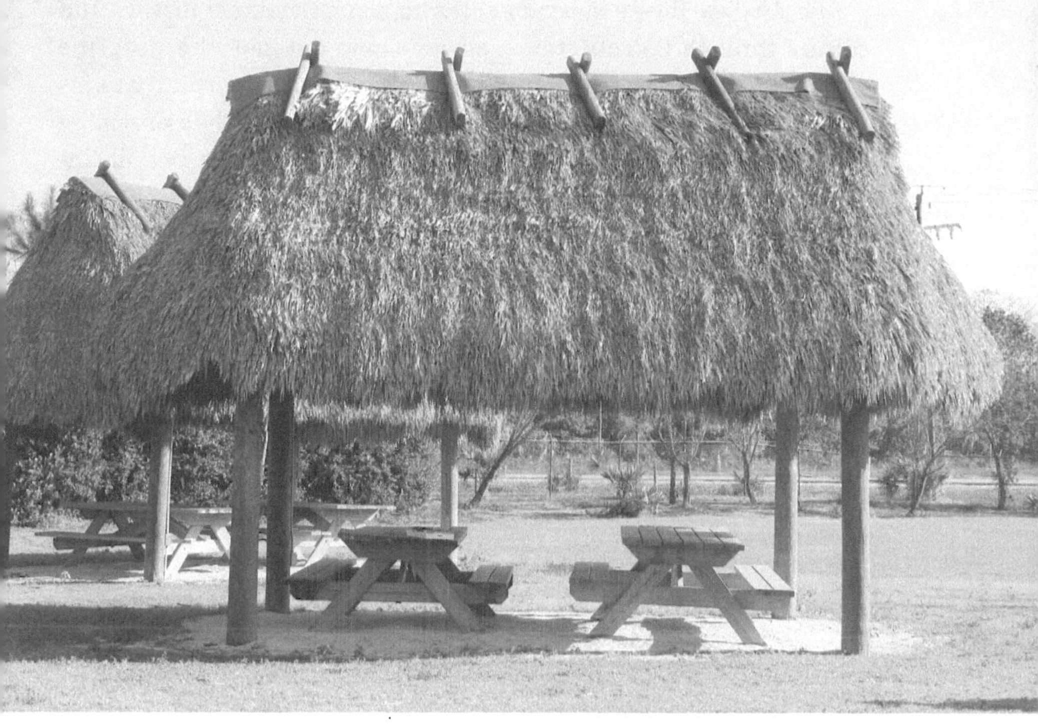

Figure 8.3. "Standard" chickee in the Ah-Tah-Thi-Ki Museum's parking lot. Photo by the author, Big Cypress Reservation, 2009.

boardwalk through a natural cypress dome, many of which contain chickees. The outdoor amphitheater is akin to a "lean-to" chickee with its sloping shed roof. This is the site of many outdoor programs at the museum, including storytelling and wildlife presentations. Though this amphitheater deviates from a traditional chickee in several ways, it provides a great setting for visitors to learn about Seminole history and culture with the backdrop of the cypress dome. The boardwalk also leads to a replica of a traditional ceremonial grounds and a Seminole village, a re-creation of the tourist camps that were set up in the early 1900s (mentioned in chapter 5). The village is an important selling point for the museum and contains six chickees, including a cook chickee. One particularly interesting thing about the chickees in the ceremonial grounds and village is that the bark is left on the uprights, which is more authentic to the old style of chickees. This detail is only seen on a few other chickees on the Big Cypress Reservation.

The Ah-Tah-Thi-Ki Museum seeks to share Seminole history and culture through its collections, exhibits, and outdoor offerings. The chickees throughout the property give visitors an opportunity to interact with a piece of Seminole architectural history while providing a shady retreat from the Florida heat. For many people (especially international tourists), this might be the only opportunity they have to ever encounter true chickees, and the chickees really complete the museum experience.

Billie Swamp Safari, located a few miles from the museum, has a multitude of chickees. At the time of the survey in 2009, this popular tourist attraction had a total of fifty-five chickees—more than any other single location on the Big Cypress Reservation. There were nine

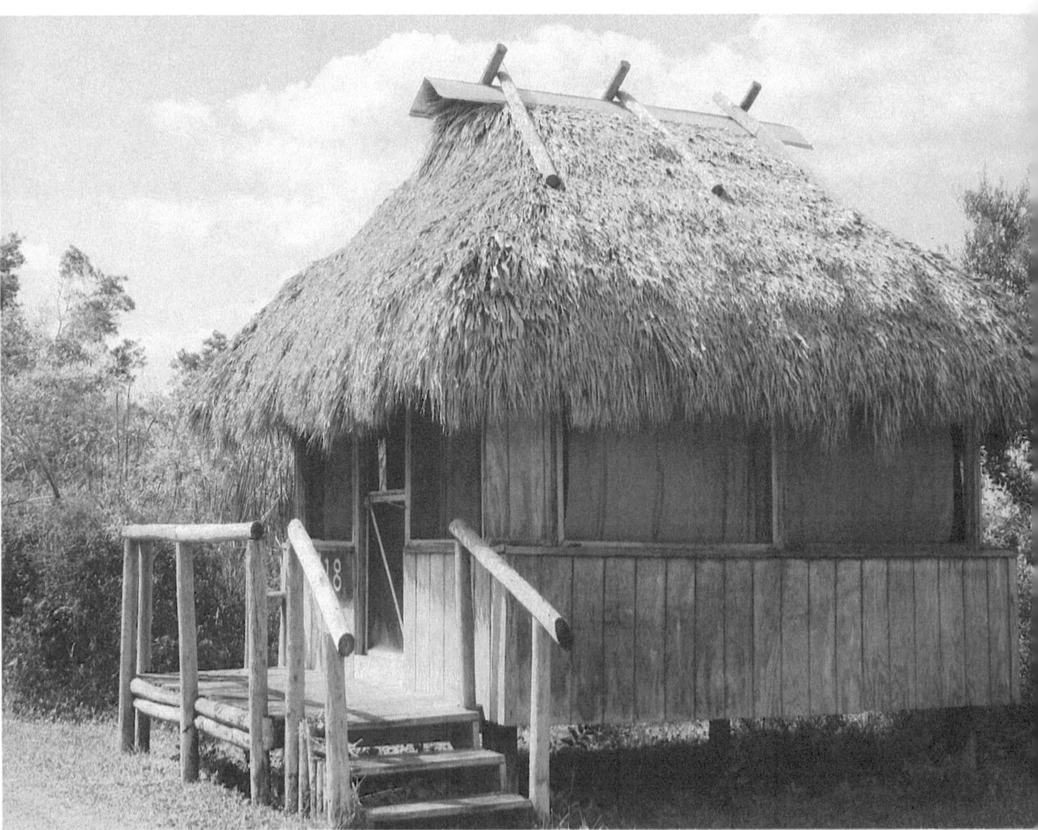

Figure 8.4. Chickee dorm at Billie Swamp Safari. Photo by the author, Big Cypress Reservation, 2009.

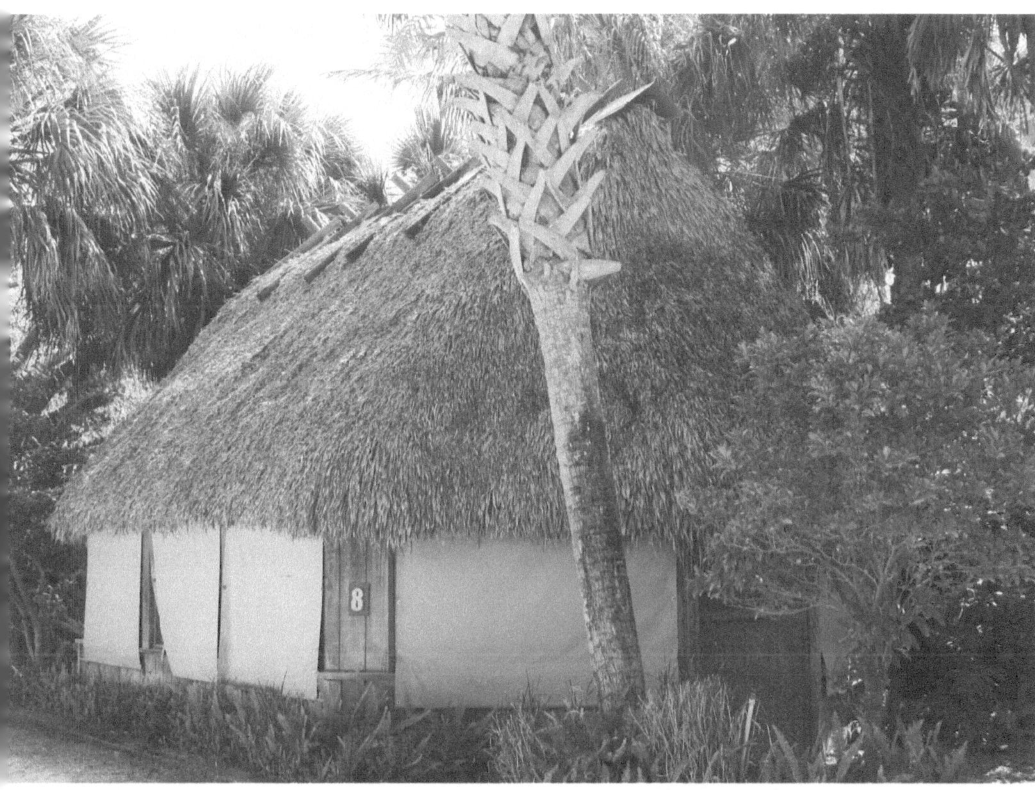

Figure 8.5. Chickee cabin at Billie Swamp Safari. Photo by the author, Big Cypress Reservation, 2009.

chickee dorms and thirty chickee cabins. The sleeping dorms were built around 1992. They are hexagonal in shape and feature screened-in windows, vertical wooden siding, and concrete floors. The dorm chickees are available to rent, and they sleep eight to twelve people each.

The cabins, also available to rent, feature wooden walls and screened-in windows, and many have a small porch. These chickees are also slightly raised off the ground. They do not have running water or electricity and try to evoke an authentic Seminole experience. Though not entirely traditional, they give visitors a feel for what it was like to live in the Everglades in a chickee.

Billie Swamp Safari contains fourteen other chickees with a variety of functions—operations office, theater, cooking, canoe storage, amphitheater, recreation, airboat ride start point, dining, and various demonstrations. Some of these chickees are enclosed with walls, while others are left open-sided. The hexagonal operations office chickee, for example, is enclosed with vertical wood siding and has aluminum windows. The amphitheater chickee features unusual construction; with its octagon shape, a series of thin, vertical pressure-treated pine poles for walls, and a smoke hole in the top, it is more akin to the roundhouse archetype or council houses seen in indigenous communities than a traditional Seminole chickee. Roundhouses were usually the site of ceremonies, and perhaps the amphitheater design was deliberate to reflect this style, but I have seen no evidence to confirm this.

Additionally, there are two chickees on the Swamp Buggy Eco-Tour—one cook chickee and one sleeping chickee (with raised platform) built in the traditional style. These two structures are only reached by swamp buggy. Tour guides give a brief history lesson as they make a

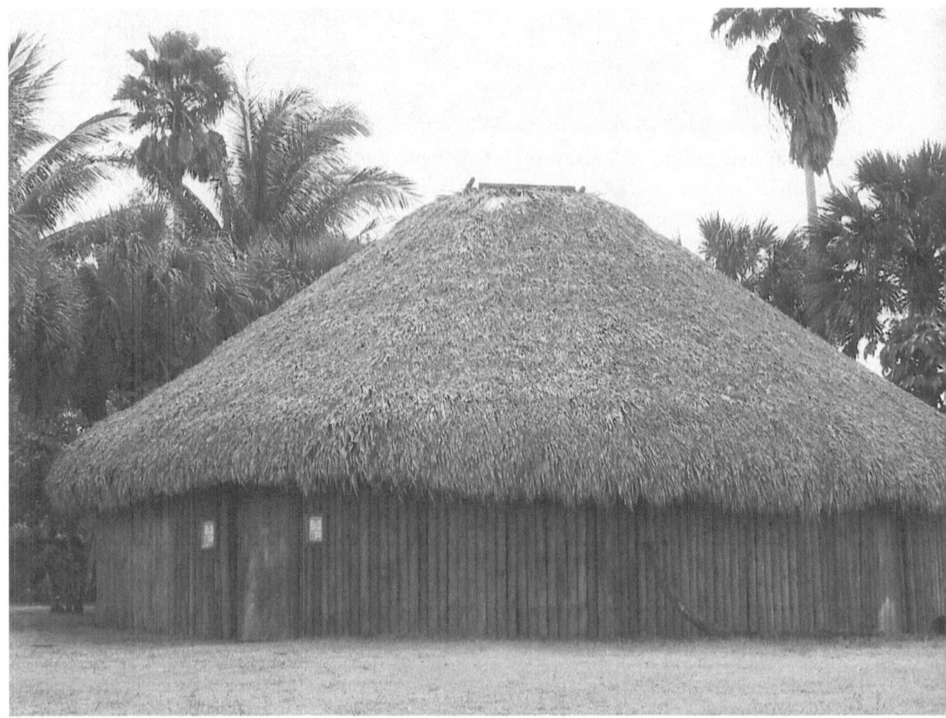

Figure 8.6. Amphitheater chickee at Billie Swamp Safari. Photo by the author, Big Cypress Reservation, 2009.

stop at these chickees. Many of the Billie Swamp Safari chickees encountered in the 2009 survey are no longer standing today, as the park has undergone renovations.

The Ah-Tah-Thi-Ki Museum and Billie Swamp Safari perhaps target two different audiences, but both places do an excellent job in presenting Seminole history and culture. Most of the other "public spaces" on the reservation have multiple chickees as well. The Junior Cypress Rodeo Arena in Big Cypress features ten chickees. The Ahfachkee School has thirteen, the RV Resort has eight, the outdoor basketball court has five, the New Testament Baptist Church and the Tribal Office both have four, the Big Cypress First Baptist Church and the baseball field both have three, the Herman L. Osceola gymnasium and the community center both have two, the Family Investment Center has one, and Sweet Tooth Restaurant has one for dining. There are two chickees at Big Cypress Landing (Sadie's), both with raised wooden plank floors, and one with a wooden ramp leading to it.

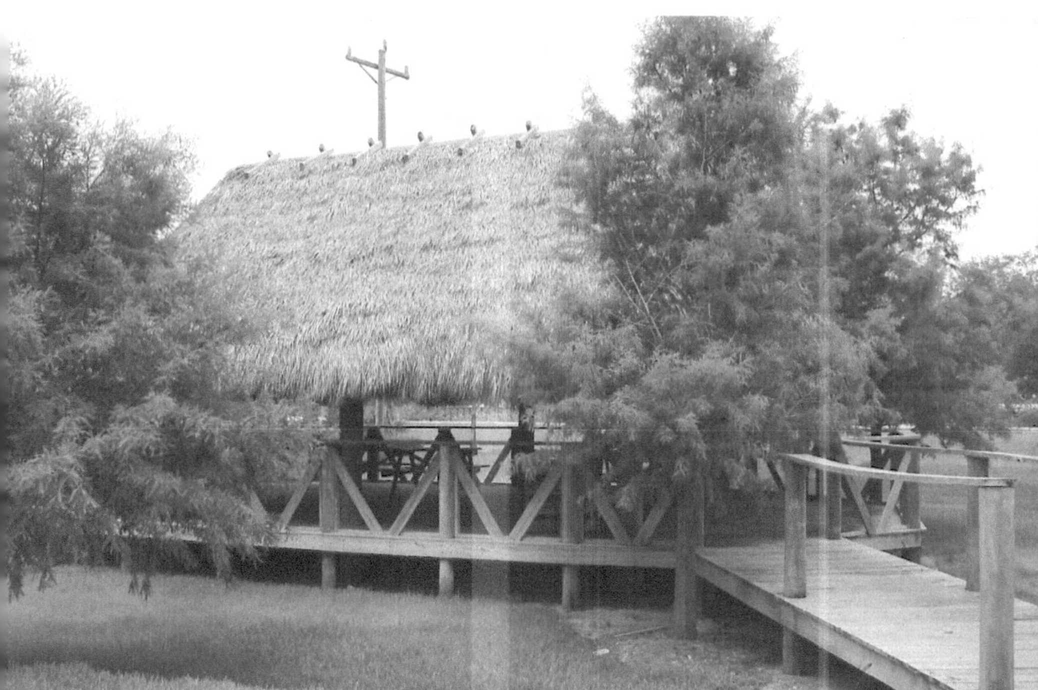

Figure 8.7. Chickee at Big Cypress Landing (Sadie's). Photo by the author, Big Cypress Reservation, 2009.

Other General Observations

Although most chickees were traditionally left open-sided, it is not uncommon today to find chickees enclosed with a variety of materials year-round. On Big Cypress, many chickees feature mesh-screen walls. Mesh screening is very common in South Florida homes as well, with most single-family homes, townhouses, and apartments provided with a screened-in patio or porch. We also encountered chickee walls made from vertical wooden panels (especially plywood or sawed wooden boards), walls featuring a combination of materials (half wood/half screen), and walls only applied to part of the chickee (wooden half-walls). In some cases the wall material is applied on the outside of the uprights so they are hidden from view, while in other cases the wall material is applied between the spacing of the uprights. Brick was the least common material for walls on the reservation, as we only saw one instance of such.

The majority of chickees we surveyed had a traditional dirt floor, but a large number featured different types of flooring materials. Poured

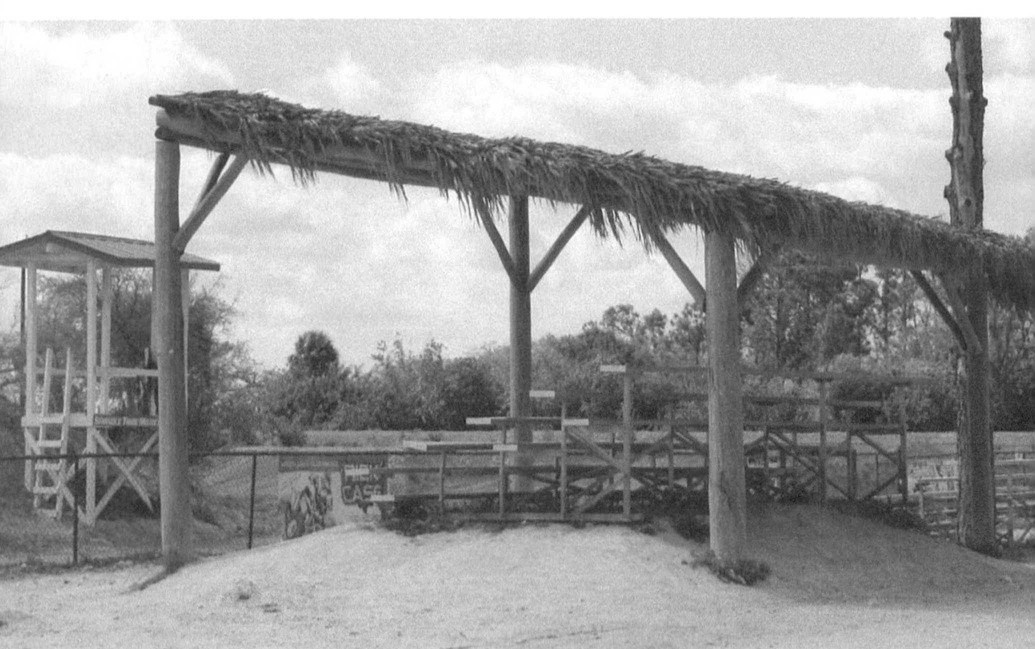

Figure 8.8. Large-scale lean-to chickee. Photo by the author, Big Cypress Reservation, 2009.

concrete was the second most common flooring type. Concrete is not only aesthetically pleasing, but it also has the added benefit of providing additional stabilization for the overall structure. We also found chickees with wooden deck floors, gravel floors, outdoor carpeting, brick floors, concrete pavers, and stamped concrete. Many of the chickees with wooden deck floors were elevated off the ground at a variety of heights. Some also had walkways and ramps made of wood similar to the chickee at Sadie's Restaurant.

Lean-to chickees with shed roofs were found throughout the reservation. Lean-tos are often used in architecture for additions to structures, and we found that to be the case with chickees as well (although we did find some free-standing shed-roof chickees). The stand-alone lean-to chickees were primarily used during the Green Corn Dance Ceremony or for temporary structures but now may also be seen as stylistic chickees on the reservations, especially for stage seating as seen at the Big Cypress Motocross Arena (the attraction is no longer open, and the chickee has been demolished).

Cook Chickees

We encountered five major variations of the cook chickee on the reservation. I devised the following classifications: full A-frame; open-ended; open-pocket (symmetrical); open-pocket with extension (asymmetrical); and open-pocket with double extensions (symmetrical). There are variations within these types as well. The full A-frame chickee is triangular from the front elevation, and the roof thatching goes all the way to the ground. The steeply angled sides meet at the top in the shape of a letter A. The open-ended cook chickee is the most traditional, with its open gable ends to allow for plenty of ventilation. The open-pocket symmetrical chickee was by far the most common type of cook chickee on the reservation. This variation is a more recent version of the cook chickee and exemplifies how the structures have evolved over the years. According to Chairman Billie, the different types of cook chickees came about because "the woman thinks up the idea for the cook chickees, and the man must come up with the means to make it happen. She made him nice clothes (including intricate designs with thin patchwork), he made her a nice chickee. The cook hut was the design that the woman wanted." The old cook chickees were

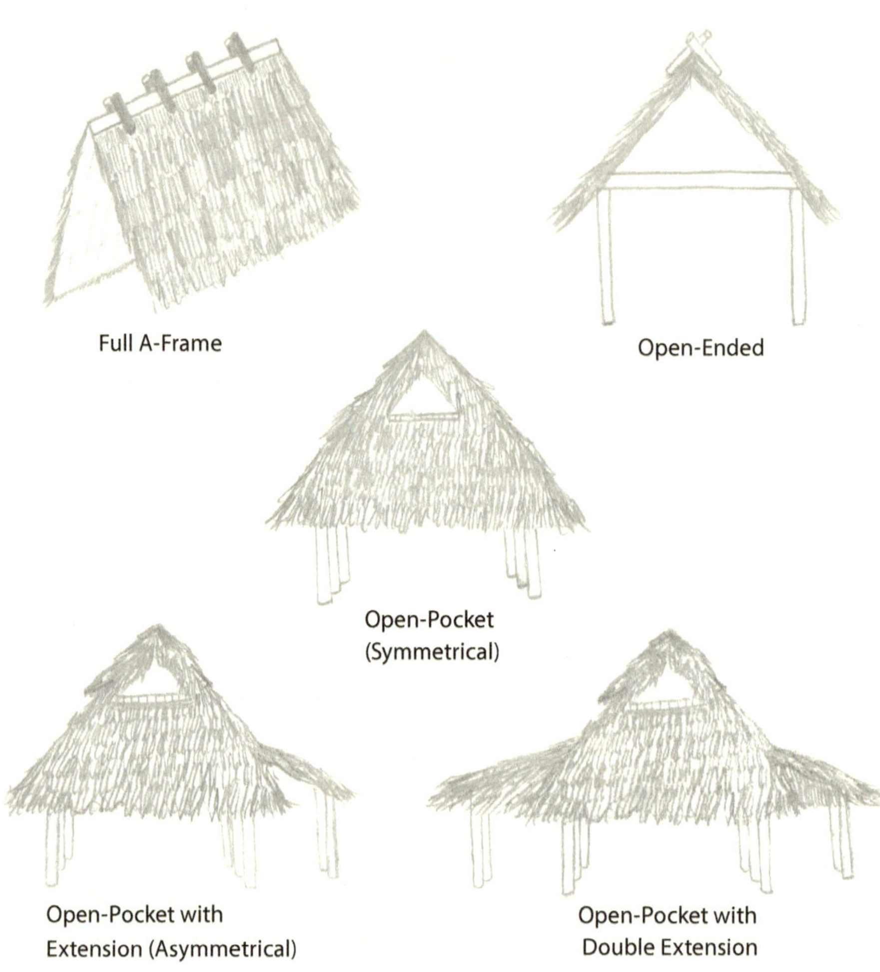

Figure 8.9. Author's sketch of a variety of cook chickees.

constructed in a way to keep dew off the fire in the woman's territory. The newer style has open pockets instead of fully open ends, which does a better job at providing sun protection.

Distinguishing Architectural Features

One of the most distinguishing architectural characteristics we encountered was the cupola. A cupola (meaning *small cup* in Italian) is a small, usually domed cap that crowns the top of a similarly shaped roof. Cupolas allow light and air into the top of a building. We only

Chickee Builder Highlight

Norman Huggins was born and raised on the Tamiami Trail. He still resides there today and is the trail liaison for the Seminole Tribal Council. He started a chickee building business when he was nineteen, honing in on the skills he learned at seven years old when he started off as a "gofer." Huggins has been in the chickee building business for thirty-one years and has built hundreds, if not thousands, of chickees. He learned how to build chickees from his uncles and his older brothers and believes that the building technique itself has not changed much over the years. The main differences he pointed out are the use of nails and uniform wood, compared to the past when builders tied all the members together and could not be too picky about their materials. He also mentioned that cook chickees are different today and that the open-pocket style became popular around thirty years ago. "Not too many people request the old [A-frame] style anymore," he said. "The old folks like those." Huggins lived in a camp until he met his wife and moved into a concrete block and stucco (CBS) house.

Huggins does not advertise his chickee building services and believes his work sells itself. He takes special care in his work so that all of the thatching is straight and all the wooden members are in good condition and uniform. He builds for the customer what he would want for himself.

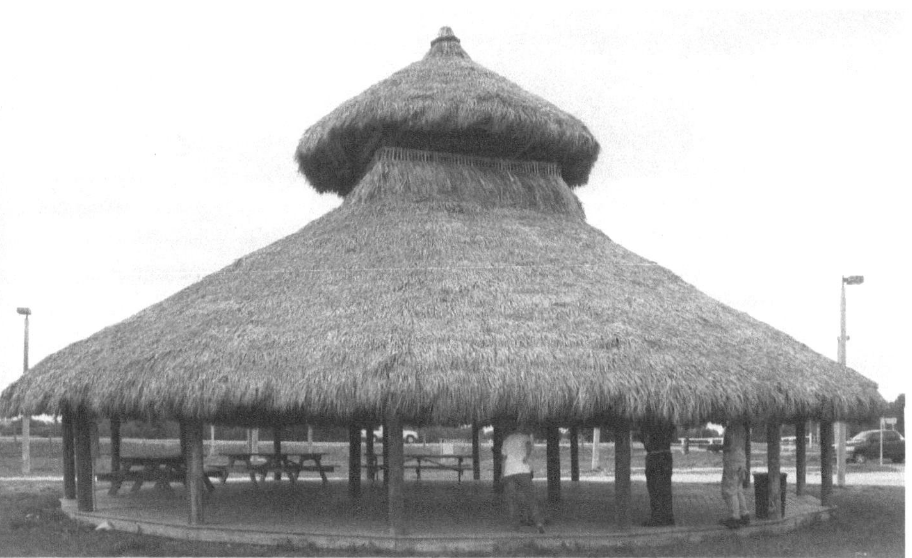

Figure 8.10. Chickee with a cupola. Photo by the author, Big Cypress Reservation, 2009.

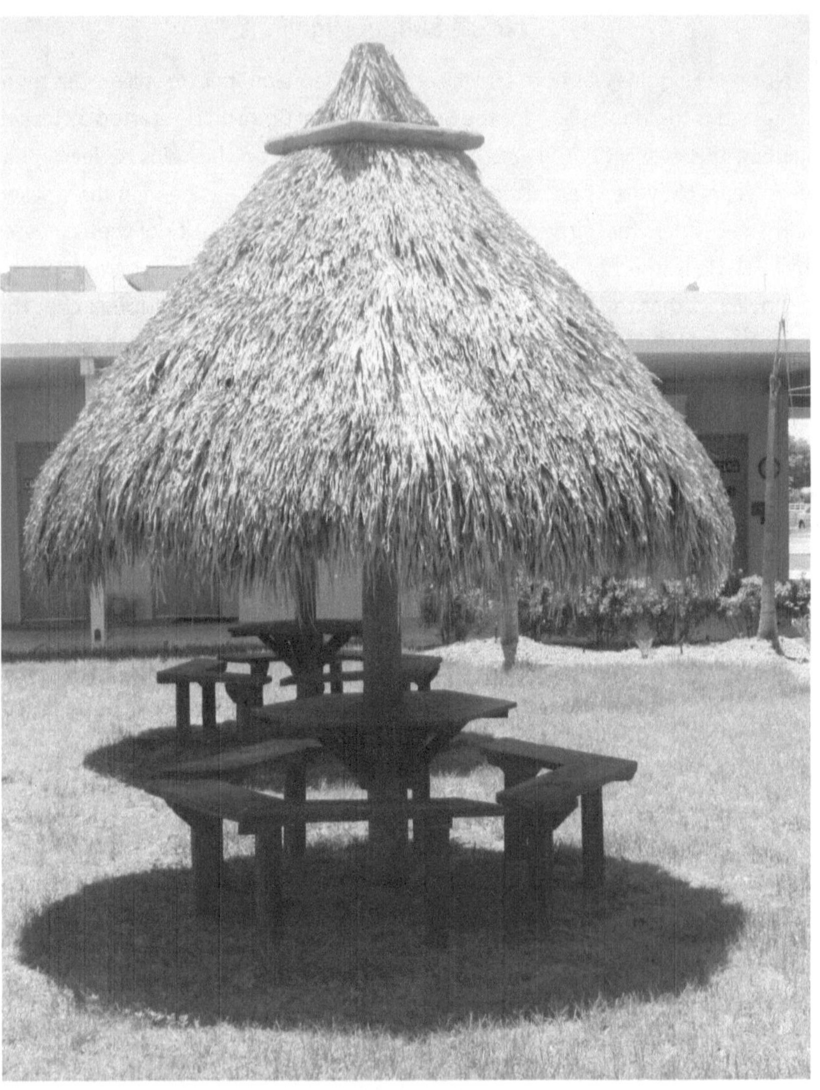

Figure 8.11. Umbrella chickee at the Brighton Charter School. Photo by the author, 2011.

recorded three chickees with cupolas, but they make quite an impression. The one featured in figure 8.10 is at the Junior Cypress Rodeo Arena. This chickee is also unique due to its sixteen-sided, nearly round shape.

Umbrella chickees look like a half-open umbrella. Because the roof comes together in a point rather than a ridge, there is no cap (metal, asphalt, tar paper) at the peak. Roof weights are still sometimes present, however. Instead of the weights being arranged in a crisscross fashion, they are often arranged in a square. The umbrella chickees feature only one central upright. They are often used for dining, for decoration, or just for shade. When used for dining, they usually have seating attached. We recorded six umbrella chickees on Big Cypress. Although figure 8.11 is from Brighton, it is a public-space chickee that is a perfect example of the umbrella style. I asked builders when the umbrella style originated, but nobody knew an exact date of origin. According to Chairman Billie, the design may have influences from African culture. Sandy Billie Jr. thought the style originated in the 1960s. In 1968, Roy Cypress Jr. and his father built seven chickees around the Miami Beach Convention Hall, including umbrella chickees.[3] I found accounts from 1977 that Johnny Tucker built three types of chickees, including the umbrella style.[4]

Chickee Builders and Unusual Requests

Throughout the survey we found numerous examples of "unusual" or distinctive chickees. It makes sense that most chickee builders mentioned the fact that they were quite accommodating in their building practices—they would build nearly any size, any design, or in any locale that the owner wanted. Chairman Billie has built chickees all over the world, but perhaps his most unusual job was rethatching the roof on Julio Iglesias's house on Indian Creek Island in Miami. The palatial home was approximately 10,000 square feet and featured an unusually low roof pitch for a thatched roof—around 4:12. The largest chickee Norman Huggins built was for the Everglades National Park, a 30′×150′ structure at the Shark Valley Visitor Center used for ticket booths, bike rentals, and so forth, that is attached to a 35′ diameter round chickee. He also built a large-scale chickee for the Miccosukee Council Grounds (45′×70′) and for the U.S. Navy in Key West (40′×70′).

Norman "Skeeter" Bowers lives on the Brighton Reservation. He learned the process of chickee building when he was around ten years old, and started helping even before that at the Green Corn Dance cer-

(Continued)

emonial grounds by handing up fans to his father. He did not have an option but to cut the fans as a child. He told me that he would rather build a chickee than build a fence in the pasture, even though it is hard work (especially when it is hot outside).

Long before Skeeter started his own chickee building business, he often cut palm fronds on the side for extra money. As a child, he received ten cents for every fan he cut, and could gather 500 pretty easily to make $50—a lot of money for a child. During his teens, Skeeter really perfected his building skills by working for Joe Dan Osceola's company during the summers. In the 1990s he built chickees all over Florida working alongside the chairman—at St. Petersburg College, at Fort Walton beach, and for doctors and lawyers throughout the state. He returned to cutting fans again as a side job in the early 2000s. In one week, he and a crew of four other men cut 35,000 fans while working from morning until night. Though he was only paid ten cents a fan as a child, the going rate at that time had increased to twenty-five cents a fan. Skeeter and his crew cut and stacked the fans and then dragged them out of the woods. It was a tremendous amount of work, but Skeeter enjoyed that part of his life. Around 2006, he started his own company, Skeeter's Seminole Huts. Presently, he contracts numerous rethatching jobs within the tribal community and builds many other chickees from the ground up. In the past, Skeeter used to do "the whole nine yards" by himself but got a little burned out because he did not pace himself. Instead of doing all the work himself these days, he now manages the company and subcontracts the labor to tribal and nontribal members.

Skeeter and his crew built a remarkable chickee at the Fred Smith Rodeo Arena in Brighton. This chickee, used for vendor stalls during events, is Skeeter's largest and proudest achievement. The structure is highly unique due to its length and because it features two 90° turns. The main section is 90 feet long and 15 feet wide, and the two smaller sections are 15′×50′ and 37′×15′. The overall structure is around 2,600 square feet and took over a month to complete. The two semitrucks full of wood needed for this structure were imported from Georgia. Skeeter's chickee would not be complete without his trademark—a small metal plaque that reads "Skeeter's Seminole Huts, 'Any Size, Any Style'" with his phone number—which he nails into the corner of each chickee he builds.

Cory Osceola (1893–1978), longtime leader of the independent Seminoles and head of a tourist camp, was a master chickee builder known for building large-scale structures. He was featured in a 1959 article in the *Miami Her-*

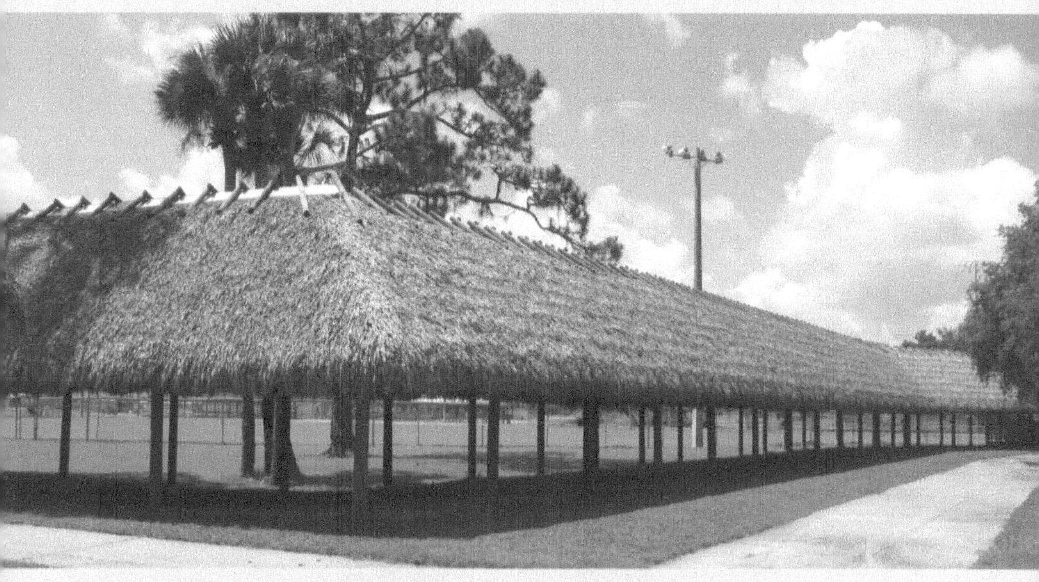

Figure 8.12. Norman "Skeeter" Bowers's largest chickee at the Fred Smith Rodeo Arena. Photo by the author, Brighton Reservation, 2013.

ald as building the largest chickee in Naples and the largest of his career. He constructed the chickee, used as a barbeque and entertainment room, with the help of his son, O.B., and Bert Cypress. They made the chickee in the traditional style using cypress and palmetto but added fire-retardant to the roof, a concrete floor, screened-in walls, and restroom facilities, all to appease Naples building codes.[1]

O. B. Osceola Sr. has carried on his father's building tradition. He said that chickee building is innate to the Seminoles: "It's in our system, Indian ways." He got his start building chickees when he was six years old with his father, handing up the palm fronds. As he got older, he graduated to doing some of the other work of the chickee building. Chickee building was his primary occupation for many years (although he also worked in air-conditioning and refrigeration installation services), and he is very well known in the Naples area and throughout Florida as a master chickee builder.[2]

The most unusual building request Ronnie Billie received was for L-shaped or U-shaped chickees. For this style of chickee, he said, you really need to know what you are doing. The connections where the sides come together are very vulnerable. Some builders staple the palm fronds at the roof intersection, which reflects poor building techniques. That area must be properly thatched. Another builder touched upon the vulnerability of this connection: "If you

(*Continued*)

apply too many fans, it cannot breathe. I put a stick underneath in the connection to give it space to breathe. Too much heat puts holes in the roof fast." That particular builder remembered that he had to rethatch the chickees on the beach built by non-Seminoles because the builders put the ribs too far apart. "Seminoles put the ribs closer together," he said.

Norman Huggins often gets special requests for chickees. He has constructed quite a few custom structures with odd shapes, but the most unusual chickee he ever built was through a live oak tree at a private residence in Coconut Grove in Miami. The homeowners were insistent that the chickee and the tree both coincide in the same location. The "tree within a chickee" concept is not as rare as it might sound, however. Skeeter fulfilled a similar request in Brighton.

1. Tom Morgan, "Seminoles Build 'Biggest' Chickee in Naples."
2. O. B. Osceola Sr., interview with Debbie Fant, November 22, 1987.

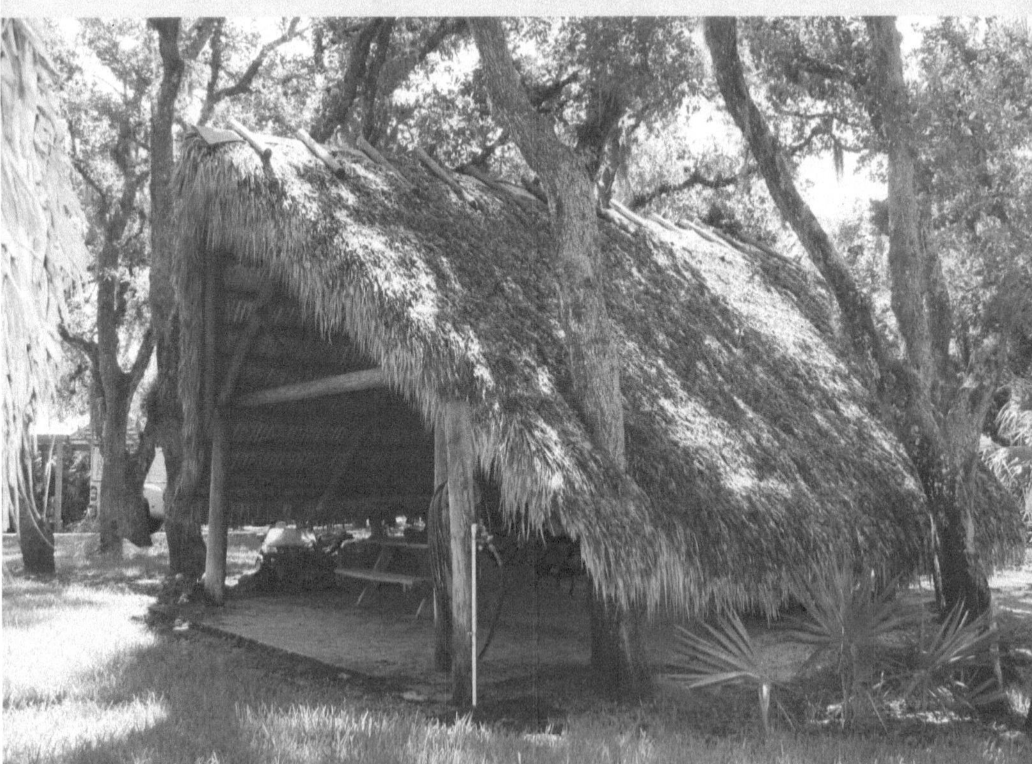

Figure 8.13. "A tree within a chickee" built by Norman "Skeeter" Bowers. Photo by the author, Brighton Reservation, 2013.

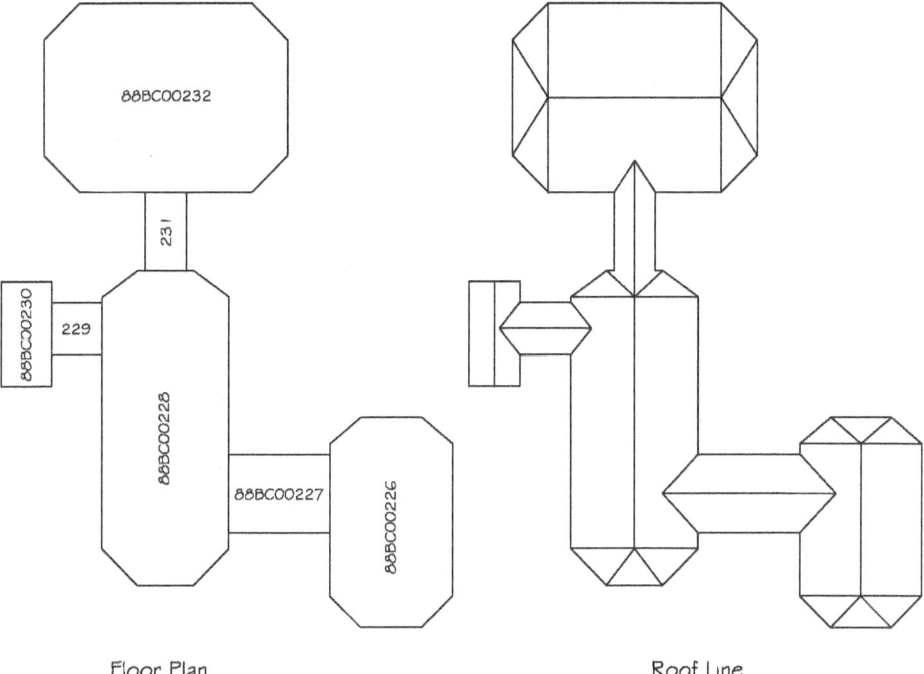

Figure 8.14. Unusual chickee example on the Big Cypress Reservation: 88BC00230 and 88BC00232 both have open-pockets, and 232 is the cook chickee; 227, 229, and 231 are connector chickees. Drawing created by the author, 2013.

Most Unusual Example

We encountered a unique chickee configuration at one home on the reservation. In this instance, seven chickees of varying sizes had been attached together. This massive chickee has areas for cooking, dining, recreation, and storage, all under one roof, with a variety of gabled and hipped rooflines. The floor plan looks like seven rectangles and hexagons attached together.

Survey Categories

Perhaps the most surprising aspect of the chickee survey was the sheer number of different uses we recorded. Forget narrowing it down to the cooking, sleeping, dining, and storage chickees of the past. I found it difficult to even narrow the list at all, and the best efforts I made

Table 8.1. Categories of usage

Category	Number on Big Cypress
Agriculture	2
Carport	9
Cooking	91
Crafts	4
Decoration	1
Dining	27
Doghouse	8
Recreation	160
Residence	2
Retail	1
Sleeping	48
Storage	106
Tourism	5
Vacant	12
Workshop	3

brought the number to fifteen main categories. This was a true effort to streamline because in actuality, there were many more specific uses. That is the beauty of chickees today—they can be built for any purpose. The possibilities are endless.

Most of the chickees we surveyed were used for recreational purposes. We saw a shift from the "basic needs" purposes as chickees have become extensions of homes, not primary residences. We also saw a large number of cook chickees, which makes sense from a cultural standpoint, where it is mandated that a camp should have a cook chickee. Norman Huggins mentioned the necessity of a cook chickee in reference to the Tamiami Trail: "Every house has a cook chickee, and eating chickee, even if they have a CBS [concrete block and stucco] structure. It's a requirement." Lonnie Billie added that the chickee is still a huge part of Seminole culture because tradition requires that Seminoles maintain both a cooking and eating chickee.

Big Cypress Chickee Builders

Although the 479 chickees on the Big Cypress Reservation had a wide variety of builders, two names came up over and over again—Lonnie

Additional Survey Notes

Another building characteristic we noted was condition. With any architectural survey, it is important to examine building condition. Again, there is some gray area about what defines each category, but within the chickee survey I set parameters for each condition and remained consistent as to how I classified each from start to finish. I used the following condition categories: Excellent Condition: chickees with a brand-new roof with palm fronds that are still a bright yellowish/tan color and either brand-new uprights or uprights that are in very good shape. Good Condition: chickees with brown palm fronds and uprights that are in good shape but show some signs of age; no holes in the roof thatching. Fair Condition: chickees in which the roof and/or uprights have moderate wear and possibly have a few minor holes in the roof. Poor Condition: chickees with numerous holes in the roof and uprights that are very worn. Ruinous: chickees that are dilapidated or falling down, with most or all of the roof missing.

We recorded 52 chickees as excellent, 262 as good, 103 as fair, 48 as poor, and 14 as ruinous. These numbers are in line with what you would expect to find in an average architectural survey. Most of the buildings during a typical architectural survey fall into the good/fair category—unless a survey is conducted as a result of a disaster (such as Hurricane Katrina, where I conducted a survey of the buildings in the Holy Cross Historic District of New Orleans, which were mostly annihilated during the storm) or in a high crime area, or if for some reason one was conducting a survey of brand-new buildings or those recently restored. It remains a natural tendency to take care of our homes and repair problems in due time unless a building is abandoned or out of use, in which case we would expect to encounter more in the poor or ruinous category.

Billie and Ronnie Billie (no relation). Lonnie Billie, from the Big Cypress Reservation, has been building chickees for twenty-five years. He grew up living in a chickee and did not move into a "modern" home until he was twelve years old. At first he mainly built them for his family (mother, sister, grandmother) and gradually established his reputation as a prominent chickee builder around the year 2000. He could not recall the number of chickees he has built over the years but remembers that the largest one he ever built was 40'×80' at a restaurant in Stuart. Lonnie learned how to build chickees from his father and builds them exactly as he was taught. Lonnie is a perfectionist when it comes to chickee building—he has to make sure that all members match and all palm fronds are neatly tucked-in. Lonnie is a versatile builder who strives to please his customers.

Ronnie Billie was also born and raised on the Big Cypress Reservation. He began working at seven years old, helping his family pick tomatoes and cucumbers for income. He grew up in a time when children were expected to do hard work. He learned how to build chickees from his stepfather in the 1960s, but remembers that he did not like it much back then. Chickee building became a business for Ronnie in the late 1990s. Ronnie takes pride in having a strong work ethic—one that he has carried with him throughout his life. He builds high-quality chickees and always stands behind his product. When business was good,

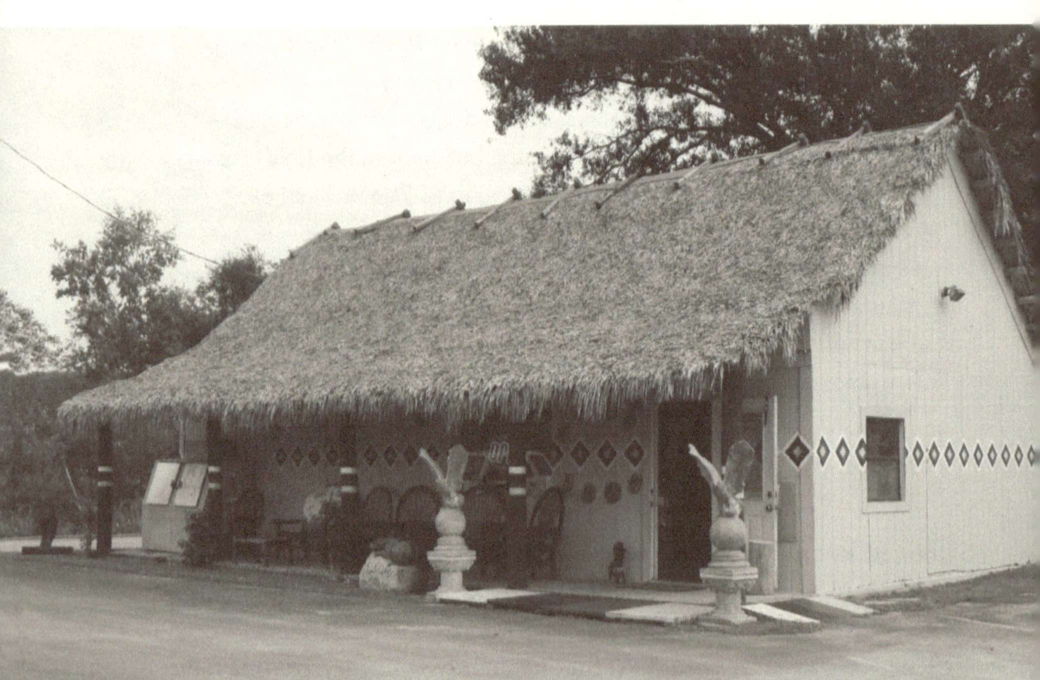

Figure 8.15. Seminole Country Gift Shop built by Ronnie Billie. Photo by the author, Big Cypress Reservation, 2009.

Ronnie used to build about six to eight chickees per month. Now, business has slowed down, and he only builds about one or two per month. "Years back only Seminoles built them," he says, and "tribal members from the reservation used to knock on my door for work." Initially he focused on building chickees on the Big Cypress and Immokalee Reservations but later expanded to other areas in South Florida. Ronnie has also built numerous chickees in the Stuart area north of Broward County.

There are several other prominent builders on the Big Cypress Reservation. Some have preferred to remain anonymous throughout this text.

Comparison to MacCauley's Remarks

So exactly how many of these 479 chickees were the 16'×9' chickees like the structures described by Clay MacCauley? It turns out that none had exactly those dimensions. Some were close—there is one 16'×8', two 16'×10', one 10'×15', two 9'×15', and eighteen 15'×10'. In fact, the most common size was 12'×12'; there were forty-eight of these on the Big Cypress Reservation, but thirty of those were the sleeping cabins at Billie Swamp Safari. That size yields the exact same square footage as the MacCauley-era chickees, though. Twenty-five percent (118 out of 479) of the chickees on the Big Cypress Reservation were 144 square feet or smaller. The second most common size was approximately 30'×20', which contains four times the square footage of the MacCauley-era chickees. There were thirty-nine chickees that size in Big Cypress. On the larger end of the spectrum, forty-three chickees were more than 1,000 square feet. Two-thirds of the chickees fell somewhere between 144 and 1,000 square feet. The chickees on the reservation are increasing in size just like the primary residences.

Another interesting modern adaptation is hurricane straps. Of course, not all the chickees surveyed were equipped with strapping, but several were, including Marty Bowers's personal chickee. When I asked why he had hurricane straps installed, he simply said they came standard from the chickee builder, and it seemed careless to build a chickee without the strapping. If we again return to MacCauley's remarks about chickee roofs, he commented: "This covering is, I was informed, water tight and durable and will resist even a violent wind.

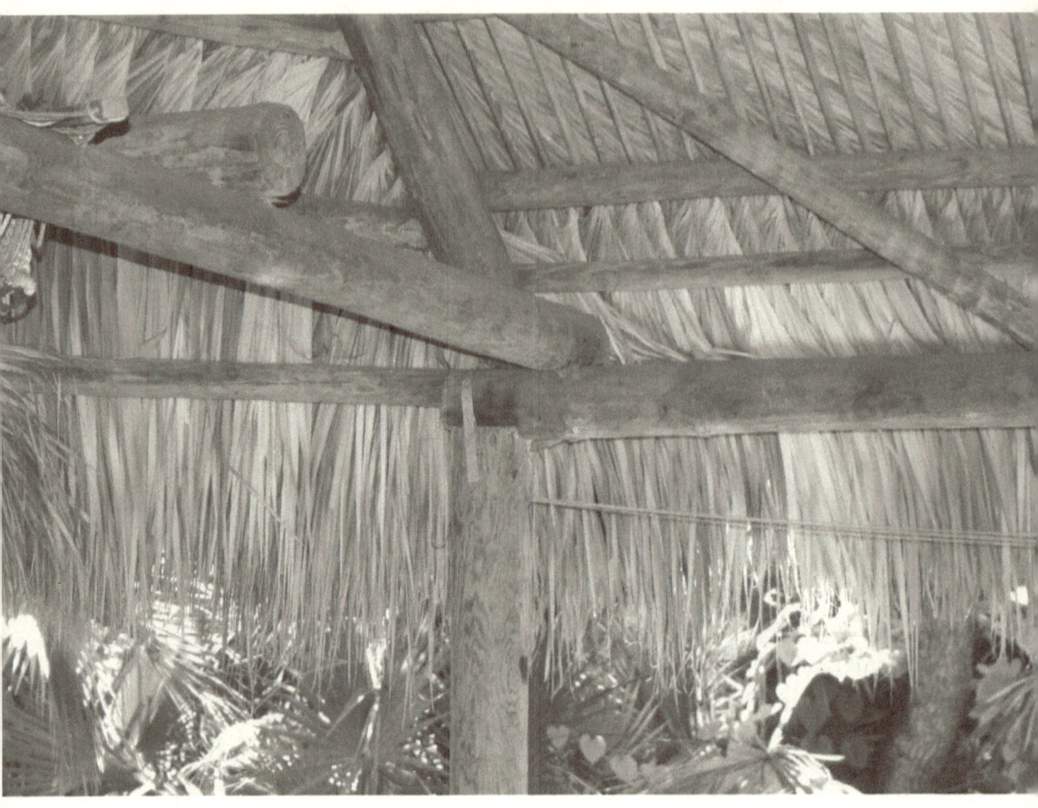

Figure 8.16. Modern chickee with hurricane straps built by Norman "Skeeter" Bowers. Photo by the author, Brighton Reservation, 2013.

Only hurricanes can tear it off, and these are so infrequent in Southern Florida that no attempt is made to provide against them."[5]

To put things into perspective, however, I doubt many South Florida homes were equipped with hurricane straps or hurricane-resistant windows over one hundred years ago. In fact, Florida did not adopt a statewide building code until 2001 (nearly ten years after the devastation of Hurricane Andrew, a Category 5 storm). New structures built since the Florida Building Code came into effect must be able to withstand hurricane-force winds and have either hurricane shutters or impact-resistant glass. The code has been amended several times to make it even stricter. Although chickees are exempt from the Florida Building Code (see chapter 2), the metal strapping makes the already sturdy chickee even studier in the case of tropical storms or full-blown hurricanes. Many builders also use poured concrete as a base to hold the uprights even more tightly in place. John Willie, a Miccosukee tribal member who was still living in a camp east of the reservation in the 1990s, told the *Sun-Sentinel* that he remembered riding out several storms in his chickee and that people used nailed wooden panels to enclose the structures during hurricanes. He did, however, evacuate his chickee during Hurricane Andrew, the most catastrophic hurricane in recent memory, which flattened parts of South Florida. Willie's chickee actually survived the storm with minimal damage to its roof, while others lost their chickees due to the 160-mph winds.[6]

There have actually been more storms in the past decade than during the 1880s when MacCauley visited the Seminoles. The number of recorded storms affecting Florida around Clay MacCauley's time in the 1880s was around thirty. That number kept dwindling until the 1960s and 1970s, when there were thirty-seven recorded each decade. From 2000 to 2009, there were fifty-five recorded storms. There were two major hurricanes during the 1880s and about two per decade (except the 1940s, with six) until the 2000s, when there were seven, five of which impacted the southern region of Florida. Seminoles have learned to reinforce their traditional structures in order to withstand the ever-changing severe weather.

Survey Summary

In 1979, Mary Elen Bundschu noted: "The Indians are not willing to change all of their native customs. Chickees are springing up in backyards of these CBS homes to allow outdoor living in the summer months."[7] The Big Cypress Chickee Survey is proof positive Seminoles have held on to this aspect of their culture, reaching a compromise of old and new within their dwellings. Chickees are just as critical to tribal culture now as they were in the previous hundred years. The overall significance of chickees has not diminished despite their changing place in Seminole society.

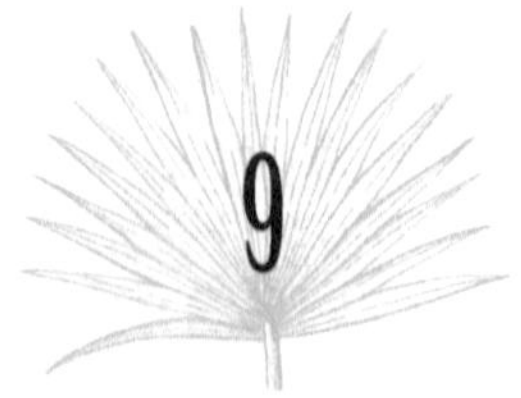

9

Chickees Today and Beyond

Driving west across the Tamiami Trail through Florida's southern interior is a flashback to decades past. Once you get out of the hustle and bustle of Miami proper, past the Miccosukee Casino on the corner of Krome Avenue and US 41, you catch a glimpse of "Old Florida." The Tamiami Trail is certainly a place where you want to drive slowly and soak in the scenery. It is a majestic place—one where you can see alligators, deer, birds, rare flowers, and native and nonnative species of trees. It is a very beautiful and, at times, desolate place.

The Tamiami Trail runs nearly 275 miles from Miami to Tampa. It cuts straight through the Everglades and through the Big Cypress National Preserve (BCNP). Amid the natural beauty of the flora and fauna, you will find hints of the commercial tourism market (many places for airboat rides, a few restaurants, parks, a casino, a fine art gallery, even a skunk ape research center). If you look closely, past gated entrances, you might even see some chickee camps that blend in almost entirely with the landscape.

The Tamiami Trail is home to many Miccosukee tribal members as well as numerous independent Seminoles. Many of the independent Seminoles who live on the trail still arrange their homes in a camp setup. Some of these camps contain chickees (typically updated with walls and modern conveniences), concrete block and stucco (CBS) or wooden homes, modular homes, CBS houses with thatched roofs, or a combination of some or all of these housing types. As Norman Huggins mentioned, the houses on the trail are required to have at least a cooking and dining chickee within the camp (as Seminole tradition and culture dictates).

As in any society, it can be both an internal and external struggle to hold steadfast to tradition with all the modern influences and conveniences in the world. Internally, the battle comes from keeping the youth educated and interested from an early age so they have a desire to keep the traditions and culture alive. It can also stem from a sudden increase in wealth (such as that generated by Indian gaming, as seen with the Seminoles). A new influx of steady funds can make it more of a challenge to hold on to tradition in a modern world. Externally, the government and other (well-meaning and not so well-meaning) people have stepped in and tried to make Native Americans change their ways and have sometimes forced them to assimilate into mainstream American society. This often came with a push toward "modern" or nontraditional houses. The Seminoles of course struggled with this throughout their history, and they are still fighting that battle today, with constant challenges to tribal sovereignty.

The struggle for the non–federally recognized tribes to hold on to their traditions while living off of federal reservation land can be viewed as a blessing and a challenge. In some ways it might be viewed as easier since they live in relative obscurity, almost free to live as they please, but certainly this way of life is more difficult to protect when challenged. In 1995, some families from the Independent Traditional Seminole Nation ran into problems with Collier County. They had been living on a privately owned piece of property (Pacific Land Company and Vine Ripe Farms, Inc.) when a fire in one of the chickees caused officials from the county to come to their camp. They had occupied this village for twelve years, hidden away from nearly everyone. County officials were not happy with what they found. The camp had been modernized to include electricity and the chickees had walls and doors, but the county officials argued that the "village does not meet electrical, plumbing and building codes." The fire was not caused by an electrical problem, as implied by the county, but had been an act of arson. The Collier County Code Enforcement Board investigator said that the camp inhabitants needed new up-to-date buildings equipped with restrooms in order to meet the county building code. "This is a matter of safety and health," he said. These Seminoles felt strongly that changing their chickees would destroy their way of life. Danny Billie, spokesperson for the Independent Traditional Seminole Nation, argued that they were healthy and had everything they needed within the camp. The chickees were not inferior to other homes, he said; they were just different. Billie stated: "They are putting our health and safety in jeopardy by enforcing foreign building codes and regulations on us."[1] Straying from traditional cultural values could impose harm more than outsiders could understand. Destroying livelihood and beliefs can be irreversible.

The battle carried on for months. In April 1996, the *Sun-Sentinel* reported that the Seminoles had just two months to prove that codes did not apply to their houses.[2] The case went to federal court, but the judge closed the case and encouraged both parties—the Independent Traditional Seminole Nation and Collier County—to pursue a settlement. In a public hearing regarding Petition CU-96-20, Collier County Community Development requested "Conditional Use '23' of the 'A' Zoning District for property located on the north side of C.R. 848 in Sec. 14, T48S, R29E." The resolution proved that the Independent Traditional Seminoles and the landowners had a multigenerational agreement for the use of the land, which was put into writing in the 1987 land lease. They also cited Title 18, Section 1151 of the U.S. Code, which defines "Indian country." Part b of the code indicates that Indian country can cover "all dependent Indian communities within the borders of the United States whether within the original or subsequently acquired territory thereof, and whether within or without the limits of a state," which means that even off-reservation, the Seminoles in question were living in "Indian country." Because the camps in question fell under the code, they were therefore not subject to the jurisdiction of the Code Enforcement Board or Collier County. The two parties reached a compromise, of sorts, on September 3, 1996—one in which the Seminoles kept their chickees on the condition that they made a few updates. The families modernized their villages by burying their electrical wires instead of having them hanging dangerously in the air and by installing electrical outlets. These two actions were enough to satisfy Collier County.[3] Resolution 96-533 was formally adopted on November 26, 1996, by a vote of 5-0.[4] It stated: "The Traditional Seminoles shall not be required to obtain County permits with respect to their use and occupancy of the lands described in Exhibit 'B' as long as their continued use and occupancy remains unchanged or essentially in the same or similar nature as presently existing." The county placed "cultural facility conditional use" determinations on the land.

This heated battle over chickees received national attention. It was featured in "The Winners and Losers of '97" section of the *Wall Street Journal* as a "winner." The short article reads: "Seminole Indians living in thatched-roof huts in the Everglades won a legal battle against bureaucrats who insisted that the native dwellings must meet modern building codes. Collier County Commissioners agreed to let 19 Seminole families stay in their 'chickees,' open-sided huts that stand on cypress poles and are topped with palm-frond roofs. Although most Seminoles live in modern housing, a few prefer to live according to ancient customs and as far from Florida's concrete jungles as possible."[5] The tone of the article shows obvious favor toward the Seminoles and points out the importance of living in chickees as maintaining culture.

This particular example shows the right to traditional usage on private lands, not in the BCNP, which undoubtedly allows customary use and occupancy. James A. Goss sums up the significance of chickees in his report for the National Park Service 1995: "To traditional Miccosukee and Seminole people, living in a chekee is the essence of still being Indian. It represents family and it represents clan. It represents separateness from the Anglo world. It represents tradition."[6] This idea rings true throughout the Seminole people.

Modern Chickees and Camps

Although the Seminole Tribe of Florida has been federally recognized since 1957 and as such governs its own affairs, the Seminoles still relied heavily on government assistance in the decades following organization. During this time, the Bureau of Indian Affairs (BIA) administered nearly all tribal programs.[7] Tribal members who reside on any of the six reservations were required to work with the Tribal Housing Authority, mentioned in chapter 7, to navigate through the myriad requirements set out by the BIA in order to build their houses and make them "habitable." As detailed in earlier chapters, from the 1950s to the 1970s there was a push to move Seminoles out of chickees and into modern houses. Chickee use and construction may have slowed down on the reservations during that period, but the practice of building and living in chickees never died out altogether.

After the gaming industry brought a newfound source of income for the Seminoles and reinforced the tribe's exercise of sovereignty, the Seminoles were eventually able to administer their own housing program. In 1996, the tribe replaced the Tribal Housing Authority with the Housing Department, which was completely controlled by the tribe itself.[8] This change ushered in an increased desire to bring traditional culture back into Seminole housing.

Just as the Miccosukee Tribe started building homes in the 1960s that incorporated modern elements into the chickee design, William Osceola, former trail liaison, worked with the Seminole Tribe's Housing Department in the late 1990s to get funding for homes for his constituents that reflected cultural values. He wanted to improve living conditions without negatively impacting traditions. These homes combined aspects of traditional camp life with modern features, such as bathhouses. The design featured thatched roofs, insulated walls with electricity (no more extension cords running all across the ground), and air-conditioning. These homes were arranged in matrilineal camps. Osceola hired Seminoles to build the chickees to increase the number of jobs for his people (and only hired outsiders as necessary). Chairman Billie strongly supported this project.[9] It is likely that this project would have been denied under the old Tribal Housing Authority, and it serves as an important example of how the tribe supports incorporating culture into architecture.

The chickee is without question a key part of the reservations today; the results of the chickee survey more than prove this point. Over the past decade or so there has been a resurgence in building and owning chickees on the reservations. The previous tribal administration encouraged a revival of chickees on the reservations and supported the cause by providing the construction and maintenance of chickees at little or no cost to homeowners. This not only benefited Seminole builders by increasing their business, but it also strengthened the chickee as a dominant symbol of cultural pride.

Other objectives within the Housing Department further reinforce the ways in which the tribe promotes traditional housing initiatives. As part of the tribe's land-use ordinance, a chickee may be used to secure a home site. Once a tribal member has been granted a home site lease, he or she has only a few years to develop it. Many tribal members put chickees on that land as a placeholder, a practice that technically works as long as the chickee is "habitable." A cook chickee, on the other hand, would not satisfy this requirement, because it is not a structure intended for habitation.[10]

There is often more structure and rigidity within the Housing Department than some tribal members would want, even today. Most traditional-minded tribal members do not want to live in planned developments or subdivisions. They would prefer to live in more scattered areas that mimic traditional camp life. The main problem with this type of habitation pattern is that there is no infrastructure where many people request to live—no roads, water, sewer, or electricity. The tribe has a limit to how much it can spend preparing a home site. According to the Seminole Tribe of Florida land-use coordinator, living on the land where the family historically lived is often more important than occupying remote areas. Not being too close to neighbors is a secondary concern.

Not only do Seminoles today build chickees on their property and try to abide by camp life as much as modern times will allow, they also incorporate traditional architectural elements into their homes. This idea is taken one step further today when we are finally starting to see modern chickees as primary homes on the reservations. Perhaps there is no better example than Chairman Billie's house on the Brighton Reservation. It is certainly a true chickee, with its palmetto thatched roof and cypress uprights, but with added modern conveniences. It is the quintessential chickee of the twenty-first century.

In order to thatch this approximately 4,000-square-foot home, it took about 27,000 palm fronds. The fronds are spaced only two inches (three fingers) apart (compared to two and a half or even three inches apart for most Seminole chickees, and even farther apart for "short-cut" jobs) to ensure the structure is completely watertight. The thatch is applied two inches thick. An interior image of the roof shows how close the ribs are and how tightly and neatly the thatching was placed. It is a true work of art, with not a single palm frond out of place. This chickee reflects a sense of pride, which is sometimes left out of chickees built as a business. Nothing is haphazard.

This home is held in place with upright posts buried five or six feet deep into the ground (compared to three for a standard chickee) and

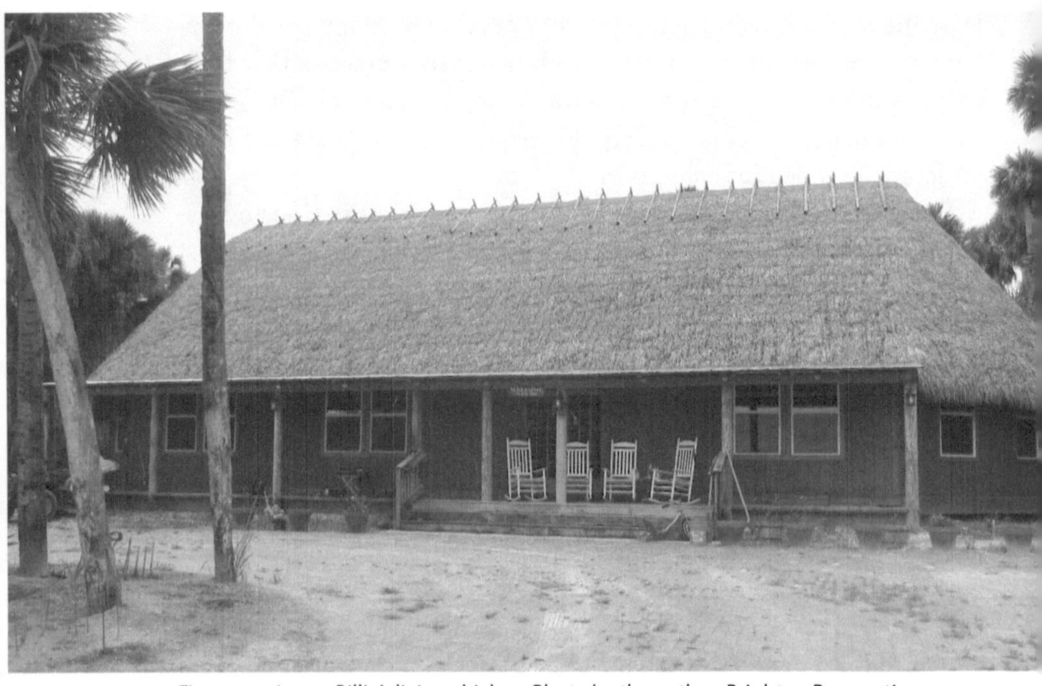

Figure 9.1. James Billie's living chickee. Photo by the author, Brighton Reservation, 2013.

secured with hurricane straps as needed. The interior space features exposed cypress poles visible within the drywall. The home has tile floors throughout and contains multiple bedrooms and bathrooms, a gourmet kitchen, and a large open living area. There are wooden decks on the front and back of the home. The chairman said the home was extremely affordable to build compared to a CBS home. On the downside, since it is air-conditioned, humidity control can be a serious issue in the summer, and the house takes on a certain earthy scent during the rain.

The chairman's home reflects a juxtaposition of old and new. It shows that while traditional small-scale, open-sided chickees have their place in society, it makes sense that chickees will evolve with changing needs of the tribe.

In addition to this living chickee, the chairman also has a camp near the main house—the only chickee camp in Brighton. He calls it his "chickee village in Brighton."[11] At his camp he has five chickees—a water station, a cook hut, one for the canoe, and two other guest

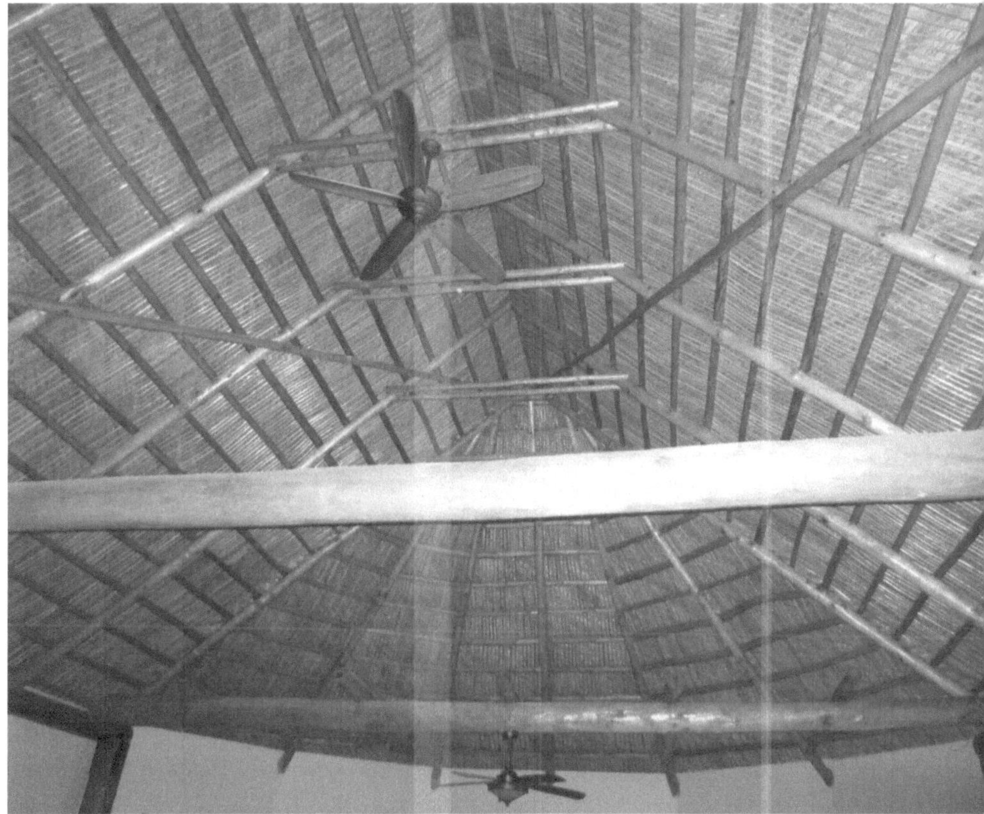

Figure 9.2. Underside of the roof thatching in James Billie's home. Photo by the author, Brighton Reservation, 2013.

chickees. When I asked why the cook chickee was round, he said because that was the style his wife wanted. Again, we see many modern influences and creative freedom. There is no true need for these to have completely open sides as seen in the cook chickees of the past.

Chickee Camps throughout Florida

The chairman and his crew also built a chickee camp at the Stephen Foster Folk Culture Center State Park in White Springs, Florida. The camp, still under construction in 2013, was ready for use during the 2014 Florida Folk Festival. The annual three-day event has taken place for over sixty years and reflects Florida's heritage. Seminoles have

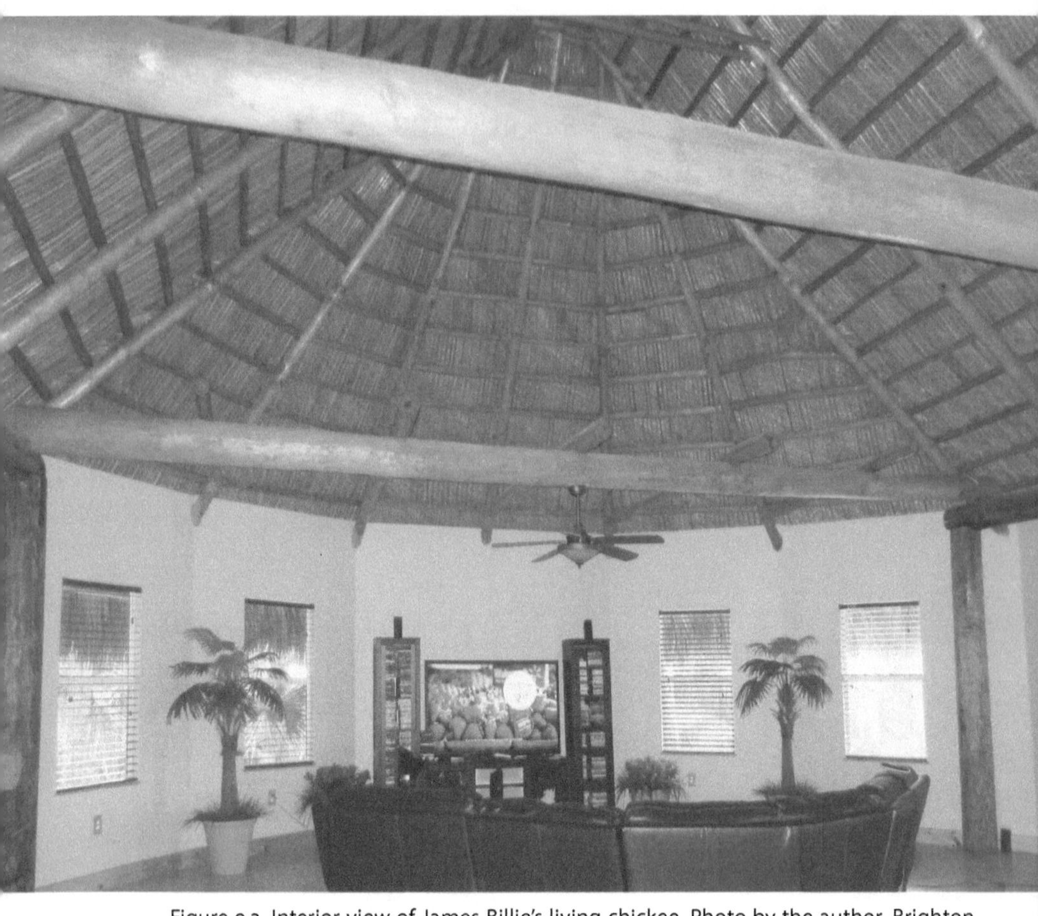

Figure 9.3. Interior view of James Billie's living chickee. Photo by the author, Brighton Reservation, 2013.

been attending the festival for decades, and they still hold a special place for the meaning of the festival. The camp serves as a place for festival-goers to learn about Seminole history and culture in an accurate setting. During the festival, tribal members cook traditional foods and make and sell crafts in this area. This camp represents one of the few places today that the average person can witness an entire Seminole camp, especially in such a northern region of Florida. The lessons to be learned here are invaluable. There are few other opportunities to showcase a Seminole camp to thousands of people over the course of a weekend.

When I had the chance to interview Chairman Billie at his home on the Brighton Reservation, it was clear that he continues to maintain a large interest in his chickee building business, although he no longer relies on it as his main source of income. He spoke about the importance of chickee building as a way of preserving his culture. Chief Jim Billie, as he is often called, lived in a chickee until he was eleven or twelve years old. He got his start helping build chickees at a very young age—at two or three years old, "handing up the leaves." I discovered that many chickee builders got their start the same way. As a child, he helped build chickees at the Green Corn Dance Ceremony but of course was not paid—this duty is an inherent part of traditional Seminole life. After he returned from serving in the Vietnam War, James Billie looked to chickee building as a source of income. His first chickee building company was a partnership with Pete Osceola, but in 1976 he started his own professional business with his wife. The first chickee he built as part of this new business was on Singer Island in Palm Beach County, Florida.

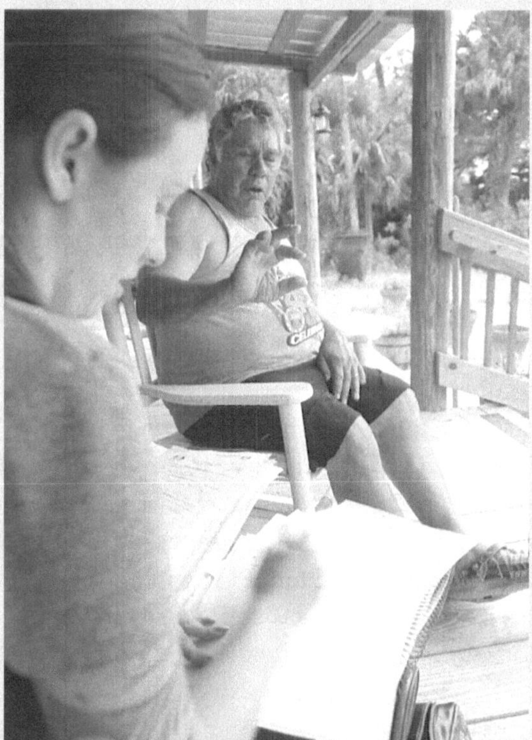

Figure 9.4. Photo of the author interviewing James Billie at his home on the Brighton Reservation. Peter Gallagher, *Seminole Tribune*, 2013.

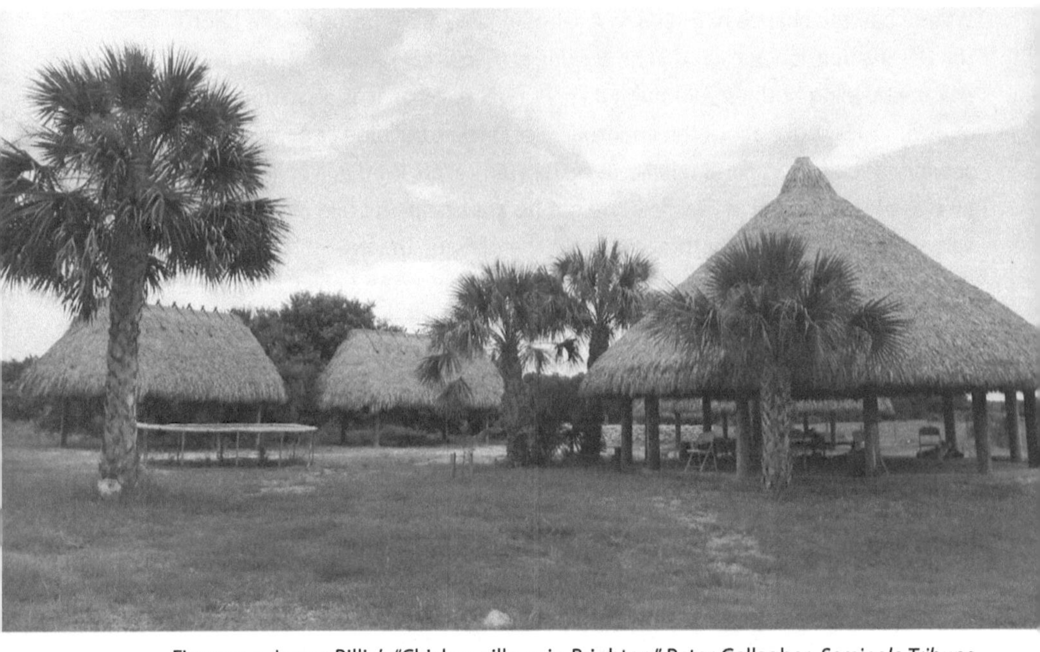

Figure 9.5. James Billie's "Chickee village in Brighton." Peter Gallagher, *Seminole Tribune*, 2013.

Tribal Youth

The builders I interviewed shared many common opinions about the future of chickee building. Since so many outsiders are getting involved in the trade, it is imperative to educate Seminole youth about preserving that inherent part of their culture. Joe Dan Osceola commented that children today are not very interested in building chickees because they are spoiled by the gaming dividends they receive. He and his son Wade had to build chickees to survive before they started receiving dividends. Wade believes that children are not too interested in chickee building these days, either, especially on the urban Hollywood Reservation. In Brighton and Big Cypress, the youth are taught chickee building in school programs. He said children these days on the reservations are spoiled with modern technology.

Wade Osceola recounted to me a story: "One day I was in my driveway skinning poles for a chickee. Some kids drove by on a golf cart and asked what I was doing. I said I was making poles for a chickee hut and they said 'Huh? What's that?' I pointed to a chickee. They

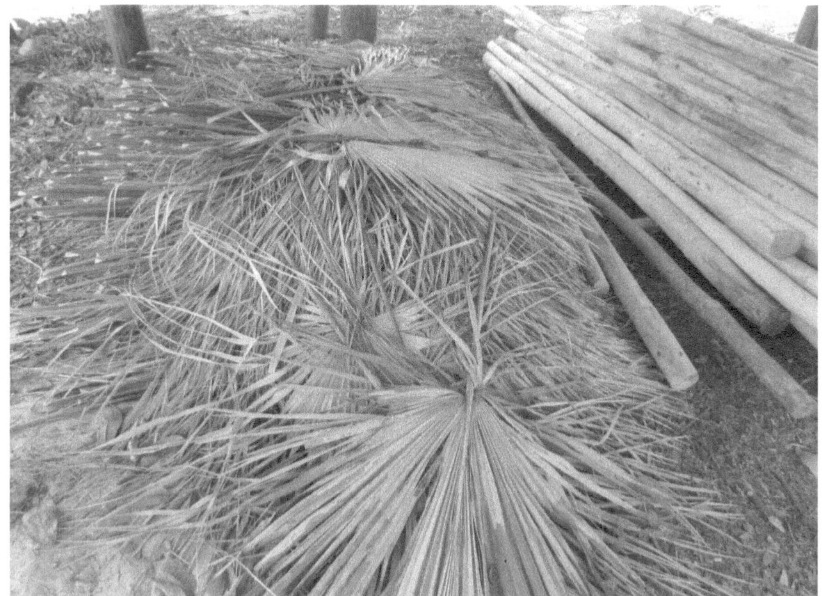

Figure 9.6. Raw building materials (palmetto fronds and cypress posts) for the chickees at the Stephen Foster Folk Culture Center State Park—the site of the Florida Folk Festival. Photo by the author, White Springs, 2013.

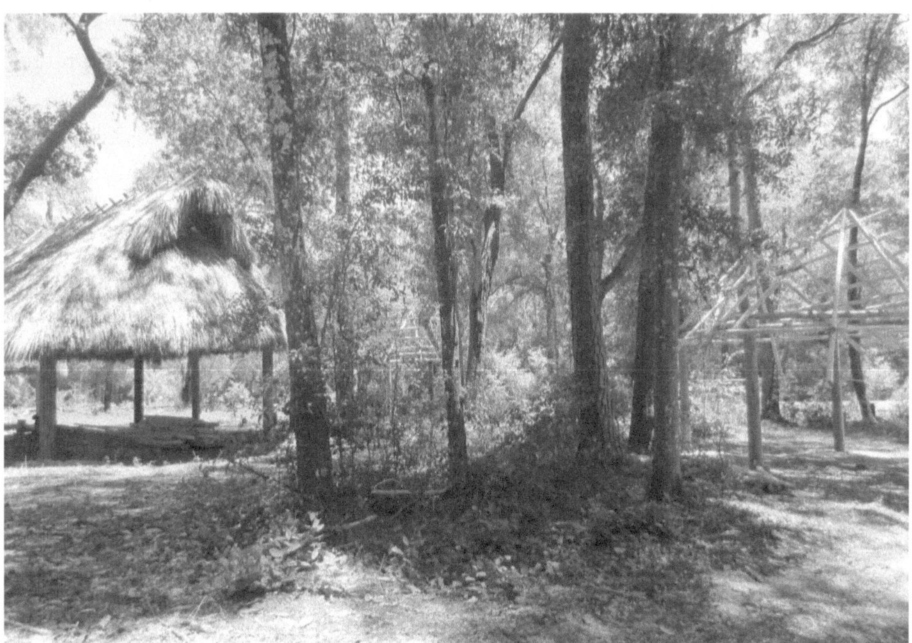

Figure 9.7. Seminole camp construction in progress at the Stephen Foster Folk Culture Center State Park. Photo by the author, White Springs, 2013.

did not even know what it was called." He did not tell me this story to speak negatively about the children, but to emphasize that times have changed.

When I asked the chairman if he thought tribal youth were interested in chickee building, he replied: "If their fathers and mothers are interested then most likely the children show an interest. . . . The younger generations have the added benefit that they can build them as big as they want . . . they have more energy and are healthier." Chickee builders are doing their part to pass on skills to their children. According to Norman Huggins, some young people are interested in chickee building, while others are not. His middle son builds chickees and helps him run his business. His youngest son does not yet know how to build them, but he wants his grandsons to learn as well. In the future, he would like to see more young people learning the trade. That is where the parents and the older generation have to come into play and teach the youth. He closed the interview by saying, "These chickees are part of our identity."

According to one builder, the true meaning of the chickee will soon be completely gone because the youth are not asking questions. They do not care enough because there are too many outside influences, and they are losing their language. "They change their hair color and do not even look like Indians," he said. "It's not the fault of the kids, though, it's the fault of the parents." His message to the children is "Don't forget the meaning of the chickee. Still live in them, still use them, because money isn't everything."

Though many chickee builders expressed that they believe that the true meaning of the chickee is dying out because the youth are not interested in preserving their culture, there is school curricula in place that teaches chickee history and/or chickee building to the students. High school students from the Brighton Reservation helped rebuild a chickee on the Okeechobee High School campus in 2001. The chickee had been built the previous year by tribal students and burned down a year later due to an act of vandalism. Eleven students from grades nine through twelve pitched in.[12] In 2002, the Brighton Summer Enrichment Program taught elementary school students how to build miniature chickees as a math assignment.[13]

The Brighton Boys Club, formed in 2012 by Lewis Gopher, has many activities on the reservation, including gathering palm fronds and rethatching chickees. During Memorial Day weekend of 2012, five members of the Boys Club rethatched a chickee at the Pemayetv Emahakv Charter School. All five of the boys were learning to thatch for the first time. Sandy Billie Jr. was there to help. As one of the young participants said, "These are supposed to be our homes. . . . I figured it would be good to know a part of me I did not know."[14]

Jade Osceola, the culture language instructor at Pemayetv Emahakv Charter School, teaches her students the history of chickees as part of the culture education program for the Seminole history class for first through eighth grade students. Her curriculum includes lessons on the materials and uses of chickees, and she discusses how chickees are used today compared to how they were used historically. She also teaches the students about the arrangement of camps, including why all chickees face the cook chickee. During our conversation, she mentioned that one of her students was upset that non-Indians build chickees because the chickee is considered the Seminole home, a family structure, and the heart of the family. That comment shows that the youth are taking a definite interest in preserving their history. Each year, eighth grade students from the charter school rethatch the roof of the chickee at the freshman campus of Okeechobee High School—the same chickee that was burned in 2001 that Jade herself helped rethatch when she was in high school.[15]

As part of Junior Archaeology Day in 2011, 2012, and 2013 (sponsored by the Ah-Tah-Thi-Ki Museum and the Tribal Historic Preservation Office), I gave a short history lesson about chickees to both tribal and nontribal students. The lesson, held under a chickee, also showed the young students how to conduct a chickee survey. All of these initiatives are teaching tribal youth about their architectural and cultural history and are hopefully sparking an interest for the future generation of chickee builders. These children may or may not someday be commercial chickee builders, but teaching them basic techniques of chickee building will help them carry on their culture.

The Future of Chickee Building

Several builders mentioned a potential shift toward more government control and commercialization of chickee building in the future. One interviewee feels strongly that the government prohibits Seminoles from living their way of life. He believes that the true meaning of the chickee is already lost: "Men were supposed to know how to do certain things: build a chickee, make a canoe, hunt, skin a deer, and always act proper when you go to another village. It is 'Indian law' to provide a chickee for his new family upon marriage." He thinks that moving into CBS houses broke up the man's role in the village. When this happened, people got lazier, and life became much easier. He believes that the chickee today does not represent what it once did; people just use them as a place for barbequing. In the future, he envisions that nobody will use the chickee in the traditional way: "They will build them for business, for BBQ, or storage."

Lonnie Billie believed that although people are implementing new materials in their chickees to prolong the lifespan, the chickee itself still represents Seminole culture. And even though moving into modern homes was not a bad thing in his opinion, Lonnie would still like to live in a chickee today, one with palmetto thatching for the walls. Bobby Henry also mentioned that he would like to still live in a chickee.

Ronnie Billie finished up his interview by saying that the focus on culture is returning. "You at least have to know your culture. Chickee building is an art form for the Seminoles." Bobby Henry concluded by saying, "Don't forget your culture, that's where you started." All authentic chickee builders, past and present, young or old, should be admired for their contribution to helping preserve Seminole culture.

Conclusion

Whether on- or off-reservation, the chickee is a symbol of cultural pride for the Seminoles. When I asked Sandy Billie Jr. how the idea of the chickee has changed over the years, he said that a chickee today is mostly a celebration house (for cookouts, parties, recreation), but it is also a reminder of what his ancestors did, what they fought for. They were once the dominant housing type for the Seminoles, and if the chairman's house is any indication, maybe chickees will be the dominant Seminole home again someday.

We may see more or fewer commercial chickee builders in the future. It is likely that more non-Seminoles will be involved in creating businesses using skills they have learned from the master builders as time goes on. But as long as chickees remain on the reservations, the culture will remain strong. The tourist camps, the public-space chickees, the festivals, and the chickee homes all help keep this part of culture alive. We are seeing new uses and new materials, but these changes ultimately do not detract from the cultural identity of the chickee.

Notes

Chapter 1. An Introduction to Native American Architecture

1. Kostof, *History of Architecture*, 17.
2. Ibid., 12.
3. Ibid.
4. Ibid., 15.
5. Nabokov and Easton, *Native American Architecture*, 17.
6. Ibid., 16.
7. Rapoport, *House Form and Culture*, 25.
8. Kostof, *History of Architecture*, 3.
9. This phrase, most commonly seen as "form follows function," was made famous by architect Louis Sullivan.
10. Nabokov and Easton, *Native American Architecture*, 16.
11. Ibid., 30.
12. Moore-Willson, *Seminoles of Florida*.
13. Ibid., 214.
14. "Indians Eager to Swap Tepees for Plumbing."
15. Holihan et al., "How Warm Is an Igloo?"
16. Nabokov and Easton, *Native American Architecture*, 320.
17. Ibid., 12.
18. Kostof, *History of Architecture*, 18.

Chapter 2. What Is a Chickee?

1. *Chiki* is the original Muscogee spelling variant. *Chikee* is a commonly acceptable spelling of the word today. *Chekee* was a popular early spelling

variants as seen in "More about Seminoles," *Miami News*, August 2, 1934. *Cheke* is the correct spelling as written in the Miccosukee language and is pronounced *chi·ge*. This version is also seen in Goss, *Usual and Customary Use*, 225.

2. Zimmerman, "Register to the Papers of Ethel Cutler Freeman," 3.

3. Freeman, "We Live with the Seminoles," 226.

4. Kirsten, *Book of Tiki*.

5. The bulk of the information for this part of the chapter comes from my interviews with specific chickee builders:

> Lonnie Billie, interview by author, Big Cypress Reservation, July 11, 2012.
> Sandy Billie Jr., interview by author, Brighton Reservation, April 8, 2013.
> Wade Osceola, interview by author, Hollywood, Fla., May 9, 2013.
> Bobby Henry, interview by author, White Springs, Fla., May 24, 2013.
> James E. Billie, interview by author, Brighton Reservation, June 20, 2013.
> Interview with anonymous chickee builder one, June 26, 2013.
> Norman Huggins, telephone interview by author, June 26, 2013.
> Norman "Skeeter" Bowers, interview by author, Brighton Reservation, June 27, 2013.
> Ronnie Billie, interview by author, Big Cypress Reservation, July 2, 2013.
> Interview with anonymous chickee builder two, July 3, 2013.
> Joe Dan Osceola, interview by author, Hollywood Reservation, July 5, 2013.

6. Hawkins, "Seminole Chickees for the Children."

7. Kirsten, *Book of Tiki*, 52.

8. Law, "Chic Chickees Spell Success for Seminoles."

9. Gallagher, "Rise and Fall of Chief Jim Billie."

10. Wade Osceola, interview by author, Hollywood, Fla., May 9, 2013.

11. Norman "Skeeter" Bowers, interview by author, Brighton Reservation, June 27, 2013.

12. Spoehr, "Florida Seminole Camp," 126.

13. Proby, "Hatching a Chickee."

14. Bobby Henry, interview by author, White Springs, Fla., May 24, 2013.

Chapter 3. The Architecture of Chickees

1. Bobby Henry, interview by author, White Springs, Fla., May 24, 2013.

2. Nabokov and Easton, *Native American Architecture*, 118.

3. Extebarria, "Indian Day Celebration Continues."

4. Sandy Billie Jr., interview by author, Brighton Reservation, April 8, 2013.

5. Goss, *Usual and Customary Use*, 116.

6. Interview with anonymous chickee builder two, July 3, 2013.

7. Sandy Billie Jr., interview by author, Brighton Reservation, April 8, 2013.

8. Wade Osceola, interview by author, Hollywood, Fla., May 9, 2013.

9. Jumper, "Oh-gu-ba-che."

10. Milton D. Thompson to John Mahon, June 25, 1975, Samuel Proctor Oral History Program Collection, 15.

11. Nash, *Survey of the Seminole Indians of Florida*, 5.

12. MacCauley, *Seminole Indians of Florida*, 45.

13. Lonnie Billie, interview by author, Big Cypress Reservation, July 11, 2012.

14. Law, "Chic Chickees Spell Success for Seminoles."

15. Spoehr, "Florida Seminole Camp," 124.

16. MacCauley, *Seminole Indians of Florida*, 47.

17. Lonnie Billie, interview by author, Big Cypress Reservation, July 11, 2012.

18. Grant Steelman (STOF fire rescue forester), personal communication with author, July 18, 2013.

19. Haase, *Classic Cracker*, 28.

20. Albert DeVane to Foster Barnes and Thelma Boltin, 1960, Samuel Proctor Oral History Program Collection, 19.

21. Nabokov and Easton, *Native American Architecture*, 117.

22. Nash, *Survey of the Seminole Indians of Florida*, 5.

23. Nabokov and Easton, *Native American Architecture*, 115.

24. Ibid., 16.

25. Ibid., 115.

26. Arnett, "Seminole Indian Clues," 147.

27. Ibid.

28. Interview with anonymous chickee builder one, June 26, 2013.

29. Whiting, "Out-of-Work Seminole Falls Back on Heritage."

Chapter 4. Seminole Architectural Roots

1. Blakney-Bailey, "Analysis of Historic Creek," 18–19.

2. Marty Bowers, interview by author, Tampa, Fla., May 28, 2013.

3. Bartram, *Travels and Other Writings*, 170–171.

4. Research by the historian Patsy West on the Miccosukee ethnogenesis for a forthcoming publication may help us prove this idea.

5. French, "Seminoles: A Collision of Cultures."

6. Hann, "Political Leadership," 188–189.

7. Ehrmann, "Timucua Indians," 176–177.

8. Bartram, *Travels and Other Writings*, 170–171.

9. Blakney-Bailey, "Analysis of Historic Creek," 106.

10. Mary Frances Johns to Tom King, May 1973, Samuel Proctor Oral History Program Collection, 10–11.

11. Bartram, *Travels and Other Writings*, 316–317.

12. W. P. Rowles, "Incidents and Observations in Florida in 1836," *Southron* (1841): 115, quoted in Weisman, *Like Beads on a String*, 120.

13. Hutchinson, "Florida Artist," 134–135.

14. Mary Frances Johns to Tom King, May 1973, Samuel Proctor Oral History Program Collection, 11–12.

15. Sturtevant, "R. H. Pratt's Report," 6.

16. Ibid., 20

17. Blakney-Bailey, "Analysis of Historic Creek," 128.

18. Ibid., 221.

Chapter 5. A Century of Evolution, 1840–1940

1. Sturtevant, "Chakaika and the 'Spanish Indians,'" 52.

2. Ibid.

3. Ibid., 53.

4. Weisman, "Chipco's House," 165.

5. Sturtevant, "R. H. Pratt's Report," 1–2.

6. Ibid., 6.

7. Ibid., 10.

8. Weisman, "Chipco's House," 165.

9. MacCauley, *Seminole Indians of Florida*, 44.

10. Ibid., 43–44.

11. Ibid., 45.

12. Ibid., 46.

13. Ibid., 47.

14. Ibid., 48.

15. Ibid., 48–49.

16. Weisman, "Chipco's House," 166.

17. Marchman, "Ingraham Everglades Exploring Expedition," 3.

18. Ibid., 13.

19. Ibid., 27.

20. Ibid., 35.

21. H. A. Ernst, "First Photo on Record Taken at Pine Island, Florida, 1850s–1930s," National Anthropological Archives, Smithsonian Institution.

22. Milanich and Root, *Hidden Seminoles*, 28.

23. Ibid., 35.

24. Kersey, *Pelts, Plumes, and Hides*, 64.

25. Milanich and Root, *Hidden Seminoles*, 57.

26. Ibid., 59.

27. Skinner, "Notes on the Florida Seminole," 64.

28. Milanich and Root, *Hidden Seminoles*, 49–50.

29. Skinner, "Notes on the Florida Seminole," 68–69.

30. Ibid., 76.

31. Milanich and Root, *Hidden Seminoles*, 50.

32. Patsy West, "Miami Indian Tourist Attractions," 200.

33. Patsy West, *Enduring Seminoles*, 12.

34. West, "Miami Indian Tourist Attractions," 202.

35. Downs, "Coppinger's Tropical Gardens," 227.

36. Kersey, *Florida Seminoles and the New Deal*, 38.

37. Downs, "Coppinger's Tropical Gardens," 228.

38. West, *Enduring Seminoles*, 84.

39. Ibid., 85.

40. West, "Miami Indian Tourist Attractions," 210.

41. Kersey, *Florida Seminoles and the New Deal*, 38.

42. West, "Miami Indian Tourist Attractions," 204, 210.

43. Downs, "Coppinger's Tropical Gardens," 225.

44. West, *Enduring Seminoles*, 26.

45. Ibid., 100–101.

Chapter 6. Seminole Camps

1. Rapoport, "Systems of Activities and Systems of Settings," 12.

2. Kostof, *History of Architecture*, 10.

3. Spoehr, "Camp, Clan, and Kin," 14.

4. Spoehr, "Florida Seminole Camp," 128.

5. Cattelino, "Florida Seminole Housing," 703.

6. Blakney-Bailey, "Analysis of Historic Creek," 93–94.

7. Patsy West, *Images of America*, 21.

8. Nabokov and Easton, *Native American Architecture*, 12.

9. Cattelino, "Florida Seminole Housing," 710.

10. Spoehr, "Camp, Clan, and Kin," 10.

11. Nash, *Survey of the Seminole Indians of Florida*, 4.

12. Spoehr, "Florida Seminole Camp," 126.

13. Tobias, "Brighton and Tampa Tribal Citizens."

14. Goss, *Usual and Customary Use*, 127.

15. Nash, *Survey of the Seminole Indians of Florida*, 4–5.

16. Garbarino, *Big Cypress*, 69.

17. Skinner, "Notes on the Florida Seminole," 70.

18. Spoehr, "Florida Seminole Camp," 124.

19. Sturtevant, "Creek into Seminole," 113–114.

20. Goss, *Usual and Customary Use*, 113–114.

21. Patsy West, "Pine Island Settlement."

22. Sturtevant, "Creek into Seminole," 113.

23. Garbarino, *Big Cypress*, 69.

24. Goss, *Usual and Customary Use*, 97–98.

25. Nash, *Survey of the Seminole Indians of Florida*, 21, 22.

26. Goss, *Usual and Customary Use*, 112–113.

27. Spoehr, "Florida Seminole Camp," 142.

28. Capron, *Medicine Bundles*, 161.

29. Ibid.

30. Goss, *Usual and Customary Use*, 115.

31. Ibid., 120–121.

32. Ibid., 126.

33. Spoehr, "Florida Seminole Camp," 126.

34. Maureen Mahoney, personal communication with author, Big Cypress Reservation, June 19, 2013.

35. Patsy West, *Enduring Seminoles*, 33.

36. Garbarino, *Big Cypress*, 69.

37. Kent, "Cross-Cultural Study," 128.

38. Patsy West, "Dressing for a Wedding."

39. Spoehr, "Camp, Clan, and Kin," 12.

40. Garbarino, *Big Cypress*, 66.

41. West, "Dressing for a Wedding."

42. Bundschu, "Housing Program for the Seminole Indians," 48.

43. Spoehr, "Florida Seminole Camp," 145.

44. Spoehr, "Clan, Camp, and Kin," 13.

45. Garbarino, *Big Cypress*, 69.
46. Skinner, "Notes on the Florida Seminole," 70.
47. Garbarino, *Big Cypress*, 69–70.
48. Skinner, "Notes on the Florida Seminole," 67.
49. MacCauley, *Seminole Indians of Florida*, 52.
50. Nash, *Survey of the Seminole Indians of Florida*, 10.
51. Spoehr, "Camp, Clan, and Kin," 14.
52. Garbarino, *Big Cypress*, 43.
53. Skinner, "Notes on the Florida Seminole," 67–68.
54. Jacob Osceola to Paul Backhouse, Big Cypress Reservation, 2012.
55. Claxton, "Report on the Conditions Observed."
56. Garbarino, *Big Cypress*, 44.

Chapter 7. The Transitional Period, 1930s–1970s

1. Blakney-Bailey, "Analysis of Historic Creek," 88.
2. Kersey, *Florida Seminoles and the New Deal*, 9.
3. Ibid., 10.
4. Covington, "Dania Reservation," 141.
5. Nash, *Survey of the Seminole Indians of Florida*, 35.
6. Covington, "Dania Reservation," 141–142.
7. Kersey, *Florida Seminoles and the New Deal*, xi–xii.
8. Kersey, *Assumption of Sovereignty*, 14.
9. Kersey, *Florida Seminoles and the New Deal*, 20–21.
10. Garbarino, *Big Cypress*, 43.
11. Kersey, *Florida Seminoles and the New Deal*, 49–50.
12. National Register of Historic Places, The Council Oak Tree Site on the Hollywood Seminole Indian Reservation, Hollywood, Broward County, Florida, National Register #12000992.
13. Kersey, *Assumption of Sovereignty*, 30–31.
14. Cattelino, "Florida Seminole Housing," 705.
15. Ibid., 710.
16. Hogan, "Indian Wives Adopt White Woman's Ways."
17. Claiborne, "On Reservations, Little Hope for Home Loans."
18. "Seminole Aid Group Plans Housing Drive."
19. "Meeting Monday to Push Home Program for Indians."
20. Cattelino, "Florida Seminole Housing," 704.
21. "Temperature Plunge Finds Seminoles Unprotected."
22. Lee Tiger to Mark Bass, October 11, 1977, Samuel Proctor Oral History Program Collection, 14.

23. Nabokov and Easton, *Native American Architecture*, 12.

24. "Another Indian Tradition Goes."

25. Lee Tiger to Mark Bass, October 11, 1977, Samuel Proctor Oral History Program Collection, 15.

26. Garbarino, *Big Cypress*, 36.

27. Ibid.

28. Judie Kannon to John Mahon, February 15, 1975, Samuel Proctor Oral History Program Collection, 9.

29. Garbarino, *Big Cypress*, 34.

30. Willie Johns, interview by author, Brighton Reservation, June 20, 2013.

31. Garbarino, *Big Cypress*, 18.

32. Bundschu, "Housing Program for the Seminole Indians," 42.

33. Tozier, "Report on the Florida Seminoles."

34. Cattelino, "Florida Seminole Housing," 705.

35. Frank, "Senior Profile."

36. Brown, "Chickees on the Way Out?"

37. Mangan, "Seminole Switch."

38. Ibid.

39. "Billie Family Leaves Chickee for House."

40. Cattelino, "Florida Seminole Housing," 705.

41. Aurilla Birrel to John K. Mahon, September 12, 1974, Samuel Proctor Oral History Program Collection.

42. "Series 1—Seminole Tribe of Florida, 1932–1970."

43. "Seminoles of Florida: Ten-Year Program."

44. Ibid.

45. Daughtrey, "Seminoles Leaving Shacks."

46. Garbarino, *Big Cypress*, 18.

47. Ibid.

48. Ibid., 18–19.

49. Cattelino, "Florida Seminole Housing," 713.

50. Aurilla Birrel to John K. Mahon, September 12, 1974, Samuel Proctor Oral History Program Collection.

51. Cattelino, "Florida Seminole Housing," 711.

52. Mary Jene Coppedge to Rosalyn Howard, April 28, 1999, Samuel Proctor Oral History Program Collection.

53. Garbarino, *Big Cypress*, 69.

54. Bundschu, "Housing Program for the Seminole Indians," 54.

55. Rapoport, "Systems of Activities and Systems of Settings," 13.

56. Hall, "'Modern Chickees' Present Big Indian Problem."
57. Van Smith, "Away with the Old."
58. Millott, "Miccosukees' Chickees Go Modern."
59. Ingle, "New Chic for Chickees."
60. Bundschu, "Housing Program for the Seminole Indians."
61. Ibid., 57.
62. Cattelino, "Florida Seminole Housing," 707.
63. Mike Morgan, "Seminoles Go Modern."
64. Cattelino, "Florida Seminole Housing," 708.
65. Aurilla Birrel to John K. Mahon, September 12, 1974, Samuel Proctor Oral History Program Collection.
66. Mary Jene Coppedge to Rosalyn Howard, April 28, 1999, Samuel Proctor Oral History Program Collection, 33–34.
67. Buster, "Mem'ries of My Dad."
68. Willie Johns interview by author, Brighton Reservation, June 20, 2013.
69. Garbarino, *Big Cypress*, 18.
70. Willie Johns, interview by author, Brighton Reservation, June 20, 2013.
71. Ronnie Billie, interview by author, Big Cypress Reservation, July 2, 2013.
72. Sandy Billie Jr., interview by author, Brighton Reservation, April 8, 2013.
73. Bobby Henry, interview by author, White Springs, Fla., May 24, 2013.
74. James E. Billie, interview by author, Brighton Reservation, June 20, 2013.
75. Lee Tiger to Mark Bass, October 11, 1977, Samuel Proctor Oral History Program Collection.
76. Aurilla Birrel to John K. Mahon, September 12, 1974, Samuel Proctor Oral History Program Collection.
77. Tribal Register of Historic Places Nomination, "Buster Twins Camp," Seminole Tribe of Florida Tribal Historic Preservation Office, 2013.
78. Lester and Laura Blain to John Mahon, 1975, Samuel Proctor Oral History Program Collection.
79. John Belmont to Tom King, February 24, 1973, Samuel Proctor Oral History Program Collection, 11.
80. Bundschu, "Housing Program for the Seminole Indians," introduction.
81. Ibid., 34.
82. Ibid., 44.

Chapter 8. The Big Cypress Chickee Survey

1. Rasmussen, *Experiencing Architecture*, 33.

2. Information from the Seminole Tribe of Florida's GIS Buildings Layer.

3. "Made in Shade."

4. Law, "Chic Chickees Spell Success for Seminoles."

5. MacCauley, *Seminole Indians of Florida*, 45.

6. French, "Seminoles Help Miccosukees Get Over Storm Andrew."

7. Bundschu, "Housing Program for the Seminole Indians,"

Chapter 9. Chickees Today and Beyond

1. French, "Seminoles: A Collision of Cultures."

2. "Seminoles Challenge Code."

3. Begay, "Hidden Tribe."

4. Collier County Board of County Commissioners, Meeting Recap, November 26, 1996, http://apps.collierclerk.com/BMR/0/doc/5389/Page5.aspx.

5. "Home Sweet Home."

6. Goss, *Usual and Customary Use*, 131.

7. Cattelino, "Florida Seminole Housing," 705.

8. Ibid., 717.

9. William Osceola to J. Ellison, June 27, 2000, Samuel Proctor Oral History Program Collection.

10. Tania Zimmer (STOF land use coordinator), personal communication with author, July 19, 2013.

11. Billie, "Around Here, It's Still *Thal-chobee-yo-ke*."

12. James, "Tribal Students Rebuild a Cultural Symbol."

13. Gannon, "Summer Enrichment Program Celebration."

14. Buxton, "Brighton Reservation Starts New Boys Club."

15. Jade Osceola, personal communication with author, July 18, 2013.

Bibliography

Books and Journals

Arnett, William T. "Seminole Indian Clues for Contemporary House Form in Florida." *Florida Anthropologist* 6, no. 4 (December 1953): 145–148.

Bartram, William. *Travels and Other Writings*. New York: Library of America, 1964.

Capron, Louis. *The Medicine Bundles of the Florida Seminole and the Green Corn Dance*. Washington, D.C.: U.S. Government Printing Office, 1953.

Cattelino, Jessica. "Florida Seminole Housing and the Social Means of Sovereignty." *Society for Comparative Study of Society and History* (2006): 699–726.

Covington, James W. "Dania Reservation: 1911–1927." *Florida Anthropologist* 29, no. 4 (December 1976): 137–144.

Downs, Dorothy. "Coppinger's Tropical Gardens: The First Commercial Indian Village in Florida." *Florida Anthropologist* 34, no. 4 (December 1981): 225–231.

Ehrmann, W. W. "The Timucua Indians of Sixteenth Century Florida." *Florida Historical Quarterly* 18, no. 3 (January 1940): 168–191.

Freeman, Ethel Cutler. "We Live with the Seminoles." *Natural History* 49, no. 4 (April 1942): 226–236.

Garbarino, Merwyn S. *Big Cypress: A Changing Community*. Prospect Heights, Ill.: Waveland Press, 1972.

Goss, James A. *Usual and Customary Use and Occupancy by the Miccosukee and Seminole Indians in Big Cypress National Preserve, Florida*. Southeast Region National Park Service and Texas Tech University, June 1, 1995.

Haase, Ronald W. *Classic Cracker: Florida's Wood-Frame Vernacular Architecture*. Sarasota, Fla.: Pineapple Press, 1992.

Hall, Nicolas. *Thatching: A Handbook*. Warwickshire, U.K.: Practical Action Publishing, 1988.

Hann, John H. "Political Leadership among the Natives of Spanish Florida." *Florida Historical Quarterly* 71, no. 2 (October 1992): 188–208.

Hutchinson, James. "A Florida Artist Views the Seminoles." *Florida Historical Quarterly* 55, no. 2 (October 1976): 134–137.

Kahn, Lloyd, and Bob Easton, eds. *Shelter*. Bolinas, Calif.: Shelter Publications, 1973.

Kent, Susan. "A Cross-Cultural Study of Segmentation, Architecture, and the Use of Space." In *Domestic Architecture and the Use of Space: An Interdisciplinary Cross-Cultural Study*, edited by Susan Kent, 127–152. Cambridge, U.K.: University of Cambridge, 1993.

Kersey, Harry A., Jr. *An Assumption of Sovereignty: Social and Political Transformation among the Florida Seminoles, 1953–1979*. Lincoln: University of Nebraska Press, 1996.

———. *The Florida Seminoles and the New Deal*. Boca Raton: Florida Atlantic University Press, 1989.

———. *Pelts, Plumes, and Hides*. Boca Raton: Florida Atlantic University Press, 1980.

Kirsten, Sven A. *The Book of Tiki*. Koln, Germany: Taschen, 2003.

Kostof, Spiro. *A History of Architecture*. New York: Oxford University Press, 1995.

MacCauley, Clay. *The Seminole Indians of Florida: Fifth Annual Report of the Bureau of Ethnology to the Secretary of the Smithsonian Institution, 1883–84, Government Printing Office, Washington, 1887*. Charleston, S.C.: BiblioBazaar, 2008.

Marchman, Watt, ed. "The Ingraham Everglades Exploring Expedition, 1892." *Tequesta* 7 (1947): 3–43.

Milanich, Jerald T., and Nina J. Root. *Hidden Seminoles: Julian Dimock's Historic Florida Photographs*. Gainesville: University Press of Florida, 2011.

Moore-Willson, Minnie. *The Seminoles of Florida*. New York: Moffat, Yard, 1911.

Nabokov, Peter, and Robert Easton. *Native American Architecture*. New York: Oxford University Press, 1989.

Nash, Roy. *Survey of the Seminole Indians of Florida*. Washington, D.C.: U.S. Department of the Interior Office of Indian Affairs, 1932.

Rapoport, Amos. *House Form and Culture*. Englewood Cliffs, N.J.: Prentice-Hall, 1969.

———. "Systems of Activities and Systems of Settings." In *Domestic Architecture and the Use of Space: An Interdisciplinary Cross-Cultural Study*, edited by Susan Kent, 9–20. Cambridge, U.K.: University of Cambridge, 1993.

Rasmussen, Steen Eiler. *Experiencing Architecture*. Cambridge, Mass.: MIT Press, 1962.

Skinner, Alanson. "Notes on the Florida Seminole." *American Anthropologist* 15, no. 1 (1913): 63–77.

Spoehr, Alexander. "Camp, Clan, and Kin among the Cow Creek Seminole in Florida." *Field Museum of Natural History Anthropological Series* 33, no. 1 (1941): 1–27.

———. "The Florida Seminole Camp." *Field Museum of Natural History Anthropological Series* 33, no. 3 (1944): 115–150.

Sturtevant, William C. "Chakaika and the 'Spanish Indians': Documentary Sources Compared with Seminole Tradition." *Tequesta* 18 (1953): 35–73.

———. "Creek into Seminole." In *Native Americans in Historical Perspective*, edited by Eleanor Burke Leacock and Nancy Oestreich Lurie, 92–128. Prospect Heights, Ill.: Waveland Press, 1971.

———. "R. H. Pratt's Report on the Seminole in 1879." *Florida Anthropologist* 9, no. 1 (March 1956): 1–29.

Weisman, Brent. "Chipco's House and the Role of the Individual in Shaping Seminole Indian Cultural Responses to the Modern World." *Historical Archaeology* 46, no. 1 (2012): 161–171.

———. *Like Beads on a String: A Culture History of the Seminole Indians in North Peninsular Florida*. Tuscaloosa: University of Alabama Press, 1989.

West, Patsy. *The Enduring Seminoles*. Gainesville: University Press of Florida, 1998.

———. *Images of America: The Seminole and Miccosukee Tribes of Southern Florida*. Charleston, S.C.: Arcadia Publishing, 2003.

———. "The Miami Indian Tourist Attractions: A History and Analysis of a Transitional Mikasuki Seminole Environment." *Florida Anthropologist* 34, no. 4 (December 1981): 200–224.

West, Robert. *Thatch: A Complete Guide to the Ancient Craft of Thatching*. Pittstown, N.J.: Main Street Press, 1987.

Oral Histories, Interviews, and Personal Communications

Bobby Henry, interview by author, White Springs, Fla., May 24, 2013.

Grant Steelman, personal communication with author, July 18, 2013.

Interview with anonymous chickee builder one, June 26, 2013.

Interview with anonymous chickee builder two, July 3, 2013.

Jade Osceola, personal communication with author, July 18, 2013.
James E. Billie, interview by author, Brighton Reservation, Fla., June 20, 2013.
Joe Dan Osceola, interview by author, Hollywood Reservation, Fla., July 5, 2013.
Lewis Gopher, interview by author, Brighton Reservation, Fla., June 20, 2013.
Lonnie Billie, interview by author, Big Cypress Reservation, Fla., July 11, 2012.
Marty Bowers, interview by author, Tampa, Fla., May 28, 2013.
Maureen Mahoney, personal communication with author, June 19, 2013.
Norman Huggins, telephone interview by author, June 26, 2013.
Norman "Skeeter" Bowers, interview by author, Brighton Reservation, Fla., June 27, 2013.
O. B. Osceola Sr., interview with Debbie Fant, November 22, 1987. Series S1622, Florida Folk Life Collection. http://www.floridamemory.com/items/show/23642.
Ronnie Billie, interview by author, Big Cypress Reservation, Fla., July 2, 2013.
Sandy Billie Jr., interview by author, Brighton Reservation, Fla., April 8, 2013.
Tania Zimmer, personal communication with author, July 19, 2013.
Transcript, Albert DeVane Oral History Interview with Foster Barnes and Thelma Boltin, 1960. Samuel Proctor Oral History Program Collection, P. K. Yonge Library of Florida History, University of Florida.
Transcript, Aurilla Birrel Oral History Interview with Dr. John K. Mahon, September 12, 1974. Samuel Proctor Oral History Program Collection, P. K. Yonge Library of Florida History, University of Florida.
Transcript, John Belmont Oral History Interview with Tom King, February 24, 1973. Samuel Proctor Oral History Program Collection, P. K. Yonge Library of Florida History, University of Florida.
Transcript, Judie Kannon Oral History Interview with John Mahon, February 15, 1975. Samuel Proctor Oral History Program Collection, P. K. Yonge Library of Florida History, University of Florida.
Transcript, Lee Tiger Oral History Interview with Mark Bass, October 11, 1977. Samuel Proctor Oral History Program Collection, P. K. Yonge Library of Florida History, University of Florida.
Transcript, Lester and Laura Blain Oral History Interview with John Mahon, 1975. Samuel Proctor Oral History Program Collection, P. K. Yonge Library of Florida History, University of Florida.

Transcript, Mary Frances Johns Oral History Interview with Tom King, May 1973. Samuel Proctor Oral History Program Collection, P. K. Yonge Library of Florida History, University of Florida.

Transcript, Mary Jene Coppedge Oral History Interview with Rosalyn Howard, April 28, 1999. Samuel Proctor Oral History Program Collection, P. K. Yonge Library of Florida History, University of Florida.

Transcript, Milton D. Thompson Oral History Interview with John Mahon, June 25, 1975. Samuel Proctor Oral History Program Collection, P. K. Yonge Library of Florida History, University of Florida.

Transcript, William Osceola Oral History Interview with J. Ellison, June 27, 2000. Samuel Proctor Oral History Program Collection, P. K. Yonge Library of Florida History, University of Florida.

Wade Osceola, interview by author, Hollywood, Fla., May 9, 2013.

Willie Johns, interview by author, Brighton Reservation, Fla., June 20, 2013.

Newspaper and Magazine Articles

"Another Indian Tradition Goes; Electric Range Now in Chickee." *Hollywood Sun-Tattler*, December 5, 1955.

Begay, Jason. "The Hidden Tribe." *Sun-Sentinel*, August 5, 2000.

Billie, James E. "Around Here, It's Still *Thal-chobee-yo-ke*." *Seminole Tribune*, April 26, 2013.

"Billie Family Leaves Chickee for House." *Fort Lauderdale News*, May 19, 1959.

Brown, Dan. "Chickees on the Way Out? 1st Seminole CBS House Nears Completion." *Miami Herald*, March 3, 1957.

Buster, Paul "Cowbone." "Mem'ries of My Dad." *Seminole Tribune*, June 10, 2005.

Buxton, Rachel. "Brighton Reservation Starts New Boys Club." *Seminole Tribune*, June 29, 2012.

Claiborne, William. "On Reservations, Little Hope for Home Loans." *Washington Post*, November 25, 1998.

Daughtrey, Rufe. "Seminoles Leaving Shacks for New Modern Houses." *Fort Myers News-Press*, November 7, 1959.

Extebarria, Susan. "Indian Day Celebration Continues under Hurricane Watch." *Seminole Tribune*, October 15, 2004.

Frank, Alexandra. "Senior Profile: Spending Time with Mary Bowers." *Seminole Tribune*, January 11, 2002.

French, Bob. "Seminoles: A Collision of Cultures." *Sun-Sentinel*, December 24, 2005.

———. "Seminoles Help Miccosukees Get Over Storm Andrew Left Reservation Powerless, Cut Off from Rescue Workers." *Sun-Sentinel*, September 5, 1992.

Gallagher, Peter B. "The Rise and Fall of Chief Jim Billie." *Sarasota Magazine*, January 2005.

Gannon, Paula. "Summer Enrichment Program Celebration." *Seminole Tribune*, July 26, 2002.

Hall, Martha. "'Modern Chickees' Present Big Indian Problem: How?" *Miami Herald*, January 8, 1965.

Hawkins, Sam. "Seminole Chickees for the Children." *Florida Living*, December 28, 1952.

Hogan, Frank. "Indian Wives Adopt White Woman's Ways." *Fort Lauderdale Daily News*, August 1, 1956.

"Home Sweet Home." *Wall Street Journal*, December 31, 1997.

"Indians Eager to Swap Tepees for Plumbing." *Orlando Sentinel*, November 21, 1956.

Ingle, Martha. "New Chic for Chickees: Young Indians Try Modified Indoor Living." *Miami Herald*, February 20, 1966.

James, Michael. "Tribal Students Rebuild a Cultural Symbol during Florida Heritage Cracker Days." *Seminole Tribune*, November 30, 2001.

Jumper, Betty Mae. "Oh-gu-ba-che." *Seminole Tribune*, October 20, 2000.

Law, Janice. "Chic Chickees Spell Success for Seminoles." *Fort Lauderdale News and Sun-Sentinel*, August 28, 1977.

"Made in Shade." *Miami Herald*, June 28, 1968.

Mangan, Pat. "Seminole Switch: Chickees Out, CBS Homes In." *Miami Herald*, November 11, 1959.

"Meeting Monday to Push Home Program for Indians." *Fort Lauderdale Daily News*, January 27, 1956.

Millott, Dan. "Miccosukees' Chickees Go Modern." *St. Petersburg Times*, December 19, 1965.

Morgan, Mike. "Seminoles Go Modern: Ancient Ways of Life Yielding to Progress as Indians Exchange Chikees for CBS Homes." *Miami Herald*, May 22, 1960.

Morgan, Tom. "Seminoles Build 'Biggest' Chickee in Naples." *Miami Herald*, October 11, 1959.

Proby, Kathryn Hall. "Hatching a Chickee." *Miami Herald*, March 3, 1977.

Rex, Lyn. "Building Business Indians Pass on Chickee Tradition." *Sun-Sentinel*, June 21, 1992.

"Seminole Aid Group Plans Housing Drive." *Fort Lauderdale Daily News*, n.d., 1955.

"Seminoles Challenge Code." *Sun-Sentinel*, January 10, 1996.
"Temperature Plunge Finds Seminoles Unprotected." *Fort Lauderdale Daily News*, February 14, 1958.
Tobias, Naji. "Brighton and Tampa Tribal Citizens Share Culture Storytelling Lessons about Seminole Life." *Seminole Tribune*, April 29, 2011.
Van Smith, Howard. "Away with the Old . . . and into the New . . . Enter 20th Century." *Miami News*, November 11, 1962.
West, Patsy. "Dressing for a Wedding." *Seminole Tribune*, December 1, 2000.
———. "Pine Island Settlement." *Seminole Tribune*, June 15, 2001.
Whiting, Bill. "Out-of-Work Seminole Falls Back on Heritage—It Helps to Pay Bills." *Miami Herald*, September 20, 1975.

Other

Blakney-Bailey, Jane Anne. "Analysis of Historic Creek and Seminole Settlement Patterns, Town Design, and Architecture: The Paynes Town Seminole Site (8AL366), a Case Study." Ph.D. diss., University of Florida, Gainesville, 2007.
Bundschu, Mary Elen. "A Housing Program for the Seminole Indians at the Brighton Reservation." Master's architectural project in lieu of thesis, University of Florida, 1979.
Claxton, W. A. "A Report on the conditions observed among the Seminole Indians of south Florida during an inspection trip to some camps in August 1930." Special Collections Florida History, University of Florida Smathers Library, Gainesville.
Collier County Board of County Commissioners. Meeting Recap, November 26, 1996. http://apps.collierclerk.com/BMR/0/doc/5389/Page5.aspx.
Gould, Eric, Grant Day, and Mike Organ. "Sustainability in Architecture: East St. Louis Action Research Project (ESLARP)." n.d. http://www.eslarp.uiuc.edu/arch/ARCH371-F99/groups/k/susarch.html.
Holihan, Rich, Dan Keeley, Daniel Lee, Powen Tu, and Eric Yang. "How Warm Is an Igloo?" Project Paper, Cornell University, Spring 2003. In eCommons at Cornell University Library, http://ecommons.library.cornell.edu/bitstream/1813/125/2/Igloo.pdf.
National Association of Home Builders/Bank of America Home Equity. "Study of Life Expectancy of Home Components." National Association of Home Builders. http://www.nahb.org/fileUpload_details.aspx?contentID=99359.
National Register of Historic Places, The Council Oak Tree Site on the Hollywood Seminole Indian Reservation, Hollywood, Broward County, Florida, National Register #12000992.

"Seminoles of Florida: Ten-Year Program." 1966. Special Collections Florida History, George A. Smathers Libraries, University of Florida, Gainesville.

"Series 1—Seminole Tribe of Florida, 1932–1970." Rex Quinn Papers, Special and Area Studies Collections, George A. Smathers Libraries, University of Florida, Gainesville.

Sherman, Sarah. "Sustainability and the Seminole Chickee." Unpublished paper, Florida International University College of Architecture + The Arts, Department of Interior Architecture, 2013.

Tozier, Morrill M. "Report on the Florida Seminoles." 1954. Special Collections Florida History, University of Florida Smathers Library, Gainesville.

Tribal Register of Historic Places Nomination. "Billy Bowlegs III." Seminole Tribe of Florida Tribal Historic Preservation Office, 2012.

Tribal Register of Historic Places Nomination. "Buster Twins Camp." Seminole Tribe of Florida Tribal Historic Preservation Office, 2013.

U.S. Environmental Protection Agency. "Sustainability Basic Information." n.d. EPA.gov. http://www.epa.gov/sustainability/basicinfo.htm.

Zimmerman, Mary. "Register to the Papers of Ethel Cutler Freeman." National Anthropological Archives, Smithsonian Institution, 1978. http://www.nmnh.si.edu/naa/fa/freeman.pdf.

Index

Page numbers in *italics* refer to illustrations.

Carrie Dilley is visitor services and development manager at the Ah-Tah-Thi-Ki Seminole Indian Museum in Clewiston, Florida. She is the former architectural historian of the Seminole Tribe of Florida Tribal Historic Preservation Office.

The University Press of Florida is the scholarly publishing agency for the State University System of Florida, comprising Florida A&M University, Florida Atlantic University, Florida Gulf Coast University, Florida International University, Florida State University, New College of Florida, University of Central Florida, University of Florida, University of North Florida, University of South Florida, and University of West Florida.

www.ingramcontent.com/pod-product-compliance
Lightning Source LLC
La Vergne TN
LVHW091141080826
845145LV00008B/2221

* 9 7 8 0 8 1 3 0 6 4 9 2 5 *